Blissful Data

*Wisdom and Strategies
for Providing Meaningful,
Useful, and Accessible Data
for All Employees*

MARGARET Y. CHU

American Management Association

New York • Atlanta • Brussels • Chicago • Mexico City • San Francisco
Shanghai • Tokyo • Toronto • Washington, D. C.

Special discounts on bulk quantities of AMACOM books are available to corporations, professional associations, and other organizations. For details, contact Special Sales Department, AMACOM, a division of American Management Association, 1601 Broadway, New York, NY 10019.

Tel.: 212-903-8316. Fax: 212-903-8083.
Web site: www.amacombooks.org

This publication is designed to provide accurate and authoritative information in regard to the subject matter covered. It is sold with the understanding that the publisher is not engaged in rendering legal, accounting, or other professional service. If legal advice or other expert assistance is required, the services of a competent professional person should be sought.

Library of Congress Cataloging-in-Publication Data

Chu, Margaret Y.
    Blissful data : wisdom and strategies for providing meaningful,
  useful, and accessible data for all employees / Margaret Y. Chu.
       p.   cm.
    ISBN 0-8144-0780-3
    1. Decision making—Data processing.   2. Management—Data
  processing.   I. Title.
  HD30.23.C4739 2003
  658.4′038—dc21   2003012530

Printing number

10 9 8 7 6 5 4 3 2 1

To family, friends, and associates.
You provided the inspiration
and material that made
this book possible.

Contents

Preface

As I was going to St. Ives,
I met a man with seven wives.
Each wife had seven sacks,
Each sack had seven cats,
Each cat had seven kits.
Kits, cats, sacks, and wives,
How many were going to St. Ives?

As a child, I longed to have a kitten. I used to daydream that I was the person in the riddle and could go to St. Ives and meet this man with seven wives, three hundred and forty three cats, and thousands of kittens. In my musings this man would offer me some kittens. How would I decide which kittens to choose?

All fantasies aside, you know that in life we are often called upon to make decisions. Depending on the decision we make, we take action. Our success depends on how well we take the right action. So it is important to be able to make the right decisions. Some decisions are easy, such as "What color socks should I wear?" Other decisions are much more difficult, and you need the right facts to assist your decision making process. You wish you had the optimum information, or the *blissful data,* to support your decisions. Blissful data are the facts and information that could help you choose your options. This data would reside in one place and be easily retrieved with the touch of a button.

In the last two decades, organizations have found that having the right information was crucial for survival in today's world of fast-paced action and changing markets. They not only needed the blissful data to make the right decisions, they also needed this data to be easily accessible to all people in the organization. Technology provided a method for organizing, storing, and retrieving massive amounts of disparate data in one location; this became known as a data warehouse.

This book is intended to help you discover the intricacies of blissful data and data warehousing, so that you know what it takes to make it work for you.

Early pioneers proved the technology worked. They showed that a data warehouse could provide access to large amounts of data that had been transformed and organized to be meaningful and useful to all employees of an organization. But data warehousing is not simple. It is also not just technical. Learn from the victories and mistakes of others and save yourself enormous amounts of time and effort in the process.

As the world market moves into the future, organizations that are prepared to face global competition, change quickly, and be flexible to market downturns and upswings will be the organizations that thrive. More and more organizations will realize their need for blissful data and data warehouses. Be forewarned, a data warehouse is in your future.

Acknowledgments

A million thanks to my sister, Rita Asia Lee, for her talented artwork and flexibility of style to complement the text of *Blissful Data.* Many thanks to our daughters, Jenn and Magdalena, for their prototypes of worms, kittens, mermaids, and sea serpents.

Enormous thanks to my makeshift editors: Gene Miller for his constant support and perseverance, my sister Gertrude Layton of Media Works (in Hong Kong), and my agent, Danielle Jatlow of Waterside Productions.

A thousand thanks to my technical support gurus, Robert and Brandon Chu, and to Jacqueline Flynn and Andy Ambraziejus at AMACOM, as well as Barbara A. Chernow of Chernow Editorial Services, Inc. And last but not least, a special thank you to Richard and Patricia Reinertson.

You've all helped make this book a reality. THANK YOU!

Margaret Y. Chu

Introduction

I've worked in Information Technology (IT) through the 1980s and the 1990s, producing computer systems for many types of business applications. Whatever the application, there was always one similar method for handling data. Data were added, changed, or deleted on one or more *databases*. One day I needed some customer data, so I began looking for a customer database. I found sixteen! Sixteen customer databases in one company? Here were riches indeed! How should I decide which customer database to use? What if I found conflicting information for the same customer on different databases? Which database contained the "truth?"

All kidding aside, it's easy to see that it is ineffective business practice for any organization to duplicate data even once, let alone sixteen times. Whenever a customer changed his or her information, such as a home address, it would have to be changed sixteen times. Inevitably the databases end up with mismatched data. Organizations didn't take long to realize that the best practice is to have ONE version of information, a centralized data warehouse of consolidated data for the entire organization to use. No more embarrassing, conflicting, and inaccurate answers to the same question. What a concept!

By the early 1990s, many companies had heard of the benefits of a data warehouse and had jumped onto the data warehousing bandwagon. You already know how the right data helps you make good decisions, but what else was so great about data warehousing? Let's look at a simple example. One day, my friend Anne was delighted to receive in the mail a beautifully embossed invitation to test drive a new luxury car. Here was an example of a target-marketing message enabled by a data warehouse. This car dealer somehow knew that Anne had a five-year-old luxury car and would probably be in the market for a new one. Their marketing ploy worked! Anne went for the test drive and drove away with a brand new car. How many more successful car sales did the dealer have that month? By knowing its customers and increasing chances for a positive sale, the car dealership had a better return for its advertising dollar. This car dealership was utilizing good customer relationship management. Therefore, understanding and better serving the customer is a huge benefit of a data warehouse.

The Internet has impacted many industries, increased the rate of change, and enabled consumers to be much more informed. But the Internet also demands that massive amounts of data be stored and accessed easily. Corporations have found that a data warehouse gives them the flexibility to adjust quickly to changing economic climates, as well as the means to improve decision-making capabilities for all levels of an organization. These innovative business corporations found that a data warehouse enabled them to keep ahead of the competition. The data warehouse then became their tool for survival. The increased rate of change in today's competitive market fuels a new generation of data warehouses. Predicting new trends and responding quickly to new opportunities and markets is an enormous benefit of a data warehouse.

How can a data warehouse help you? We all use data. Your effectiveness and success is measured by how well you turn that data into information and take the right action. With blissful data you become empowered to make better decisions. Having the facts to support your decision-making strategies places you on the road to success. Blissful data provides the tool for such optimum information, enabling decision making to occur at all levels of an organization. With knowledge and understanding of the business of the organization, every employee is able to increase his or her productivity, thereby increasing profits for the organization. The enrichment and empowerment brought about by enhanced decision making capabilities by employees are other important advantages brought about by a data warehouse.

A data warehouse can provide benefits to the publisher who receives thousands of documents in a single month, to the farmer who needs to know when to rotate crops, to the medical researcher who tracks hundreds of experiments, to the Naval commander who decides which regions to navigate, to the governor making policy decisions, and definitely to the business analyst looking at sales breakdowns. In other words, having the right information to make decisions and plan for the future is for you and me and everyone in between!

So we all need information, and a data warehouse of blissful data can deliver that information. End of story? Not quite. Unfortunately, realizing that you need blissful data in a data warehouse is only the beginning. There are many hurdles to overcome, roadblocks in your way, detours that will impede your progress, and easily made wrong turns that will necessitate backtracking.

This book takes you on a journey of discovery that pushes through all the hype, the jargon, the myths, and the misconceptions so that you understand the intricacies of blissful data and the challenges of data warehousing. Learn from the victories and mistakes of others to seize the gain and sidestep the pain!

Margaret Y. Chu

CHAPTER 1

What Is a Data Warehouse?

Why Should You Care?

AXIOM 1

Data, data everywhere, but none for you to use!

Have you ever had a great idea that could have brought your organization significant value, but you pushed it aside because you could not get the correct data? I once knew a business analyst, named Robert, who was always full of good ideas. At one time, Robert had an idea that could have significantly increased productivity in his business division. Robert got really excited about this idea, but his boss told him to first research some numbers and figures to support his proposal. So, with the blood pounding in his ears, Robert started to gather the data to make his case, only to come across many barriers.

Some of the brick walls he encountered were:

- Some data were too difficult to access.
- When he analyzed the data he could access, he got some inaccurate answers. He wasn't sure if he could trust the data.
- Sometimes he found too much data (i.e., data duplicated in different places with conflicting information).
- Cryptic naming conventions and strange codes made the data difficult to decipher.
- Some of the reports he obtained didn't have the data in a usable format.
- Certain functional areas wouldn't share their data.

After facing quite a few roadblocks in trying to access and understand the data, Robert wrote up his data requirements and asked John in information technology (IT) if he could create a report to extract the data he needed. "Oh sure!" said John, "But it will be quite a while before I get to it. I have eight other priority projects right now, so you'll just have to wait your turn!" By now the pounding in Robert's ears had faded to a murmur. He went back to his desk and got back to his stack of daily work. The great idea soon became as historic as a paleontological fossil. After a while, Robert stopped trying to push his ideas. No one seemed to listen, and there were just too many barriers in the way.

Robert is not alone in his quest for the correct information. Organizations have found that data by itself is useless because information alone does not make an organization profitable. Benefits are realized only when data are evolved into information that drives better decision making and strategic action. This optimally organized information should be not only for strategic decision makers in top management, but it should also be available to all employees of an organization. With such empowerment, employees such as Robert can drive maximum productivity. Not only can he produce more in his day-to-day activities, but when a bright idea occurs he can act on it, with potentially tremendous results. Imagine the combined impact where each employee contributes increased value to an organization!

So what data do organizations seem to be lacking? How are these data different from the vast quantities of information that organizations use to run their day-to-day business? Why is it so difficult to attain? How does an organization achieve the goal of optimally organized information? What are the pitfalls and barriers that must be overcome? What tools, best practices, and guidelines are available to increase chances of success? What can be learned from others who have succeeded and those who have failed?

This book addresses these questions one at a time. But for now, let's look at the first question: What data do organizations seem to be lacking? When you think about successful organizations, the answer to this question is simple: Organizations need optimized information that drives maximum productivity. I call this optimized information blissful data.

What Are Blissful Data?

Well, then, how does one define blissful data? Blissful data consist of information that is accurate, meaningful, useful, and easily accessible to many people in an organization. These data are used by the organization's employees to analyze information and support their decision-making processes to strategic action. It is easy to see that organizations that have reached their goal of maximum productivity with blissful data can triumph over their competition. Thus, blissful data provide a competitive advantage. All organizations need blissful data to be victorious into the future.

I know what you may be thinking—data are data, every organization has tons of data, and the data just need to be managed so that it doesn't take too long to access. I used to think along the same lines until I began to work closely on the requirements for an informational system with a business manager named Peggy. Peggy had an in-depth knowledge of the business of her functional area. She was always thinking of ways to improve processes and bring value to the company. However, more often than not, like Robert's, Peggy's bright ideas were lost by the absence of the correct data to sustain them. At other times, she found too much data, customer data duplicated in multiple places, with some matching and other mismatching information. Peggy and her group often had to make assumptions on which data were more accurate. Naturally, their assumptions were not always correct. This guessing game sometimes resulted in bad decisions. Trends and variations were often missed because the data took too long to gather and analyze, decisions had to be made in haste, and there was never time to go back and evaluate what went wrong. In short, Peggy knew her group was not as accurate or effective as they could be. They had too many of these data problems.

From Peggy I learned that data for analysis were very different from operational data used in day-to-day workings of the company. Business clients and strategists clearly needed data that had been consolidated and optimized by going through a transformation and organization process. She helped me realize the need for blissful data. Together, we designed an informational data system to help alleviate some of her group's data problems.

A few years later, computer technology enabled a new methodology. It provided the ability to store large amounts of dissimilar data in one location with the means to access the data in a reasonably quick fashion. The availability of low-priced computing power also made this technology economically feasible.

The method became known as data warehousing, and it utilized a storehouse of data called a data warehouse.

It seemed that Peggy's dreams had been fulfilled—because the data within a data warehouse are BLISSFUL DATA.

A data warehouse of blissful data can provide the solution to many business problems in various industries across the world. However, it is not as simple as it sounds. As we shall see, a data warehouse of blissful data is not that easy to achieve. Let's start at the very beginning and define a data warehouse in more detail.

REMEMBER

Blissful data consist of information that is accurate, meaningful, useful, and easily accessible to many people in an organization for their decision making purposes.

What's a Data Warehouse?

Let's break down the term. Data is the plural of datum, which is a piece of information. A warehouse is a place for storing goods. Combining these two definitions, we can surmise that a data warehouse is a place for storing pieces of information. This seems to be a reasonable definition; data warehouses have been broadly defined as "centralized storage sheds of related data." But what does it all mean? What is a centralized storage shed of related data?

We already know that the warehouse is not a brick-and-mortar building but an imaginary place on a computer for lots of important data. This imaginary place is in a centralized location. The quantity of data is large and they are blissful data. Therefore, these data are used often to make decisions and take action. In addition, there are two more characteristics of the data in a data warehouse:

1. Each piece of datum is tied or combined with other pieces of data, so they are "related."
2. These data have happened in the past (there is no recording of data in the future) and, therefore, once recorded, doesn't change

With these characteristics in mind, it can be said that data warehouses have been around for a very long time, in fact as long as human beings have roamed the earth. How can that be, you say? Computers haven't been around for thousands of years! Well, they have, if you consider the human brain to be a computer and its memory to be a data warehouse!

Let's look at the analogy of your memory as a data warehouse. You have memory cells that retain past experiences and a retrieval mechanism to recall

Figure 1-1 Your memory is like a data warehouse.

these experiences (as depicted in Figure 1-1). All the experiences are meaningful and related to you, have happened in the past, and shape your values and thoughts in every decision you make. Your memory can be defined as:

> *"A data warehouse is a set of computer databases specifically designed with related, historical blissful data that assist in formulating decisions and taking action."*

> ". . . a store of past experiences and information that help you make decisions and take action."

We already know that blissful data are used in decision making and taking the right action, but I like to emphasize this in the definition of a data warehouse:

> ". . . a set of computer databases specifically designed with related, historical blissful data that assist in formulating decisions and taking action."

What do you think of when you see the term "database?" I often think of a database as a file cabinet full of folders, each folder containing some data. The folders can be indexed by last name so if data on Zelinski are required the folder called Zelinski is found and its data retrieved easily. This points to a database being a place to a store a bunch of data. But that's what a "data warehouse" breaks down to. What makes data warehouses different from databases? How are data warehouses special? Aren't they just a large collection of databases?

An easy way to realize the differences between data warehouses and databases is to go back to my analogy of your memory. What makes it special? That's an easy question, you say, "My memory is full of my past experiences." Bingo! Just as your memory uniquely relates to you, a data warehouse contains data that have been specifically designed to relate to a specific organization. They are unique and meaningful to that organization and reflect its business. Blissful data for one organization are never the same as those of another. Therefore, consider a data warehouse as the memory of an organization.

Just as you use past experiences to make decisions and plan for the future, an organization uses its blissful data to formulate decisions and strategize for the future. Thus an organization's data warehouse provides a competitive advantage; it is a key element for the organization to move victoriously into the future.

The original definition of the term "data warehouse" is attributed to William H. Inmon, considered by many to be the father of data warehousing. In 1990, he defined a data warehouse as:

> "A subject-oriented, integrated, time-variant, and nonvolatile collection of data in support of management's decisions."[1, p 29]

We'll look at Dr. Inmon's definition more closely in Chapter 8. For now, let's think of a data warehouse as the memory of an organization and go on to find out more about the characteristics of a data warehouse.

 REMEMBER

"A data warehouse is a set of computer databases specifically designed with related, historical blissful data that assist in formulating decisions and taking action."

Did You See a Data Warehouse Today?

"I saw one once," said Piglet. "At least, I think I did,"
he said. "Only perhaps it wasn't."[2, p 56]

In A.A. Milne's book about a boy named Christopher Robin, a bear named Winnie the Pooh, and a pig named Piglet, Pooh and Piglet decide to set a trap for a heffalump. They had only one problem: They didn't know what a heffalump looked like. In their minds, it had two characteristics: It was big and scary. Similarly, a data warehouse, too, could be big and scary. Thus it is important to understand what constitutes a data warehouse. All data warehouses have some common characteristics.

We already know that a data warehouse is not just another computer repository of data; it is a total environment of CHANGE, INTEGRATION, ENRICHMENT, and FLEXIBILITY. It contains large volumes of blissful data that are used in decision making and taking the right action. Let's go back to the memory analogy. What are some of the characteristics of your memory?

■ Your memory works as a part of your brain. Your brain is the portion of the central nervous system that resides in the vertebrate cranium (a.k.a., your skull). So your brain is like a computer, your skull the hardware platform, and your central nervous system the network. Similarly, a data warehouse exists as part of a computer on a hardware platform. This platform can be a mainframe, a set of servers, or a PC or workstation. The computer network makes everything work together.

■ Your memory contains many memory cells. This collection of cells makes up a database. In addition, you have a built-in "database management system (DBMS)" to operate your memory cells. In a data warehouse, the DBMS is the computer software that organizes, operates, and manages the data.

■ In addition to your built-in DBMS, you also have the ability to retrieve data in your memory. When this retrieval system doesn't work you basically

Figure 1-2 Could this be a data warehouse?

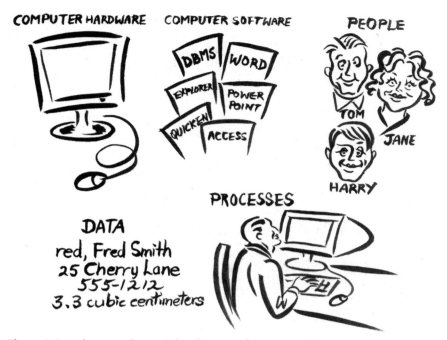

Figure 1-3 A data warehouse is hardware, software, people, data, and processes.

"lose your memory"; in other words, you simply "forget." In a data warehouse, another item of computer software called a . . . a . . . ("I forget . . . oh yes!") an application is used to access the data. There are many types of applications that allow you to query the data warehouse, obtain the selected data, and receive the information in the format specified. Because these applications allow you to interface with the data warehouse, they are called end-user interfaces.

- Each memory cell contains a previous experience, something you've learned or believe. That is, each memory cell contains some data. Over the years, your memory has collected huge amounts of information. These special data influence all the decisions you make. Similarly, a data warehouse contains large amounts of data that are used for analysis and making decisions.

- The data in your memory could very possibly exist elsewhere. That is, a sibling or friend could have shared an experience, a book, a TV show. Sometimes, hundreds or thousands of people share a memory. This duplication of experiences is a very good thing. Similarly, the data in a data warehouse also exist elsewhere. Usually, they come from data in the day-to-day operations or from something as simple as a hand-written list. At first I thought that this duplication of data in the source system and data warehouse was a waste of resources. This is not so. Think about how many people can share remembrances of an event. Each will have a different perspective of the event, all having a bearing on the true happenings of the event. Just as you play a crucial role in your memory, people are an important aspect of a data warehouse.

■ A funny thing happens when people try to recall the memory of an event. Two people may remember it very differently. Their various perspectives cause their minds to process events differently. People tend to focus on and remember what matters to them; they "transform" the event. Similarly, data in a data warehouse also go through a process of transformation. The place where data originates from is known as the source system. Operational systems often provide large amounts of source data. But data in operational systems exist for the purpose of running the day-to-day business of the operation; they are not well suited for analysis and decision making. Therefore, the data must go through a process of transformation (explained in Chapter 4), before being loaded to the data warehouse. A data warehouse involves many other types of processes, too. Thus, processes are an important characteristic of every data warehouse.

In summary, then, a data warehouse is made up of hardware, software, special data, people, and processes. This is depicted in Figure 1-3.

REMEMBER

A data warehouse is an entire environment of change, integration, enrichment, and flexibility! It consists of a combination of hardware, software, data, people, and processes.

What Are the Key Benefits?

Organizations know that to survive in the 21st century, they must have a competitive advantage. A data warehouse of blissful data provides this advantage. By using the data warehouse every person in the enterprise can access the information to assess risk and make decisions. A data warehouse can be used to bring the necessary information to all levels of an organization. With decision making no longer limited to management, every employee can respond to customer requests, questions, and demands. By providing an increased level of customer service, every employee contributes to an organization's success. Successful organizations have customers coming back again and again. These organizations don't just survive, they thrive!

Figure 1-4 Data warehouses can bring pots of "gold."

Organizations with successful data warehouses found many benefits. Some of the general benefits are:

1. The ability to predict new trends and shifts in the marketplace and the flexibility to adjust and respond quickly to these changes.
2. The capability to intimately know and hence better serve the customer.
3. The means to facilitate employee knowledge and complete understanding of the entire business of an organization.
4. The capacity to promote increased productivity per employee, resulting in increased profitability for an organization.

You can also read about many data warehousing success stories. These organizations used a data warehouse to bring them pots of "gold," also known as significant revenues[3]:

- A major retailer reports improving customer service, thereby increasing sales by over 20% in just 6 months to more than $315 million.
- Another retailer uses a direct marketing campaign that results in a 400% return on investment (ROI) in a pilot study.
- A small insurance company lessens its claims by 20% for a $250,000 savings.
- A government agency saves millions by detecting billing fraud violations.

Therefore, by being able to adapt quickly to changing markets, having increased levels of customer service, and with enhanced knowledge and productivity of employees, organizations have found that a data warehouse can increase profits and boost sales. It's no wonder so many organizations tried to emulate these successful pioneers and jumped onto the data warehousing bandwagon.

REMEMBER

Data warehouse pioneers proved that data warehouses could bring in pots of "gold" in increased revenues.

Should Jack Jump Over the Candlestick?

Jack be nimble,

Jack be quick,

Jack jump over the candlestick.

A data warehouse enables employees of an organization to predict new trends and shifts in the marketplace. It allows the organization to be flexible enough to adjust and respond to these changes quickly. The ability to query directly (discussed in Chapter 8) the data in the data warehouse empowers employees to make decisions and take quick action.

Taking the right action can bring tremendous profits to an organization. Consider Jack from the nursery rhyme, illustrated in Figure 1-5. Jack makes decisions every day based on facts and values. With the right information, Jack can leverage his assets, analyze risks, make a decision, and take action. Jumping over a candlestick doesn't need much thought, but Jack does not have to be the president or CEO of an organization to make decisions. The outcome of these decisions could be tremendously valuable. I'll use this nursery rhyme to illustrate Jack's decision-making process. First, Jack assesses the height of the candlestick; he knows how high he can jump, weighs the possibility of getting burned, and then, whatever his motivation (money, fun, boredom, fear, bravado?), makes the decision to jump. Now instead of assessing candlesticks, suppose Jack was assessing a new marketing campaign. He gets information about the buying habits of his customers from his data warehouse. Jack finds the best markets he should target. He goes ahead with the campaign and obtains lucrative results. By assessing the right information Jack makes good decisions.

A successful data warehouse provides information to many people at all levels of an organization. Imagine the combined efforts of people like Jack

Figure 1-5 Jack makes a decision to jump.

making decisions and taking action. By empowering the workforce, the organization becomes more flexible and can adjust quickly to market upswings and downturns. In addition, employee capabilities are enriched, resulting in increased productivity and profitability.

REMEMBER

A data warehouse enables employees of an organization to be able to predict new trends and shifts in the marketplace. It allows the organization to be flexible enough to adjust and respond quickly to these changes by empowering employees to make their own decisions and take action.

Why Serve the Customer Well?

A data warehouse provides the capability to intimately know and hence better serve the customer. It allows detailed analysis by providing the capability to slice and dice (discussed in Chapter 8) the data. This allows for comparisons, trends, and forecast evaluations that enable employees to predict the buying habits and patterns of the customer.

> *"The most valuable asset of any company is its reputation in the marketplace, how it is known to its customers."*
> BRIAN TRACY[4, p 192]

Customer relationship management (CRM) was one of the biggest buzzwords of the 1990s and it's still buzzing! Every seminar, industry magazine, or speaker has something to say about the latest and greatest methods to satisfy and retain customers. A customer who is treated well and likes your product will keep coming back. What better place to collect and integrate customer data than a data warehouse? Therefore, a centralized data warehouse has become synonymous with CRM.

Some examples of how successful data warehouses have made customers happy are shown in Table 1-1.

As shown in Table 1-1, a data warehouse offers capabilities to a wide range of industries. Organizations use information from a data warehouse to offer special discounts to customers, target buyers for custom products, detect fraud, obtain higher returns from marketing campaigns, bring additional products to customers, integrate best methods, maximize yield, and cross-check claims. By delighting customers, organizations enjoy increased sales, improved market share, and boosted profits. Better returns result in savings that can be passed back to the customer, further increasing customer satisfaction and brand allegiance.

REMEMBER

A key benefit of a data warehouse is to intimately know and hence better serve the customer.

Are There Poisonous Gases in the Sky?

A data warehouse facilitates employee knowledge and understanding of the entire business of an organization. It can bring unimagined benefits to the organization. The

> *"Imagination is more important than information"*
> ALBERT EINSTEIN[5, p 136]

With a Data Warehouse	Without a Data Warehouse
Vacation/Travel: You are offered a $200 discount coupon for a cruise in April for your 10th wedding anniversary.	No one remembers your wedding anniversary except your spouse (maybe).
Retail: Your 15.5-year-old son cruises Internet sites for a brand new luxury sports coupe with custom wheels and spoiler. Two weeks later he gets an e-mail from an auto vendor offering a used sedan with a spoiler at a price that is not astronomical. There is no way that he would get a brand new luxury sports coupe, but perhaps he gets the used sedan.	There is no way he would get a brand new luxury sports coupe (some things don't change).
Telecommunications: A wireless phone makes use of Call Detail Records (CDRs) to generate thousands of alerts. These alerts are analyzed against customer information and payment history from the data warehouse. Early fraud detection reduces account loss by more than 60%	Higher phone charges due to fraud. Undetected fraud adds millions of dollars to the bottom line.
Finance: A credit union pitches its auto-lease product to its members. By analyzing variables in its data warehouse, letters are sent to the 15,000 most likely prospects. This targeting pitch results in a 4.5% response rate, at a cost of $40 per new lease customer.	Random mailings result in a 1% response rate, at a cost of $175 per new lease customer. Lease and mailing costs are passed on to the customer.
Transportation: A major airline company sends its most frequent flyers customized packages for flights, hotels, car rentals, or first class upgrade coupons, generating more revenue and loyal customers.	Customer may easily switch to a different carrier.
Education: Teaching methods are matched with test scores by region. The most effective teaching methods are shared within the state and within the country. The future citizens and leaders of the country win.	Little or no integration of effective teaching methods.
Agriculture: Farmers capture data to create detailed maps that show which plots produce the biggest yield, and which plots need more fertilizer, herbicide, or pesticide.	Farmers have to work a lot harder and make quite a few more guesses.
Government: The U.S. Internal Revenue Service obtains additional tax revenue of $70 million by finding incidents where both divorced parents were claiming their children as dependents.[7]	Loss of revenue to the IRS. Happier divorced parents?

Figure 1-6 Soar to new heights.

power of advanced analysis (discussed in Chapter 8) could bring about the Joseph-Michel Montgolfier of the 21st century. Let's see what this amazing man found over 200 years ago.

Humanity has benefited from those with great imagination! Regardless of your industry, imagination can fuel a revolution. Look at Montgolfier, the 18th-century French paper maker whose imagination literally went up in smoke! Watching smoke rise up his chimney, Montgolfier said to himself, "If the smoke was captured in a paper bag, the bag should rise too. With enough smoke, the bag should be able to carry something else with it as well." Voila! The idea for the hot-air balloon was born.

What Einstein didn't state was that imagination must be followed by information. Montgolfier needed information to get his idea off the ground (excuse the pun), such as:

- Was there something better than paper bags?
- Was taffeta coated with resins strong enough?
- What size should the balloon be?

- Were there poisonous gases in the sky?
- How much weight could the balloon carry?

On November 21, 1783, Montgolfier realized his dream. His seven-story tall balloon took off with a young pilot aboard. It flew from the gardens of the royal palace to a location beyond the Seine, a distance of 5 miles. And that is how a paper manufacturer from France, letting his imagination soar, set civilization on the road to human flight, from balloons, to airplanes, to rockets, and ultimately, as Buzz Lightyear in "Toy Story" would say, "to infinity and beyond!"

What untapped potential do you have? What information is hiding in your organization ready to spring out and fuel your imagination? The world is full of people with vivid imaginations that must be supported by information. Blissful data captured in a data warehouse provide this information. As employees increase their knowledge and understanding of the entire business of their organization they too could get ideas like Montgolfier's and make discoveries not even imagined today. Data warehouses have the potential to leverage the next generation of balloons, airplanes, and rockets, to take us to infinity and beyond!

R EMEMBER

Data warehouses enrich employee knowledge and understanding of the entire business of an organization. This can lead to unimagined benefits!

Why Couldn't Some Data Warehouses Fly?

Making haste, rushing off, flying at top height,
But beware of dangers just out of your sight;
Or before you know it, you come down with a thump!
That hard work and effort all tossed in the dump.

GERTRUDE LAYTON

Now we know what a data warehouse is, what it can do, and what it looks like. It seems like many organizations would benefit from having one. What's stopping them? Read on . . .

The Data Warehousing Institute (DWI) states a failure rate higher than 70% percent[7] for data warehouse endeavors. Some even go as high as 90%. Why are failure rates so shockingly high for such projects? A lot of people would shake their heads knowingly and say, "Ahhhh, yes, the technology is quite

Figure 1-7 Not all data warehouses could fly.

complex." I used to think technology was the big bottleneck, too. I know now that it isn't about the technology or even about getting the right data. Surprisingly, it's about the people!

Remember the story about the three pigs? One built his house out of straw, the second built his house out of wood, and the third built his house out of brick. Only the brick house stood up to huffing and puffing by

> *. . .Or I'll huff and I'll puff*
> *And I'll blow your (data ware-) house in*
> THE BIG BAD WOLF

the Big Bad Wolf. Suppose this wolf had bad allergies and the straw and wood caused him to sneeze? Is it his fault that these pigs picked such shaky material for their homes? Perhaps long-lasting homes secure from wolves were not their objectives. Ease, cost, or time constraints may have been the driving factor. Or, perhaps the first two pigs were afraid of earthquakes and did not want bricks to come crashing down on them. Whatever the pigs' objectives in building their homes, they needed to have considered all the risks.

Data warehouse endeavors require close consideration of many potential risks. Such endeavors involve a lot of people, various objectives, and high levels of change. Success requires massive amounts of communication and integration. The Big Bad Wolf is everywhere. Ironically, many data warehouse failures are caused by the three "Ps":

1. Politics – Data warehouses are cross-functional endeavors, and the rules of stovepipe (discussed in Chapter 3) organizations no longer apply. It's no longer "our way" and "our data" but "share and share alike." (Discussed in Chapter 4)
2. Power – Data warehouses have heavy upfront costs and time requirements from client communities. Culture, organizational structure, and sponsorship from both business and IT play important roles in cost justification and overcoming resistance (discussed in Chapters 5 and 6).
3. People – A fear of change and lack of knowledge of the advantages of a data warehouse will cause resistance such as, "I know how to do my job and don't need to waste time using a data warehouse."

Therefore, data warehouses are all about "change." Horizontal work structures replace the traditional vertical and hierarchical organizations. Changes are required in traditional roles and relationships; IT and the business must perform as partners and strive toward a common goal. Such change also involves "integration." New roles and responsibilities need to be combined with existing ones. Integration of data, business rules, and requirements means breaking down age-old barriers and frequently overcoming resistance. On top of these social changes are technical changes. New products, methods, and processes mean constant vigilance and training. People often resist change, resulting in confrontations, conflict, and misunderstandings. The amount of change and integration required by data warehouses makes it easy for data warehouses to fail.

REMEMBER
Politics, power issues, and people problems cause the failure of many data warehouse endeavors.

A Cakewalk? Not!

I worked in IT through the 1980s and 1990s, blissfully producing computer systems for many types of business applications. Over the years I worked with dozens of data bases but I still was struck unawares by my first encounter with a data warehouse. Let me relate what occurred. At the time, I was excited to gain an opportunity to work on a forecasting project that would use data from a data warehouse. This data warehouse did not yet contain the forecasting information, but the business clients had already begun working with specialists in the enterprise data management (EDM) group of IT to add these data from multiple source systems.

EDM would handle all the technical aspects of the data warehouse, as well as the transformation of the source data. EDM assured my forecasting logistics project team (FLPT) that there should be no problem with the data being available in 6 months. FLPT could just concentrate on the forecasting requirements and count on having its data available from the data warehouse.

FLPT set about gathering its forecasting design requirements with regular status meetings with EDM. At first, good progress was made and all seemed well. But, meetings with EDM began to become less and less regular. One day I heard some disquieting news about the data warehouse from the logistics business clients. Strange rumors went around which included:

- Business clients were unhappy with the data warehouse because response times were too slow.
- Some functional groups felt that data values in the warehouse were skewed to certain business functions; they did not trust the data and would not use the warehouse.
- Other areas said they were never asked what they needed from the warehouse so it lacked critical data and to them was useless.
- Some said that the data in the warehouse contained errors; they could not trust the data.

At the first opportunity, I asked EDM what problems were being encountered. How did this affect the data for the forecast project? EDM mentioned "politics," "dirty data," "nonexistent metadata," and "sponsorship issues." I found such terms quite confusing. There seemed to be a lot more to building a data warehouse than I had imagined. It certainly was not just a large database; it was an entire environment, one of many changes.

Many more negative events started to occur, including:

- Key EDM people left the company.
- A lack of funds caused EDM to stop work temporarily.
- The quality of the data was so bad that six people were hired just to fix data.
- Expertise on the data was missing; these data were not understood and could not be validated.
- Major policy changes took place, such as budgeting problems and data ownership issues.
- Surprising political issues came about; the logistics group would not share their data, and EDM had to create certain duplicate data for FLPT.

These significant events had a tremendous impact on the forecast project. After 6 months there were no forecasting data available. FLPT had to stop in its tracks and take over the data warehouse function for the forecasting data expansion. This caused a domino effect with additional events going awry. FLPT, not surprisingly, could not deliver the forecasting project on time. Why did so many things go wrong? In hindsight, I realized that the goals and objectives of EDM and FLPT were not in synch. The goals for the data warehouse expansion and the forecasting project should have been tied, yet they were handled as two separate projects. Without a common clear goal or definition of the objectives, there was no chance of success. More data warehouses fail from a lack of definition of the objectives than all other reasons combined.

I also realized that many involved with the data warehouse endeavor had unrealistic expectations that contributed toward its failure. Some common unrealistic expectations of a data warehouse are:

1. A data warehouse can be created with little or no idea of how it will be used.
2. Data can be copied into a data warehouse "as is," without cleansing and transformation.
3. Unrealistic schedules without a preliminary analysis of the work involved.
4. A data warehouse is magical and will solve all our problems.
5. A data warehouse is a one-time shot; once it is set up we will not have to change or maintain it.
6. A data warehouse can be set up on a shoestring budget.
7. A small data warehouse can be created and added onto later.
8. A data warehouse belongs to IT so business clients don't need to get involved.
9. The IT staff can read a book and set up a data warehouse with no outside help.
10. The project manager can handle the data warehouse project in addition to regular daily responsibilities.
11. All the latest and greatest hardware and software tools from multiple vendors can be used straight out of the box, without adequate training or learning experiences.

Unrealistic expectations about the purpose, objectives, time and effort, cost, and complexity of a data warehouse can lead to its failure.

REMEMBER

More data warehouses fail from a lack of definition of the objectives than all other reasons combined. Unrealistic expectations will also lead to data warehouse failure.

The Rest of the Story

You've now seen how benefits of a data warehouse can enable phenomenal successes. You've also seen that successful data warehouses are not that easy to achieve. The remaining chapters discuss the intricacies of achieving data warehouses of blissful data in more detail. Use this book as your stepping stone into the world of business intelligence and move victoriously into the future.

Chapter 2: Data Warehouses, Data Marts – What's In a Name?

> **AXIOM 2**
>
> The power of two: The amount of data in a given organization can double every year.

Rome was not built in a day, and neither can a data warehouse be. As data volume kept increasing, quick solution data marts came about. Chapter 2 cautions against some of the easy pitfalls that lead to short-sighted solutions and long-term problems.

Chapter 3: Myths and Misconceptions – What Should You Eradicate?

> **AXIOM 3**
>
> Once you get rid of "unrealistic expectations," you'll get more "unrealistic expectations."

With any type of change there is resistance. Data warehousing requires many changes. Many barriers and misconceptions must be overcome for data warehousing success. Chapter 3 distinguishes data warehouse facts from the fallacies to eradicate fears, break down barriers, and manage expectations.

Chapter 4: What Are Dirty Data? – Where Do Dirty Data Come From?

> **AXIOM 4**
>
> Dirty data are like dirty laundry: Every organization has some dirty data.

Organizations use operational systems to handle day-to-day work. These operational systems create large volumes of operational data. Operational data, however, cannot be copied straight to a data warehouse as this can cause errors. Chapter 4 describes the types of dirty data and steps to take to prevent a data warehouse "disaster."

Chapter 5: Politics – Who Owns It Anyway?

> **AXIOM 5**
>
> Build it and they may NOT come!

Issues of people, power, and politics come with implementing cross organizational change and integration. Organizational cultures, leaders, structure, and the important role of the data warehouse sponsor all play a part in overcoming these issues. Chapter 5 describes the recommended organizational structures and guidelines necessary for the integration of business rules and metadata to keep stakeholders involved and committed to data warehouse success.

Chapter 6: Politics – Who's Going to Pay?

> **AXIOM 6**
>
> The right investment of a data warehouse can bring significant business value!

Switching to a data warehouse overnight (Big Bang) just does not work. Smaller steps and rewards must be planned along the way to show continued value for the involvement. Chapter 6 discusses the aspects of hard and soft return on investment (ROI) to demonstrate the *investment* of a data warehouse and how costs are justified in terms of benefits.

Chapter 7: Project Management – Is It the Silver Bullet?

> **AXIOM 7**
>
> The three Rs of data warehouse project management: recommunicate, recommunicate, recommunicate.

Data warehouses involve high levels of change, integration, and enrichment within stakeholders. Continuous planning, executing, and control must take place. Chapter 7 describes the fundamentals of project management and how its disciplines of process groups and knowledge areas can contribute toward data warehouse deployment success.

Chapter 8: Data Modeling – Why Model the Data?

> **AXIOM 8**
>
> Make the model fit the business, not the business fit the model!

Technology is the tool used to deliver the data warehouse. Chapter 8 defines the major elements of a data model and the impact of a good data model on performance. Discover the capabilities a data warehouse can deliver, from simple queries to advanced analysis. Summarize the knowledge you've acquired.

Chapter 9: Case Studies – Is There a Light at the End of the Tunnel?

> **AXIOM 9**
>
> Seek new heights by agreeing to agree!
> Case Study 1: The Good. Case Study 2: The Bad and Ugly.
> Chapter 9 guides you into the exciting possibilities that lie ahead.

REMEMBER THIS!

✔ Blissful data consist of information that is accurate, meaningful, useful, and easily accessible to many people in an organization for their decision making purposes.

✔ A data warehouse is a set of computer databases specifically designed with related and historical blissful data that assist in formulating decisions and taking action.

✔ A data warehouse is an entire environment of change, integration, enrichment, and flexibility! It consists of a combination of hardware, software, special data, people, and processes.

✔ Data warehouse pioneers proved that data warehouses could bring in pots of "gold" in increased revenues.

✔ A data warehouse enables employees of an organization to predict new trends and shifts in the marketplace. It allows the organization to be flexible enough to adjust and respond quickly to these changes by empowering employees to make their own decisions and take action.

✔ A key benefit of a data warehouse is to intimately know and hence better serve the customer.

✔ Data warehouses enrich employee knowledge and understanding of the entire business of the organization. This can lead to unimagined benefits!

✔ Politics, power issues, and people problems cause the failure of many data warehouse endeavors.

✔ More data warehouses fail from a lack of definition of the objectives than all other reasons combined. Unrealistic expectations will also lead to data warehouse failure.

CHAPTER 2

Data Warehouses, Data Marts

What's in a Name?

AXIOM 2

The power of two: The amount of data in an organization can double every year.

Have you ever had that rundown feeling caused by the truckloads of data relentlessly coming your way via e-mail, voice mail, flyers, documentation, reports, and innumerable requests for more information? If you don't have the resources to organize and structure these data, they have little value. Data are only as good as the information they provide and the action that results. Optimum value is received from data that provide the right information to drive maximum productivity.

Chuck was familiar with that rundown feeling. On some days he felt as if he'd been run over by a steamroller! Let's take a peek into Chuck's work life: His boss had just requested a revenue analysis for a new product, a VP was calling him for a report showing low performers by region, and he already had five other projects on his plate. How could he get it all done on time? Each of the requests required analysis of multiple reports, summarization and consolidation, and quite a few conversions as well. After pulling another all-nighter, he was ready to throw down his badge and quit.

"Why can't they ask questions on the day-to-day operations?" grumbled Chuck. "Those answers are already available in daily, weekly, or monthly reports and require little analysis. But, to carry out their requests I have to gather data from multiple sources, match codes, and analyze certain values," he sighed. Nervously, Chuck raked his fingers through his hair, and said, "I wonder if they know how often I play a guessing game?"

I certainly didn't envy Chuck's position and wondered what would happen the day his luck ran out. What Chuck needed was to have all the right data in one place, synchronized, and ready to go. He could then create reports in any format he desired and analyze the data. What Chuck needed was to have blissful data available in a data warehouse.

Unfortunately, Chuck's difficulty in obtaining useful data in a timely manner is a common challenge at many organizations. Organizations have no shortage of data. With the advent of computers, operational systems could churn out truckloads of data in a single day. But businesspeople such as Chuck found that operational data were not very useful for analysis and comparisons. They needed the data to be organized into meaningful reports that provided answers to their business questions. Obtaining such reports posed another problem: it took a long time. It involved a process in which businesspeople had to write up their requests, wait for IT to accept, prioritize, schedule, develop, and eventually produce the reports. If the requestor was lucky or had a high priority, this process could take a week or two, if not; the report would arrive as much as months later, if at all. IT always had a backlog of requests.

Thus, the idea of being able to question directly a data warehouse of blissful data and obtain answers in a few seconds seemed almost magical. Naturally, organizations rushed to implement this magic potion. Unfortunately, as you know, many did not succeed. Some organizations encountered roadblocks and pitfalls too difficult to overcome. Others created embarrassing debacles that were no longer discussed. Yet others started and ended up with something quite different from what they were expecting. Many organizations found enterprise-wide data warehouse of blissful data to be a greater challenge than they had ever imagined.

About the mid-1990s a new solution called a data mart appeared. A data mart was touted to be quicker and cheaper to build than a data warehouse. It still contained blissful data to provide quick answers to business questions. A data mart seemed like an ideal resolution for organizations' informational needs. But was it? Let's go back to Chuck to answer this question.

Some people would say that all Chuck needs is a data mart and not a data warehouse. Before deciding on whether Chuck needs a warehouse or a mart, some questions must be considered. Does he need to get answers to a specified set of departmental queries? If so, then a data mart is a good solution. However, if Chuck and other businesspeople must answer a variety of queries that require cross-functional views of the data of the entire company then a centralized data warehouse is the solution. Such centralized data warehouses came to be known as enterprise data warehouses (EDWs). Therefore, determining the business needs is the critical first step to be taken before deciding whether a data mart or EDW should be built. In either case, all data warehouses or data marts must contain blissful data.

The common element in EDWs and datamarts is data. Let's look at the aspects of data, the definition of data marts, and the similarities and differences between data marts and EDWs.

Do You Have Truckloads of Data?

Data can be found everywhere. Think about your memory. We use data within our memories so frequently, we don't even realize that we are accessing and employing data. But problems come about when volumes of data are so large that required information cannot be quickly or easily obtained when needed. Organizations realized that data must be optimally organized and available in order to provide information that is used to drive maximum productivity.

What is the power of two? A lot more than the power of one, of course, but let's see how powerful it can be. There once was a king who happened to be indebted to one of his knights. He asked the knight to name whatever he wanted. The knight said, "A piece of gold on the first square of a chessboard, multiplied by two on the second square, the gold on the second square multiplied by two again on the third square, and so on, until all squares on the board are covered with gold." Well, thought the king, that isn't too bad, so he said, "Your wish is granted!" This king totally underestimated the strength behind the "power of two." To see what the savvy knight knew, let's look at the first eight squares:

1. The first square would have 1 piece of gold.
2. $1 \times 2 = 2$: The second square would have 2 pieces of gold.
3. $2 \times 2 = 4$: The third square would have 4 pieces of gold.

4. 4 × 2 = 8: The fourth square would have 8 pieces of gold.
5. 8 × 2 = 16: The fifth square would have 16 pieces of gold.
6. 16 × 2 = 32: The sixth square would have 32 pieces of gold.
7. 32 × 2 = 64: The seventh square is already overflowing with gold.
8. 64 × 2 = 128: You get the idea.

As shown in Figure 2-1, a very large number of gold coins are obtained by multiplying pieces of gold by two for each square of a chessboard. The sixth square already would contain 32 pieces of gold. Soon the chessboard is overflowing with gold coins. By the time the 64th square of the chessboard is covered, the knight would be a very rich man indeed!

Fortunately, organizations don't need kings to give them data. As organizations perform and track their day-to-day work, large quantities of operational data are generated. In addition, data are available from external sources, such as statistical bureaus, market research or survey results, laboratories, retailers, and consulting firms. But organizations find that data by itself do not provide much value: These data must be turned into information and used to drive better decision making processes to take the right action. Only with the right action will an organization become more profitable.

Studies have indicated that the amount of data in an organization can be expected to double every year.[8] This means that after 5 years an organization could have 16 times the data it started out with. It is no wonder that databases start overflowing with data. Organizations need a method to structure and arrange this data to make it useful to their employees.

Remember

Organizations obtain large amounts of data from their day-to-day operations. These data grow quickly in volume and can double year after year.

Figure 2-1 Organizations are rich in operational data.

Where Should You Go?

He got to the crossroads, but it was all dark
Seeking a signpost, there was no mark.
How to move forward . . . turn left or right?
Despite his huge hurry, he was stuck alright.
　　　　　　　　　　　GERTRUDE LAYTON

Data have been around for a long time. In the 1960s and 1970s computer capabilities increased to handle large amounts of data. During these early days of data processing, it was easy to know what to do with data. Computer applications pulled data in, combined or modified the data in some way, produced various reports, and then either replaced, discarded, or sent the updated data to other processes. These operational data were used or created by the day-to-day processes of the operational systems.

As the operational data grew, doubling and quadrupling over time, electronic files and databases contained larger and larger amounts of data. Operational systems processed the vast amounts of data on large computer mainframes.

Figure 2-2 The road to the right action was dark and unmarked.

Mainframe systems were extremely busy and often taxed to their limits. Although many daily, weekly, and monthly operational reports were generated, there were very few resources available for data analysis and informational reporting.

Although stacks of reports were printed, business analysts found that these operational reports didn't contain the information they needed for data analysis and comparisons. They needed optimum data to support their decision making for choosing the best action. These analysts found they either had to pull the data they needed from many different sources (which took days and weeks) or request a special report from information technology (IT) (which took weeks and months). Just like Chuck in Figure 2-2, they often felt they were playing a guessing game and making decisions in the dark.

During my earlier years in IT, I once met two business clients named Alex and Amy. Alex managed a finance group while Amy supervised a sales group. Alex and Amy often needed ad hoc reports to analyze market conditions and compare historical sales and outcomes. They made requests for these special reports to the IT department. However, IT was often busy with high-priority operational systems development and maintenance. They also often had a large backlog of report requests. Alex and Amy often had to wait weeks if not months to get responses to their requests. When they eventually got their reports from IT, the data were often outdated or market conditions had changed. They wished they had a better way to get the information they needed.

Well, one day in the late 1980s Amy did find a better way. She had just obtained a new product called a "personal computer." With a little help, she found out how to extract data from the operational systems and various other sources and send it to her PC. By taking a "snapshot" of the operational data she needed every week, Amy soon had a history database of sales data. Amy used these history databases to answer her regional sales analysis questions. She could now create informational reports quickly and easily. Amy no longer had to wait for IT to create reports for her analysis and decision support.

Amy had discovered a new way to structure data to make it useful for analysis and planning. By creating an "informational data" environment on her PC, she could report and analyze data, predict trends, and quickly adjust her forecasts to adapt to changes in the business. Although Amy didn't know it, she was performing on-line analytical processing (OLAP, discussed in Chapter 3). The informational data helped increase her forecast accuracy, improve her productivity, and access the correct data to support her decisions. Amy became very effective in her job by using two types of data:

1. Operational data for day-to-day work.
2. Informational data to analyze and report on situations for future planning and support data to back up her decisions.

Amy soon shared her method of extracting data from various sources, combining, and reformatting it to her PC databases for informational analysis and reporting with Alex. Alex set up a similar process for his finance and accounting data. By synchronizing the time of their extracts from the operational systems, Amy and Alex obtained snapshots of data with the same timestamp. Now Amy and Alex could share their data and perform even broader analysis and comparisons. These two pioneers had discovered the benefits of data sharing for increased productivity. Amy and Alex were ahead of their time in obtaining and using informational data for analysis, planning, and decision support.

REMEMBER

In the 1980s, it was found that two types of data were needed: operational data for day-to-day work and informational data for analysis, planning, and decision making support.

How Do You Choose the Right Action?

Making up your mind is a hard thing to do,

Especially when it may be all wrong for you

Tossing this way and that, should you stay out, should you go in?

Just what should you risk, to make sure you win?

　　　　　　　　　　　　　GERTRUDE LAYTON

Savvy people have found that making the right assessment and taking action can be a challenge fraught with risks. They needed to have the necessary facts and figures to evaluate outcomes and make decisions on which option to select. Operational systems contained data that changed often with no record of the prior values of data. Operational data were not well suited for analysis, comparisons, and decision making support.

The time was ripe for a new type of system, an "informational data" system. This system would be separate from the overloaded operational systems and would utilize data from various sources. These data would be combined and integrated into informational data. People like Andrew in Figure 2-3 would use these systems of data for analysis, planning, and decision making support. Hence, they came to be called decision support systems (DSSs).

DSS contained characteristics that were very different from operational systems. I'll define some of these characteristics with an example. In the mid-

Figure 2-3 Take the right action.

to late 1980s, I designed an informational data application called the Parts
Ad-hoc Reports System (PARS). PARS utilized a relational database technology
that allowed on-line access to the data using a query capability. Some of the
characteristics of PARS were:

- Operational data were copied and saved to a new medium at regular time
  intervals (in PARS, data were copied daily).
- PARS included a timestamp showing the date and time the data were
  last saved.
- No changes to the PARS data were allowed; the data could only be ac-
  cessed. Each day a brand new copy of the data was saved.
- The PARS data consisted of data from multiple operational databases.
  These operational databases were the source systems to PARS.
- Queries (discussed in Chapter 8) could be submitted against the PARS.
  These queries could be submitted from a terminal or PC by multiple
  analysts. The answers to these queries were displayed on the terminal or
  PC screen as a report.
- Common queries were saved and shared by many business clients in the
  department.
- The answers to the queries assisted business clients when making deci-
  sions in their daily work and in analysis of the data.

PARS was a big success with the business clients. They enjoyed the ability to submit queries and obtain answers so quickly and easily. They no longer had the long turnaround time for report requests from IT. In addition, PARS provided a single location for their data; they no longer had to go searching through multiple operational reports, file cabinets, and spreadsheets. They were able to get data in minutes whereas previously they had to spend hours if not days gathering the data they needed. This time was more productively spent in analysis, comparisons, and gaining better understanding of the data. These business clients were soon clamoring for expanding PARS to further applications and capabilities.

Recall Amy's PC system of informational data? Amy's system was similar to PARS in that informational data were captured for analysis activity and decision support. Both PARS and Amy's PC system were predecessors to full blown DSS. As computing capabilities grew, DSS matured and evolved into sophisticated environments, providing cross-organizational views to informational data that enabled enterprise-wide strategic decision support. A broader term was needed to encompass the many products and processes for any activity dealing with accessing, analyzing, and synthesizing information. This term came to be "business intelligence." Data warehouses, data marts, and DSS all fall under the umbrella of business intelligence.

REMEMBER

DSSs contain informational data for analysis, planning, and decision support. DSSs and data warehouses fall under the umbrella of business intelligence.

What's a Data Mart?

Rub-a-dub-dub

Three persons* in a tub,

And how do you think they got there?

The butcher, the baker, the candlestick maker—

They all jumped out of a rotten potato!

'T'was enough to make a fish stare.

---

*Revised from "Three Men in a Tub."

Many organizations are made up of various functional groups or departments, where each department has an area of focus. The departmental function usually becomes the name of the group (e.g., finance, sales, human resources, inventory, and parts). Operational systems are often built around these departments. In the nursery rhyme about the butcher, the baker, and the candlestick maker (depicted in Figure 2-4), there is little in common with these three functions as they each tend to focus on their own products. Similarly, there may be little or no interaction and data sharing between departments of an organization. They function as independent units with imaginary walls around them. As we shall see, this departmental focus makes it easy for data marts to come about, but first let's look at some definitions.

A data mart can be considered a type of data warehouse built for a defined set of functions. Thus, there are two types of data warehouses, a data mart and an EDW.

You will find that people will call an EDW a data warehouse and a data mart a data warehouse. Both names are correct; hence, the name does not matter. The key point to emphasize is that a data mart differs from an EDW in its focus and purpose. The question to be asked is, "What's the business need?" If the business need is for cross-functional use with shared organizational data, then an EDW is the answer. If the business need is solely for departmental use with clients requiring specific functionality, then a data mart is

Figure 2-4 Various departments have different areas of focus.

the answer. Further comparisons between an EDW and a data mart appear later in this chapter, but for now all you need to remember is that a data mart is a type of data warehouse built for a particular purpose.

In Chapter 1, I also made the analogy of a data warehouse being like a memory, with a storage and retrieval system for data. Your own personal memory has the ability to retain past experiences, facts, and figures and recall these items with ease (most of the time). This memory can also sort and structure hundreds of subject areas or categories. Some of these categories could be family, sports, work, or hobbies. Every decision you make is based on a combination of one or more of these categories. In other words, your entire memory is a simplified EDW in that it's able to support multiple functions and subjects. Your focus can switch from subject area to subject area such as butcher, or baker, or candlestick maker; make queries; and obtain answers.

Let's apply this analogy to a data mart. What if you had to plan a huge event, like your Dad's 80th birthday party? This big event would be the family reunion of the century! To focus, you take every piece of datum on family, caterers, photographers, banquet halls, past reunions, etc. in your memory and move it out into a submemory called Pops80. You use Pops80 to make all the decisions about the birthday party. Basically, Pops80 is a simplified data mart!

To keep matters straight, we need a definition. So if you consider your entire memory as a simplified data warehouse, we've already defined a data warehouse as:

> "... a set of computer databases specifically designed with related, historical blissful data that assist in formulating decisions and taking action."

Keeping the purpose of Pops80 in mind, the definition of a data mart could be:

> "A data mart is a type of data warehouse with data specifically designed for a defined set of functions."

 R*EMEMBER*

There are two types of data warehouses: data marts and EDWs.

Definitions:

- "A data mart is a type of data warehouse with data specifically designed for a defined set of functions."
- "An enterprise data warehouse is a set of computer databases specifically designed with related and historical blissful data that assists in formulating decisions and taking action."

Will It Be Done by Half Past Eight?

> *Cobbler, cobbler, mend my shoe.*
> *Get it done by half past two.*
> *Half past two is much too late!*
> *Get it done by half past eight.*
> *Stitch it up, and stitch it down,*
> *And I'll give you a half a crown.*

Data marts appeared on the scene in the mid-1990s. This was about the same time that the first blush of attraction with data warehouses had worn off. Although many companies had had phenomenal success with data warehouses, other organizations found that an EDW took too long to create and was too expensive to achieve. Many people thought the data mart was the better solution. To them, data marts were cheaper and quicker to implement and use. Just like the cobbler in Figure 2-5, who had to work under time constraints to produce results, they saw the data mart as a quick solution to their informational data needs.

I'll go back to the example of Amy and Alex to explain how data marts come about and the problems they could cause.

Amy and Alex had created crude informational systems on their PCs. But, although their PC informational systems worked well they were often constricted by the size of their databases. Amy found that she could keep only 2

Figure 2-5 People often work under time constraints.

months of weekly data on her PC. She longed to perform analysis over longer spans of time. One day, Amy was interviewed by Tom from IT. Tom told her that IT was building an EDW and he needed to know the types of data and information requirements utilized by Amy's functional area. Amy was thrilled to hear such news and looked forward to the day the EDW would be available. She heard that this "magical" warehouse would store 10 years of historic data and be the solution to all her informational data needs.

However, 6 months went by, and then a year. Tom was always busy when Amy tried to contact him. She heard that the IT team was wrestling with something called "dirty data" problems. Amy continued with her daily work, patiently waiting to see this warehouse soon.

One day Amy bumped into her friend, Tessa. Tessa told Amy about a wonderful solution her group had obtained. This solution was a data mart! Tessa explained that a data mart was like a small data warehouse. She told Amy that her management had given up waiting for IT to create the EDW and gone out on their own to get a consulting firm set to up their data mart. It had taken a little more than 6 months. Amy was intrigued. This data mart sounded like the better solution. Perhaps she should be talking to the consulting firm, too.

As Amy found out more about Tessa's data mart she became more convinced it was the right solution. She learned that Tessa's data mart existed separately from the operational systems. Therefore, the analysis of data could be performed without impacting the operational systems. She also found out that there are two types of data marts:

1. Dependent data marts that get source data from an EDW.
2. Independent data marts that get source data from operational systems and/or other external media.

Tessa's department's data mart was an independent data mart. Because the EDW was not available, the independent data mart appeared the way to go. Amy went to her boss with the proposal of a data mart creation for her department and upon approval and funding began discussing requirements with the consultants.

 REMEMBER
There are two types of data marts: dependent and independent.

What Frightened Miss Muffet?

Little Miss Muffet
Sat on a tuffet

Eating her curds and whey;
Along came a spider,
Who sat down besides her
And frightened Miss Muffet away!

Spiders like Charlotte in the children's book "Charlotte's Web" are great artists. In this book Charlotte spells out phrases on her web about a pig named Wilbur and saves him from a trip to the bacon factory.[32] Although I've never found any words spelled out in spider webs, I am amazed at the intricate works of art spiders can create. But no one likes spider webs in a data warehousing environment. Just as Miss Muffet in Figure 2-6 was frightened by a spider, spider webs in data marts are scary. They cause a sticky mess. Let me explain what I mean by spider webs, how they come about, and the trouble they can cause.

Tessa was advocating an independent data mart, which was a good solution for her departmental requirements. The data were extracted from the operational applications and the data mart was designed to solve a focused set

Figure 2-6 Spiders can be scary.

of functions for Tessa's organization. It worked independently from an EDW or any other data mart.

Independent data marts are a temptation. Suppose Chuck (from the beginning of this chapter), Amy, Alex, and Tessa all work in different functional groups of the same corporation. Once Chuck, Amy, and Alex see the ease and time savings with which Tessa obtains information for analysis and decision support, they too will clamor for similar capabilities for their own functional groups. Who can blame them? I, too, would be ready to jump on any shortcut that had all the correct, well-synchronized data residing in one place, making it easy to access and evaluate. They all needed data marts of blissful data. The data marts would be significant value in getting the right answers for their specific sets of questions, thus helping them in their departmental analysis, decision making, and planning.

Suppose Chuck, Amy, and Alex all get independent data marts created for their groups. Now there are four data marts that must be loaded with data from source systems every night. What do you think will occur? Recall that source data often come from operational systems. The source data for each of the independent data marts overlap often and must be extracted from the same operational databases. Therefore, the finance, sales, human resources, inventory, and parts databases are accessed one or more times per night to extract data for the data marts. Figure 2-7 is used to illustrate this nightly process. Extraction of data is indicated by the arrows in Figure 2-7. The crossing and interlacing of these arrows soon begin to look like an intricately tangled spider web.

Let's take a look behind the scenes: Multiple independent data marts create an environment that is difficult to manage and hard to maintain. Some problems encountered are:

- The source data are accessed multiple times, wasting time and resources.
- Any errors in the source data are replicated in the data mart/s.
- Different interpretations of data values could occur.
- The source data are being copied at different times. Because operational applications are consistently changing data values, nonmatching values in the data marts will come about.
- Because the data marts are independent, they will contain business rules (see Chapter 5) that neither match each other nor conform to the goals of the enterprise.
- There will be no single source of information. Stovepipe (discussed in Chapter 3) operational applications are being recreated into stovepipe data marts.
- Sharing of knowledge, information, or metadata (defined in Chapter 5) across data marts does not exist.

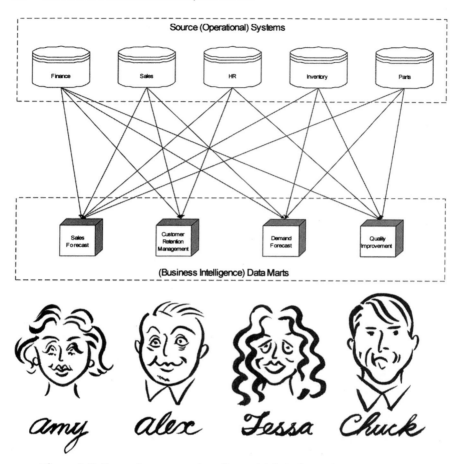

Figure 2-7 Extracting source data for multiple independent data marts.

- A design or physical change in an operational application will propagate multiple data mart changes.

As you can see, independent data marts result in wasted resources, duplicate efforts, misinterpretation of data, and replication of errors. There is little or no sharing of data, knowledge, or resources. The result will be functional operational systems duplicated onto the platform of a data mart. Without standardization or common practices, multiple versions of the "truth" will exist. How will you know which version is right? Dozens of hours will be spent to attempt to untangle the errors that come about. Beware of spider webs. Multiple independent data marts may looks like a quick solution, but they will cause long-term problems.

R*EMEMBER*

Independent data marts offer a quick solution to departmental needs. However, multiple independent data marts in an organization can cause long-term problems with no easy solution.

How Do You Prevent Spider Webs?

Independent data marts can and do provide significant value to many organizations. The crevasse occurs when multiple independent data marts are created where little or no data sharing or communication occurs. Unfortunately, many organizations have the misconception that multiple independent data marts can one day (when they have the time) be integrated to form an EDW. That day will never come (see Truth of Myth in Chapter 3). But there is a method to prevent spider webs . . . and still provide the functionality and speed of data marts.

Suppose there is a central group responsible for planning and organizing the data warehouse environment for the organization. This central group works with all the departments in the organization; it obtains the source data requirements, integrates the data, and loads it into a consolidated storage medium or EDW. Notice that this central group doesn't have to work with all the business units at the same time and build the entire EDW all at once. No, this central group works with a key functional area first, so the EDW first contains a small set of subject areas. As their knowledge, expertise, and experience grow, the EDW is expanded with additional subject areas. As the EDW expands additional dependent data marts are built. This central group continues to work with the departments in the organization to set up dependent data marts, eventually reaching the goal depicted in Figure 2-8.

Consider an environment with an EDW and several dependent data marts, as in Figure 2-8. Figure 2-8 no longer contains the "spider web" depicted by the tangle of arrows in Figure 2-7. This environment is much easier to manage and fewer problems are encountered. Some of the advantages of this environment are:

- Source data are accessed once.
- An error in the source data needs to be fixed only once.
- Because data are accessed and interpreted once, interpretations are consistent.
- Only a single set of business rules exist and the rules conform to the goals of the enterprise.
- The enterprise data warehouse provides a single source of information; there are no more conflicting and inconsistent values.
- Knowledge and information are shared.

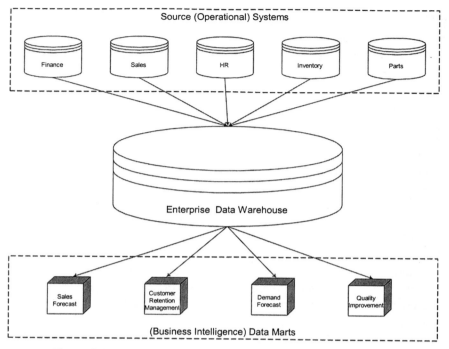

Figure 2-8 Enterprise (common view) data warehouse approach.

- A design or physical change in an operational application will incur a single change to the EDW.

In summary, the advantages of an environment with an EDW with dependent data marts are that source data are only accessed once, errors are more easily fixed, business rules and data are consistent, and there is sharing of knowledge and information. This environment enables a single version of the "truth."

REMEMBER

Utilizing a single central group for control and consistency to create an EDW with dependent data marts brings about an environment of sharing with a single version of the "truth."

To Data Mart or Not to Data Mart?

I wish there were a set of hard and fast rules to say, "This is when you should build a data mart. . . . and this is when you shouldn't build a data mart." But, there are no such rules.

■ TABLE 2-1 ■ **A Comparison of Data Marts versus an Enterprise Data Warehouse**

Data Mart (DM)	Enterprise Data Warehouse (EDW)
1. Defined set of functions – solves a specific set of departmental/ industry problems	1. Multifunction use – solves a multitude of problems (enterprise wide)
2. Departmental clients	2. Enterprise-wide clients
3. Mostly tactical decision support	3. Strategic and tactical decision support
4. Typically smaller volumes of data within the context of the enterprise	4. Large volumes of data
5. Some data can be detailed, most data summarized.	5. Data at highly detailed levels
6. Queries are usually repetitive.	6. Queries may be one of a kind (ad hoc).
7. Response times on most queries take just minutes or seconds.	7. Response times on some queries could take hours.
8. Data typically organized and catered for the department, enabling speedy access	8. Data typically organized to reflect the business rules of the enterprise

Quick solution independent data marts are a temptation! In a society pressed for time, we are all like Tessa, advocating solutions that can be delivered in 6 months. But first the purpose and focus of the data warehouse must be determined If it is to solve a defined set of functions then perhaps all you need is a data mart. Just like my hypothetical example of the memory subset data mart called Pops80, if the focus is to plan a bang-up reunion for my father's 80th birthday party then all I would need is a subset of my entire memory.

The main differences between a data mart and an EDW are summarized in Table 2-1. These differences are provided as guidelines to help you determine when a data mart may be the right solution for you.

1. Defined set of functions versus multifunction use – What business needs are to be solved? As an example, a data mart would focus on a departmental need to create a monthly parts demand forecast, while an EDW would provide answers to dozens of business divisions who have forecasting, planning, marketing, and a variety of other business intelligence needs.

2. Departmental clients versus enterprise-wide clients – Who are the clients of the data warehouse and how many are there? A data mart would have a specific number of clients who either belong to the same department or perform similar functions. An EDW provides varied information to be used by a multitude of groups performing vastly different functions.

3. Tactical versus strategic decision support – What business needs are to be solved? Wait – that was the first question above. It is so important it bears repeating. The information in a data mart is usually constrained to help clients with their short-term, tactical decisions. Using the example of the monthly parts demand forecast data mart, an analyst uses the same query every month to decide how many air conditioners should be ordered for a certain vehicle model, region, and month of the year. With the EDW for the dozens of business divisions, the queries are constrained only by the creativity and knowledge of the clients. As the clients become smarter and their knowledge increases they jump to more creative queries that expand the horizons and profits of the business. The results of queries could bring about new strategies not even dreamed of today.

4. Smaller versus larger volumes of data – What subject areas does the data warehouse address? A data mart targets a small number of subject areas to perform a defined set of functions, whereas an EDW contains a wide number of subject areas. The data mart would then only contain a subset of data that may be in an EDW.

5. Summarized data versus highly detailed levels of information – How will the data in the data warehouse be utilized? A data mart performs a set of discrete business functions, for example, creating a monthly parts demand forecast. The parts ordering data are captured daily and for the data mart summarized to the monthly level. The EDW for the parts forecasting subject area must keep data at the lowest level of detail (i.e., daily) for a rich history for planning and analysis.

6. Repetitive queries versus ad hoc queries – What types of analysis will clients be performing against the data warehouse? A data mart performs a set of discrete known business functions. The clients submit the same queries against the data mart every month. The EDW for parts forecasting is used for complex analysis that may shed light on surprising information and unexpected relationships.

7. Response times on queries may be seconds/minutes versus hours – What performance requirements do clients have for the data warehouse? The data in the data mart have been designed and optimized for a predefined set of functions, resulting in speed and access flexibility. The high-volume, high-detail, and ad hoc nature of analysis against an EDW all lead to slower response times for queries.

8. Data organized for speed versus data organized for business strategy – What types of data in the data warehouse will the clients want to see together? In a data mart, the data that is often accessed together are designed to coexist together, known as denormalization. This enhances access speed. On the other hand, the data in an EDW are organized to reflect the business rules of the organization. A business rule is in general a statement that defines or constrains some aspect of the business. An EDW could reveal relationships between data previously unknown (usually called unknown unknowns).

REMEMBER

Some guidelines for recognizing a data mart are:

- A data mart focuses on a defined set of functions.
- A data mart usually has a limited number of clients who perform similar functions.
- A data mart supports tactical decision making.
- A data mart typically contains a smaller volume of data within the context of the enterprise.
- A data mart may contain summarized data.
- Repetitive queries are often used with a data mart.
- Response times on queries from data marts are usually seconds/minutes.
- Data in data marts are typically organized for access speed.

REMEMBER THIS!

✔ Organizations obtain large amounts of data from their day-to-day operations. These data grow quickly in volume and can double year after year.

✔ In the 1980s, it was found that two types of data were needed; operational data for day-to-day work and informational data for analysis, planning, and decision making support.

✔ DSSs contain informational data for analysis, planning, and decision support. DSSs and data warehouses fall under the umbrella of business intelligence.

✔ There are two types of data warehouses: data marts and EDWs.

Definitions:
- "A data mart is a type of data warehouse with data specifically designed for a defined set of functions."
- "An enterprise data warehouse is a set of computer databases specifically designed with related and historical blissful data that assist in formulating decisions and taking action."

✔ There are two types of data marts: dependent and independent.

✔ Independent data marts offer a quick solution to departmental needs. However, multiple independent data marts in an organization can cause long-term problems with no easy solution.

✔ Utilizing a single central group for control and consistency to create an EDW with dependent data marts brings about an environment of sharing with a single version of the "truth."

✔ Some guidelines for recognizing a data mart are:

- A data mart focuses on a defined set of functions.
- A data mart usually has a limited number of clients who perform similar functions.
- A data mart supports tactical decision making.
- A data mart typically contains a smaller volume of data within the context of the enterprise.
- A data mart may contain summarized data.
- Repetitive queries are often used with a data mart.
- Response times on queries from data marts are usually seconds/ minutes.
- Data in data marts are typically organized for access speed.

CHAPTER 3

Myths and Misconceptions

What Should You Eradicate?

AXIOM 3

Once you get rid of "unrealistic expectations," you'll get more "unrealistic expectations."

Have you ever had someone yell at you for making changes? I have. One occasion that stands out happened a few years ago. I had worked on a large computer application for the allocation and distribution of certain stock keeping units (SKUs). With the successful implementation of the project, the project team was jubilant. But, a week or two after implementation as I was visiting a client site, a business analyst approached me and demanded in a loud voice, "Why did you change the allocation method? It was working fine before. Why couldn't you have left it alone?"

It was easy to see that this analyst, Peter, was the type of person who says, "If it ain't broke, don't fix it." Such an attitude stems from the reluctance to face change. The "fear of change," along with the "fear of public speaking" and the "fear of dying," are the three great human fears. I understood that Peter was afraid these new changes would affect his job function. He felt threatened by the fact that he was being pushed out of his comfort zone—or worse, he feared he could be pushed out of his job. Peter hadn't been involved on the project and he felt blind sighted when all his familiar processes were replaced by new methods without much warning. When viewed from his perspective, Peter's fears were reasonable and should have been foreseen.

Data warehouses require significant change. They involve changes in technology with new products and tools, many changes in industry processes, and even changes in traditional structures and methods. The traditional method of IT creating an application and deploying it to businesspeople to use it no longer works. A data warehouse built in a vacuum with little input or involvement from the business clients will stand lonely and unused. Business clients must be involved from the very beginning. Data warehouse endeavors must always be a joint effort between the business and IT.

For change to take place successfully, every stakeholder, from business client to the CEO, of an organization must have a clear vision of the goal, see the benefits of reaching the goal, and have their expectations met and managed. Successful organizations know that business clients who are involved and educated from the start have a greater commitment and buy-in to see the endeavor to successful completion.

One of the first steps in managing expectations is to get rid of notions that may already exist. Finding out the underlying reasons for resistance to change is not easy. Let's see how it can and has been done.

Do You Resist Change?

Like Peter, we've all resisted change. With a data warehouse, there will be lots of change. Many people will not want to change their familiar methods and there will be

> *"The more important your cheese is to you the more you want to hold onto it."*[9]

power struggles and resistance. Resistance will be expressed in the form of excuses. Some excuses you may hear are:

1. I don't have the time.
2. Our data are sensitive so we can't share it.
3. Our VP does not believe in data warehousing.

4. We've always done things this way.

5. Our people are already trained in our way of doing things.

6. We don't need to see Accounting's data; we keep our own records.

7. We're understaffed and don't have anyone to put on this project.

8. Our data must stay this way; there is no way we can change.

How do you overcome this resistance to change? According to Kotter,[10] to implement change, there must first be a vision, then there must be people who have a strong belief in being able to achieve the vision to help implement this vision, and finally people must be given some motivation to change. Therefore, to implement successfully the changes a data warehouse brings there must be three prime factors:

1. The vision of a data warehouse – Educate all stakeholders of how and what problems the data warehouse will solve. Demonstrate real-life examples of the benefits and advantages realized by similar organizations. There must be constant reinforcement of the value a data warehouse brings to the organization.

2. The right sponsors – Obtain change agents to help share the vision and level set expectations. These change agents must also extricate underlying fears, misconceptions, myths, and fallacies surrounding data warehouses. Once these barriers are understood, the change agents can work to overcome each one.

3. People motivated to change – There must be the right incentives for people to want the change of a data warehouse. With frequent feedback, rewards, and milestones celebrated, people begin to taste success. As their fears are eradicated they will come to accept or even embrace change.

 REMEMBER

People resist change. To overcome resistance to change brought about by a data warehouse, people must first be educated about the benefits of a warehouse, their fears eradicated, and incentives to change must be provided.

Who'll Choose the Direction?

The harder you throw, the faster the ball,

The higher it flys the greater the fall

So make sure you know . . . when making your throw . . .

In which direction it should go!

GERTRUDE LAYTON

Figure 3-1 Change agents lead the way.

Change agents are leaders who make change happen. They are people who believe in their own ability to attain the goals as well as motivating others to stretch themselves and reach to attain the goals. Thus, not only do they embrace change, but they help others overcome their resistance to change. As depicted in Figure 3-1, a change agent points people in the direction of the change. Change agents exist at all levels. A data warehouse needs both business and IT change agents to assist in sharing the vision, leading the way, and motivating others to change. The more change agents who exist within the stakeholders of a data warehouse endeavor, the better the chances for success.

I've mentioned stakeholders a couple times. Who or what are the stakeholders? Stakeholders are anyone or any group impacted by an endeavor. The impact could be positive or negative. Business client stakeholders are the final word on the success or failure of the endeavor; therefore, their expectations must be managed well.

Keep in mind that a data warehouse endeavor impacts a lot of people in the organization. It could have hundreds—perhaps thousands—of stakeholders. The trick is to identify key stakeholders, find the change agents within these stakeholders, and use these stakeholder change agents to spread the word, advertise the benefits, address concerns, and set expectations throughout the organization. Let's identify the key stakeholders for a data warehouse:

1. Industry/business clients – The primary people who will use the data warehouse. You have the final word on the success of the data warehouse. The more you use the data warehouse, the more you can achieve. Once you understand the possibilities, responsibilities, and challenges in your hands you can reach a potential greater than you ever imagined.

2. Executives and managers – The organization's leaders. You are the champions of the data warehouse. Without your support, the data warehouse won't fly. As leaders and visionaries you need to know and understand all the tools and techniques available to you. Two main stakeholders here are the executive sponsor and the project sponsor.

3. Information technology (IT) staff – The team who will deliver and support the data warehouse. You are the lifeblood of the data warehouse. Without your technical expertise the data warehouse will not perform and will die a quick death.

4. The project manager and the core project team – The team that consists of both business and IT members. You are the lifeforce driving the data warehouse. Deliver milestones every 30 to 45 days to keep the interest and involvement of the business units. Use these occasions to recognize and celebrate successes of the project team.

These people are the right sponsors to make the data warehouse a reality. It becomes imperative to find effective stakeholder change agents to drive the change every successful data warehouse requires.

Another factor in implementing change is to provide the right incentives for people to change. People always want to know what they stand to gain from making a change. WIIFM (pronounced "whiff-em") stands for What's In It For Me and is discussed in Chapter 6. People want to know their WIIFM. Once they know what the incentives are, they decide whether to make the change or resist it. People like to make up their own minds. Therefore, it becomes imperative that the right incentives for people to make the change toward a data warehouse are provided. This brings to mind a joke about a psychiatrist. (This joke is so bad that it sticks in my mind.) How many psychiatrists does it take to change a light bulb? Answer: Just one, but the light bulb must really want to change.

Organizations that are ready for a data warehouse must really want to change. At some organizations, the level of "pain" of getting the right information is so high that the despairing business clients are ready for anything. They feel that anything, ANYTHING, must be better that what they have now. Be wary of such

> *"When you get sick and tired of being sick and tired you'll change."*[11, p 137]

conditions! These organizations may be so desperate they'll jump to any short-sighted solution that will cause long-term problems. Instead of taking baby steps for success, they'll try to run and fail dismally in their haste. Keep in mind that a clear business need must exist for a data warehouse to succeed. Only when the organization is ready to change with well planned business objectives will the data warehouse be a successful business solution.

REMEMBER

Stakeholders are people or groups who may be positively or negatively impacted by an endeavor. Key stakeholders for data warehouse success are business clients, executives and managers, and IT staff.

One Line to Pay (OLTP)?

Actually, change is like time; it keeps on occurring. The means of handling data have undergone significant changes over the decades. One such method is common in operational systems. It is called on-line transactional processing (OLTP). OLTP involves making updates to data, such as adding, changing, or deleting one or more pieces of data.

Do you find yourself standing in line often? All too frequently, there seems to be only one line to pay or make some transaction. We make numerous transactions in our daily lives, buying our lunches with our credit cards or getting cash at the ATM. In today's electronic age, we use OLTP so often it's a common daily occurrence. Remembering OLTP as One Line to Pay makes this acronym easy to recall.

We already talked about operational systems in Chapter 2. An operational system is any manual or automated process that supports the day-to-day work of the business. It's easy to see that operational systems are critical for the organization to function. This is quite logical as organizations make their money from their daily operations, i.e., "the show must go on." If any part of the show or system breaks down, it brings day-to-day operations to a grinding halt. Organizations lose customers when they cannot handle their daily operations. Let me illustrate this with a simple example.

Suppose you need some cash but forgot your ATM card; this means you have to go to your bank branch on your lunch hour. You rush to get there, only to see a long line waiting for a single bank representative at an open window. You sigh and get in line, somewhat like the one depicted in Figure 3-2. After waiting patiently, your turn finally arrives. The bank's computer system breaks down just as you begin to cash your withdrawal check. The bank is unable to complete the transaction and you leave in disgust. If that happens too often, you'll soon switch banks. How many customers can the bank afford to

Figure 3-2 On-line transaction processing.

lose before it has to shut down? For an organization to keep its customers, operational systems must work smoothly and consistently.

Operational systems are built around functional applications such as banking, airline reservations, sales, and finance. The data that feed these applications are usually transactional in nature. For example, suppose you visit a car dealership and buy your 16-year-old son Brandon a new luxury car. Next you go to your bank and take out a loan. Finally, you call your insurance company and have heart failure when you find out how much more your insurance premiums will cost with the addition of a new car and a male teen driver.

In a single day you have completed three transactions (maybe four if you also had to check into your medical center).

Each of these three transactions can be handled in one of two ways. For example, at the bank you would have had to fill out an application. The loan processor then either told you that an approval would take a couple of days or approved you right away. In the first case, the bank is collecting all the transactions for the day and processing them at night; this is called batch transaction processing. The second scenario uses an on-line facility where approvals are obtained right away. This method is known as on-line transaction processing (OLTP).

On-line transaction processing uses a computer process that is part of the operational system. These processes are fine-tuned to give responses in seconds or subseconds.

REMEMBER

OLTP stands for on-line transaction processing. This is a method for conducting business by processing transactions against operational systems right away.

A Pig or a Hog?

> To market, to market, to buy a fat pig.
> Home again, home again, jiggety jig.
> To market, to market, to buy a fat hog.
> Home again, home again, jiggety jog.
> To market, to market, to buy a plum bun.
> Home again, home again, market is done.

As a child, I never knew the difference between a pig and a hog. A quick look in my dictionary tells me that both pigs and hogs are mammals of the *Suidae* family. Just like there are two types of mammals in the suidae family, there are two types of data, operational and informational. While both of these are "data," they're really quite different and used for totally different purposes. Let's examine each in more detail.

In the previous section, you experienced a busy (and expensive) day buying a car, getting a loan, and changing your insurance. But, look behind the scenes and you will see that your three transactions triggered a flurry of activity and a variety of applications at the car dealership, bank, and insurance company as well. Each transaction carried with it some new or changed data. Operational data were changed at the point-of-sale as well as the inventory, accounting, sales, loan, billing, and insurance databases. Therefore, operational data have these key characteristics:

- Undergo frequent change.
- Contain values that are up-to-date just at this point in time.
- Belong to a certain functional application.

In addition to all the data changes that took place, new data were also being created. For example, customer relationship data such as your age, gender, the members in your household, other cars in the household, as well as demographic data such as the city and region of the dealership are captured. These data eventually become source data to an informational data system. Thus operational systems produce large amounts of operational data.

 REMEMBER
Day-to-day operations create lots of operational data that are frequently updated.

Other Lines Available-Purposefully (OLAP)?

Although there often are vast amounts of operational data produced daily, business clients like Amy (from Chapter 2) have found that these operational data are not well suited for analysis and comparisons of historical results. Amy started saving copies or snapshots of the operational data on her PC for analysis. Without realizing it, she had designed an on-line analytical processing system (OLAP). By making copies of operational data and formatting the data for her particular business function, she found **O**ther **L**ines **A**vailable-**P**urposefully. That is, Amy no longer had to wait for IT and could create informational reports herself for her departmental purpose. By analyzing the informational data in these reports she found the right facts to help her make decisions for her particular business functions.

Amy had found the value of "informational data": the right data at the right time to help make the right decisions. Informational data have these key characteristics:

- Once loaded, updates to the data are not allowed.
- Were accurate at a certain time in the past.*
- Organized by subject area.*
- Consistent* and integrated.*

---

*See Chapter 8 for additional information.

Although operational data and informational data are both data, they have different characteristics and are used for very different purposes. Operational data are used in day-to-day operations while informational data are used for analysis and decision support. Informational data became the basis for decision support systems (that were introduced in Chapter 2). OLAP became the primary access and reporting tool for DSS. OLAP is a common activity when using DSS and data warehouses.

Hold it! Where do blissful data fit in? Blissful data consist of information that is accurate, meaningful, useful, and accessible to many people of an organization for their decision making purposes. This definition points to all informational data being blissful data. But this is not necessarily correct. Blissful data are data that have been transcended to a higher level of precision for the many people that access it. This level is reached through a transformation and cleansing process discussed in Chapter 4.

Remember

OLAP stands for on-line analytic processing. Informational data are the right data at the right time to help make the right decisions. Blissful data are informational data that have been transcended to a higher level of precision for the many people that access it.

What Myths Should You Eradicate?

Like the age-old myths of mermaids and sea serpents, myths and misconceptions are rampant in data warehousing. This is due to the political nature of a data warehouse. Organizations that have had a data warehouse failure dislike talking about their failure, and organizations that have succeeded don't want to give away their secrets and endanger their business advantage. Thus failures and successes are rarely discussed leading to assumptions and guesswork. Misinterpretation and misinformation cause misconceptions to come about that could cause your data warehouse endeavor to fail. Just like sailors had to watch out for the mythical sea serpent in Figure 3-3, be wary of the dangers misconceptions can pose.

Recall the problems encountered by having multiple independent data marts in a single organization in Chapter 2? This is a pitfall many organizations fall into. If 3, or 4, or 10 functional groups of an organization created their own independent data marts, there would soon be an abundance of data marts duplicating the same data over and over. This sounds like the operational systems where each functional group had its own databases. Soon there would be as many disparate data marts as there were operational systems in the organization. If each of these data marts contained customer data, there would soon be numerous copies of customer data in the data

Figure 3-3 Myths are common in data warehousing.

marts. Which customer data would be correct? It would be impossible to tell.

Does this sound familiar? Recall that I once came across 16 customer databases in one organization. I didn't know

> "*W*hen we fail to learn a lesson, we get to take it again . . . and again . . . and again!"[22, p 37]

which had the optimum information. Just like 16 databases presented no single version of the truth, 16 data marts will present no single version of the "truth." Independent data marts foster repeating the same mistakes of operational systems. They simple duplicate old problems onto a new platform. Learn from mistakes made in operational systems and avoid making the same mistakes with informational data.

The best way to avoid making costly and embarrassing mistakes is by learning from the blunders of other organizations. Let's look at some common myths and misconceptions that have come about in relation to data warehouses and see which are true and which are false.

Truth or Myth?

A Data Warehouse Can Leverage Tremendous ROI

FACT. Return on investment (ROI) calculations take the ratio of overall benefit or savings to cost to find the value of the investment (ROI is discussed in Chapter 6). The International Data Corporation found that after 3 years average ROI was better than 400% for 45 major companies. Although this statistic is impressive, keep in mind it could be even higher with intangible benefits from a data warehouse. These intangible benefits are difficult to measure, and include such benefits as:

- Enhanced customer relationships.
- Ability to adjust quickly to changing economic climates.
- Improved decision making capabilities at all organizational levels.
- Flexibility to "change" in the industry.
- The cost of not "changing" or being slow to change.
- The value of clean, consistent, colocated data.
- All-around greater levels of satisfaction.
- Increased efficiency and productivity.
- Recognized leadership and prestige in the industry.

Return on investment calculations are often based on tangible profits or cost savings in proportion to the effort or investment. Many intangible benefits are difficult to measure and may or may not be included in the ROI.

A Data Warehouse Is an Architecture

FACT. According to Jill Dyche,[12, p 4] "Any separate hardware platform – be it a mainframe computer or a PC – that enables a businessperson to make a decision can be considered a data warehouse." Now you know that I mean computer architecture rather than building architecture. When I think of a data warehouse, I visualize a big box with lots of smaller, irregularly sized boxes within it and lots of people interacting with one or more of these smaller boxes. Each of the smaller boxes is a subject area (discussed in Chapter 8) and the big box is the entire data warehouse. In my imagination, it could look like the National Jigsaw Puzzle Competition in Chicago, where people gather around tables, frantically fitting jigsaw pieces into place. Sometimes the piece fits; for others they have to try again. Eventually all the pieces are completed and the entire puzzle is finally in place. Recall that the data warehouse is an entire environment and the people and processes who interact with it are an important part of this environment. Just as the jigsaw puzzle had to be built, so too must a data warehouse. A data warehouse is thus indeed an architecture.

However, the fact that a data warehouse is computer architecture causes yet another fallacy—that data warehousing is a technical solution and therefore only an IT department problem. Business client groups or business analysts think they don't have to be involved until the end of the project. They think that once IT creates the data warehouse a training session or two will take place and they'll be able to carry on from there. Unfortunately, it doesn't work that way. Data warehousing is very different from the traditional data processing systems of the 1970s and 1980s. Without the full involvement and support of business clients and key stakeholders from the beginning, the data warehouse endeavor will not catch on and will die a quick death.

A Data Warehouse Is an Ongoing Process

FACT. This is a tough one. There are dangers in calling a data warehouse a process because that implies that it never ends. Many people would not even want to get started without an end in sight. Others would say that ROI can't be calculated because there is no way to determine the eventual cost for an ongoing process. By tradition, such a process would mean a straight line graph showing performance as time marched on. This is NOT what an ongoing process means for a data warehouse. With a successful data warehouse, instead of a straight line graph of continuous improvement as seen in Figure 3-4,

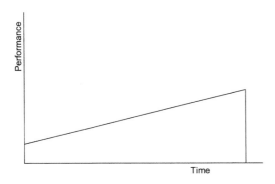

Figure 3-4 Continuous improvement graph.

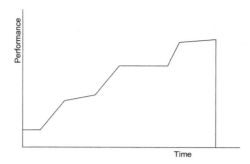

Figure 3-5 Innovation graph.

improvement over time would appear as an innovation graph with many bumps and jumps showing periods of massive improvements followed by periods of slower activity as seen in Figure 3-5. Each of these jumps denotes a significant value increase to the organization. Each big bump or jump is a milestone project with a definite beginning and end. It is imperative that each milestone is well defined with measurable goals and objectives.

A Data Warehouse Is Expensive to Build and Maintain

FACT. During the early days of data warehousing, it was whispered in awe that the average data warehouse costs $3 million to build and 3 years to complete. Even if those averages were correct at that time, they have since changed. Making the customer wait 3 years for an investment of $3 million certainly would be unacceptable. However, data warehouses do require a commitment and could mount up significant costs. Your costs will vary greatly depending on your goals, amount and quality of data, size and location of the warehouse, number of business clients to use the warehouse, as well as skills of the IT developers, processes already in place, and involvement and cooperation of the business units.

But stop! STOP thinking about the "cost" of a data warehouse; instead, think about the "investment" of a data warehouse. Ask "If I had the right information what would it be worth?" Once the costs of a data warehouse are compared to its potential benefits and returns, you'll find it a worthy investment. A data warehouse is not just a new tool or another technology system; it is a total environment with expanded capabilities and opportunities. Simply stated, "Can your organization survive without one?"

A Data Mart Is a Small Data Warehouse

FALLACY. Actually, this is another tough one. A data mart is a type of data warehouse and is typically smaller than that other type of data warehouse, the enterprise data warehouse (EDW). However, I would caution against calling a data mart a small data warehouse because the purpose of a data mart is so different from that of an EDW. A data mart focuses on a specific set of business problems, while an EDW serves as the cross-sectional view of the entire endeavor. At one organization a single data mart may be larger than another endeavor's EDW. It would be as wrong as calling an orange a small pomelo (a citrus fruit like a large grapefruit)!

In addition, what is a "small data warehouse?" Somehow the fallacy grew in the world of data warehousing that "bigger means more information and, therefore, better." I once saw a company proudly declaring that its data warehouse consisted of 40 terabytes (1 terabyte = 1 trillion bytes; see below). Would 40 terabytes be the key factor rather than the number of business problems that are solved? Definitely not.

What's so great about a terabyte? Let's go back to the power of 2. In the beginning there were databases of just $2K^2$ or $2 \times 2K = 4K$ (kilobytes), then 2^3K or $2 \times 2 \times 2K = 8K$, then 64K, and so on. Soon even kilobytes (2 bytes^{10} = 1024 bytes or 1 kilobyte, rounded down to 1000 bytes) weren't enough and megabytes became common (2 bytes^{20} = 1,048,576 or 1000 kilobytes, or 1 million bytes. To remember, think M for mega and M for million). Next came gigabytes (yes, you got it—2 bytes^{30} = [oops, my calculator couldn't count so far] 1000 megabytes, or 1 billion bytes). Giga can only stand for gigantic. In 1999, a 23-terabyte data warehouse appeared, with a terabyte consisting of 1000 gigabytes, or 1 trillion bytes. The next term is a petabyte, which consists of 1000 terabytes. What next? Will we then have a gazabyte from the word gazillion, a term used by kids to denote infinity? Or perhaps an infabyte from the word infinity?

Now that we know something about bytes let's get back to the size of a data mart, for which there are many definitions. Some say a data warehouse of less than 50 gigabytes qualifies as a data mart; others use 100 gigabytes as the upper limit. Yet others combine the number of clients and size to determine a mart versus a warehouse. For example, they may say 20 clients of a 50-gigabyte database make it a mart whereas 40 clients of a 50-gigabyte database defines a warehouse. Actually, neither size nor the number of clients matters! The major determining factor for a data mart is that it contains data to solve a functional focus. A data mart can contain several thousand gigabytes or as little as five gigabytes of data.

A Data Mart Can Be Added to and Can Grow into an Enterprise Data Warehouse

FALLACY. It is easy to think this is true. With the pressures to conserve budget and show results every couple of months, we often want to believe this fallacy is true. Data warehouses are expensive. It is a lot easier to get funding for a data mart this year, get another few hundred thousand next year, and another hundred thousand the year after that. Lots of people will want to start small with a data mart, adding more functionality when further funding becomes available. In fact, by chopping the data mart into small enough pieces the cost of the project will be able to creep beneath the radar. That is, large cost justifications, detailed profit analysis, and signature approval from an army of executives can be avoided.

I've fallen into this trap myself. It's logical to think, "I'll build a data mart first to solve this business-specific requirement, and then add the next business-specific requirement and then the next, until the entire business of the enterprise has been captured." Why shouldn't this work? Isn't building an enterprise data warehouse like building a new international airport for a busy city like Chicago? If you don't have the financial backing to build the vast airport in one go, you start off small, building a terminal and runway for small cargo and private airplanes. This is done in 6 months and everyone is happy. More money comes in so you add on domestic short-segment flights. Then the runway gets too congested and another is built. Next you need arrival and departure gates for the passengers, but your terminal building is not the correct height and you spend a lot of money revamping it. After long delays the airport finally works for regional domestic passenger and cargo flights. Eventually, you get more financial backing and you're ready for the big kahuna, the large international jets and flights. What do you find?

- The runways are not long enough for these large planes to take off and land.
- Wind shear or tunnels from the large planes will cause problems for smaller planes on adjacent runways.
- There is no more land to accommodate the larger terminal building, so another terminal building has to be built on the opposite end of the newly lengthened runway.
- The roads leading into and out of the airport are insufficient for the increased traffic.

- In the case of a major accident or disaster, there is no access for emergency crews to reach the airport due to gridlock on the roads.

I apologize to all of you who build airports. I certainly don't, as you can tell from my fictitious example, but you get the idea. You cannot take a data mart and keep adding to it, expecting to eventually get to an EDW.

Let me throw a spanner (or a wrench—they are the same) into the works. Ready? After giving you my above example, I am going to say that it is possible to start small with a subset of the business data and grow into a data warehouse. How? Do what successful airport builders have done. First come up with the plan for the entire airport, and then build it in stages. If the site for the airport is well chosen and allows for expansion (both in terms of passenger traffic, new equipment, and types of aircraft), then it is possible. Similarly, come up with the plan for your EDW and then build it, one subject area at a time. But, you must keep the end goal in mind and plan accordingly.

Data Marts Can Be Integrated to Form an Enterprise Data Warehouse

FALLACY. If only this were true, the world of data warehousing would be so much simpler. A single department usually drives data marts. By keeping costs low, these departments don't need to go through time-consuming approval and resource allocation processes. They hire outside resources that may use nonstandard or proprietary technologies and set up a data mart in 6 months. After a couple more departments follow suit, problems begin when there is no longer a single version of the truth. Why can't we try to combine these independent data marts into an EDW? Imagine the following scenario:

> A city contracts three independent firms to each build an airport. There are no restrictions other than that costs have to be within the budget and the airport has to be able to handle specified traffic volumes in terms of jets, cargo, and customers.

The results could be an airport that exists on the east side of town handling the domestic passenger and cargo jets. The other two airports are coincidently both on the north side of town but have flight paths that cross.

Yikes! What's the city to do? Each firm thought their airport was a success and demanded to be paid. After all, the airports were completed within the budget and met the specifications for traffic volume for types of jets, cargo, and passengers. The city finally had to hire a consultant to see what pieces of these airports could be salvaged, if anything. Next the replanning, tearing down, rebuilding, and reworking have to begin. At the same time, a lot of time, money, and resources had already been spent. By trying to save money in the beginning, how much more money must now be spent? The city would have been far better off to have planned its needs from the start and controlled the work of the three independent firms.

Just like trying to incorporate three totally different airports into one is extremely difficult to accomplish, the lack of a single vision or overall plan will result in independent data marts that are virtually impossible to integrate.

What Barriers to Change Must You Extricate?

Now that many of the myths and misconceptions about data warehouses have been cleared up, let's take a look at other barriers that surround data warehouse endeavors. As you will see, data warehousing endeavors are again different from traditional endeavors. Matters such as unrealistic expectations, the level of pain currently being experienced by the business units, the level of involvement the business units are willing to commit, and the culture and structure of the organization can place barriers in the path of data warehousing success.

In planning a traditional project, one of the first tasks is to interview stakeholders and find out their data requirements, skills, and knowledge. In data warehousing, it becomes even more important to talk to stakeholders not only to determine their skills and knowledge but also to gain a full picture of their motivation to change. Not only must their informational analysis needs and requirements be extricated but also their EXPECTATIONS. It is important to find out what business clients are expecting from the data warehouse.

I once worked with a business manager named Kathy. Kathy had incredibly unrealistic expectations. Some of them were:

- A data warehouse could be built in 3 months and used by everyone in the organization.
- It could function out of a box (a packaged solution).
- The first iteration of a data warehouse would solve all the organization's problems right away.
- Data quality issues were minor issues and could be frequently bypassed.
- A data warehouse could be completed by the IT department and turned over to the business units overnight.
- A project manager was needed only part time on a data warehouse project.
- The project team could read a book and successfully deploy a data warehouse.

As you can tell, many of these unrealistic expectations are due to missing education about the total package of a data warehouse. People such as Kathy have the misconception that a data warehouse is simply an enormous data-base. They don't realize that a data warehouse is an entire environment of change, integration, enrichment, and flexibility. Beware of people such as Kathy because their lofty expectations can cause endeavors to be viewed as fail-ures, although there is no way even the most talented team could have met the expectations. Unrealistic expectations must be extricated and eradicated con-sistently and continuously for better chances of data warehousing success.

One of the major barriers to change is "time"; people don't have the time to get involved. The level of involvement the business units are willing to com-mit depends on the culture of the organization and the executive sponsor for the data warehouse (both discussed in Chapter 5). A culture of friendliness and helpfulness will contribute to a higher level of involvement from the busi-ness units to the success of the data warehouse.

A key element toward data warehousing success is early involvement of the business units. The business units must partner with IT to make the ware-house happen. One of the best ways to get your industry/business clients in-volved early is to meet with them early and often. The first meeting could be to determine their current information requirements and the level of pain they are experiencing. Because a data warehouse involves many cross-functional groups, this initial meeting or gathering of stakeholders is an important step toward the goal of a successful data warehouse.

As the stakeholders meet, they discover many new or unfamiliar aspects of people and the organization. I call this the discovery stage. During this stage, stakeholders' needs, problems, expectations, requirements, problems, and pain thresholds are extricated. Not only do stakeholders feel involved, but they in turn discover new aspects of the business and develop a better understanding of the overall functioning of the organization. In addition, similarities and differences between their efforts and those of cross-functional groups are un-covered. Last but not least, they gain insights into overall corporate and orga-nizational goals and strategies. The discovery stage is mandatory for data warehousing success. More importantly, the discovery exercise sets the stage and foundations for cross-functional activities, such as:

1. Evaluating data quality. If data are invalid, inaccurate, or redundant, they are considered dirty (Chapter 4). Establish the process to validate and clean data to pave the way for data warehousing success.

2. Clearly defining and reaching agreement on business rules (Chapter 4) and subject areas (Chapter 8).

3. Beginning to keep and continuously update the store of metadata (Chap-ter 4). Metadata are data about each piece of data. They tell the per-

son accessing the data warehouse the meaning of that piece of data, where it comes from, how often it may change, who owns it, and any other pertinent information. Metadata are invaluable for data warehousing success!

Data warehouses require cross-functional groups to work together to assess data quality, integrate business rules, and define metadata. A culture of change, sharing, and respect for others facilitates and speeds the pace of the three cross-functional activities.

Involvement and agreement are keys to data warehouse success.

 REMEMBER

The discovery stage is a preliminary and important step in getting stakeholders involved early. It sets the stage for the cross-functional activities for evaluating data quality and reaching agreement on business rules and metadata.

Are You in a Stovepipe?

Oh, the grand old Duke of York,

He had ten thousand men;

He marched them up to the top of the hill,

And he marched them down again.

And, when they were up they were up;

And when they were down they were down.

But when they were only halfway up,

They were neither up nor down.

In the nursery rhyme about the Duke of York, we don't get a good idea about the organizational structure of his 10,000 men. He could have had 10 generals, each general to lead 999 men in a vertical unit. In that case, they would have looked like 10 long pipes going up and down the hill. Many organizations today are structured in various vertical units to support the different day-to-day operations. Each vertical unit focuses on particular functions and their structure looks like side-by-side stovepipes. Hence, these vertical units have come to be known as stovepipes, while the organization is called a functional or stovepipe organization.

A stovepipe organization has certain advantages. It allows workers to focus on a single piece of the business. It also allows for the day-to-day operations to be partitioned into functional pieces. It also has disadvantages: Stovepipes create a mindset of real or imaginary boundaries that in turn serve to set up barriers between people and resources. Often, there is little trust, communication, and interaction between the stovepipes, generating an "us versus them" mentality.

Because of these disadvantages, stovepipe organizational structure will cause a barrier to the cross-functional involvement and commitment requirement of a successful data warehouse.

REMEMBER

Functional or stovepipe organizations contain vertical units to perform certain functions. The lack of sharing, interaction, and communication between stovepipes can cause a barrier to data warehousing success.

Do Stovepipes Burn?

The functional groups within these stovepipes track their own functions and readily create their own independent data marts. Barriers and boundaries are placed between stovepipes. Beware! These aspects will deter data warehousing success.

Imagine what could happen when people in stovepipes are asked to start working together. They must now perform the cross-functional activities for evaluating data quality, integrating business rules, and defining metadata. Will there be power struggles and resistance? Absolutely! Conflict arises in every endeavor; huge conflicts arise when functional groups try to overcome boundaries and barriers of a stovepipe organization.

Barriers and boundaries created by the vertical nature of stovepipe organizations have burned many companies and contributed to data warehouse failure. Stovepipes can cause many burns, so take care to overcome the problems they can cause. Chapter 4 discusses the issues of dirty data, business rules, and metadata and offers steps for overcoming these barriers.

REMEMBER

Many conflicts arise when functional groups try to overcome boundaries and barriers of a stovepipe organization.

REMEMBER THIS!

✔ People resist change. To overcome resistance to change brought about by a data warehouse, people must first be educated about the benefits of a warehouse, their fears eradicated, and incentives to change must be provided.

✔ Stakeholders are people or groups who may be positively or negatively impacted by an endeavor. Key stakeholders for data warehouse success are business clients, executives and managers, and IT staff.

✔ OLTP stands for on-line transaction processing. This is a method for conducting business by processing transactions against operational systems right away.

✔ Day-to-day operations create lots of operational data that are frequently updated.

✔ OLAP stands for on-line analytic processing. Informational data are the right data at the right time to help make the right decisions. Blissful data are informational data that have been transcended to a higher level of precision for the many people that access it.

✔ A data warehouse can leverage tremendous ROI - FACT.

✔ A data warehouse is an architecture - FACT.

✔ A data warehouse is an ongoing process - FACT.

✔ A data warehouse is expensive to build and maintain - FACT.

✔ A data mart is a small data warehouse - FALLACY.

✔ A data mart can be added to and can grow into an EDW - FALLACY.

✔ Data marts can be integrated to form an enterprise data warehouse - FALLACY.

✔ The discovery stage is a preliminary and important step in getting stakeholders involved. It sets the stage for the cross-functional activities evaluating data quality and reaching agreement on business rules and metadata.

✔ Functional or stovepipe organizations contain vertical units to perform certain functions. The lack of sharing, interaction, and communication between stovepipes can cause a barrier to data warehousing success.

✔ Many conflicts arise when functional groups try to overcome the boundaries and barriers of a stovepipe organization.

CHAPTER 4

What Are Dirty Data?

Where Do Dirty Data Come From?

AXIOM 4

Dirty data are like dirty laundry; every organization has some dirty data.

Have you ever been hit with "dirty" data? I'm pretty sure you have. Although the term may be new, you will probably recognize one or more of the following inconsistencies caused by inaccurate or dirty data. Dirty data are responsible when:

1. You get letters from the bank addressed to Mr. Bobbie Jones although you are a female.
2. Your 8-year-old son receives an invitation to apply for a credit card with a limit higher than yours.

3. You receive duplicate mailers, one addressed to William T. Smith and the other to Bill Smith.
4. Your grandmother gets an invitation to join a kindergarten on her 104th birthday.
5. You receive a traffic ticket in the mail even though you were nowhere near the intersection where the ticket says you ran a red light.

These examples may seem humorous and trivial and for the most part you can ignore them. You may be thinking, "What's the big deal? I can deal with dirty data." But, what if you keep being billed for the traffic ticket? Or, you lose your good driver insurance discount because the company says you have a moving violation ticket on your record? Now, the dirty data become not only irritating but also starts costing you time as you try to sort matters out. Somehow, you'll have to prove that the ticket was sent to you in error to get it off your record.

Let me introduce you to my neighbor Paul, who works at a bank and is very familiar with dirty data. This bank often sends me preapproved credit card invitations and other promotional material in duplicate: one piece of mail addressed to Margaret Chu and a second addressed to Mr. M. Chu.

One day I asked Paul why his bank was wasting money by sending out duplicate mailings and why address me as "Mr.?" Paul apologized, shuffled his feet, and said that the bank's data were incomplete, missing, or just plain wrong. When their data warehouse was built a couple of years back, data from the different functional groups were simply combined and copied into the warehouse. Now the inaccurate and incomplete data had increased a hundredfold. Obviously more than one record existed for me in the warehouse: Along the way, M. Chu had been coded as being "male" and as such I had become Mr. M. Chu. Although my initial, last name, and address matched in both records, the bank and its system had not figured out that Margaret Chu and M. Chu were the same person and hence duplicated mailings.

Paul was embarrassed and uncomfortable talking about these bad data. Asked what the bank was doing to correct these problems, Paul reluctantly admitted that he was the data steward responsible for cleaning up the mess. But, instead of cleaning it up, the mess was bogging him down. He was discouraged by the resistance he encountered at every turn. None of the functional managers would talk to him about their dirty data issues; they all thought it was "someone else's" problem.

Poor Paul had a tough situation on his hands. All he wanted was to be some place far, far away.

What Are Dirty Data?

Let's define dirty data as: "... data that are incomplete, invalid, or inaccurate."

In other words, dirty data are simply data that are wrong. If we went back to our analogy of our memories being a data warehouse, the analogy for a piece of dirty datum is an "incorrect memory." Somehow the wires in our brains get crossed and mistakes are made. For exam-

> "**D**irty data contain incomplete, invalid, or inaccurate values."

ple, you may remember that Patti lives at the west end of Humming Bird Lane, so you make a left turn from Heritage Place. After an unsuccessful search you turn around and eventually find Patti's house to the east of Heritage Place. For some reason you inaccurately recalled the location. This incorrect memory resulted in the wrong decision to turn left. Dirty data work the same way. Incomplete or inaccurate data can result in bad decisions being made. Thus, dirty data are the opposite of blissful data. Problems caused by dirty data are significant; be wary of their pitfalls.

Looking at the different aspects of dirty data, let me first give you an example of what dirty data *aren't*. I once worked at an organization where there were a ton of meetings. During one of these meetings, the subject of dirty data came up. "Oh! We know all about dirty data," said operations manager Mike. "The unexpectedly large volumes of data that we had to deal with when we converted to the new distribution system really put us in a bind." No, Mike. You've missed the mark! Unexpected large volumes of data are a planning snafu, not dirty data.

Now, here's an example of what dirty data *are*. At yet another meeting, the issue of dirty data came up again. The distribution system that Mike mentioned contained data on the hundreds of different accessories for vehicles. Dealerships could send in their monthly orders and the accessories would then be delivered to the appropriate destination. But, incorrect destination codes in the database caused hundreds of car mats to be delivered to a small dealership in South Florida. This new dealership needed only a dozen sets of floor mats to start off their inventory and certainly had no need for the truckloads of mats that arrived. Little did this dealership know that its destination code had become the default destination code for every dealership with a missing or invalid destination code. In the meantime, other dealerships throughout North America were waiting with growing frustration for their floor mats to arrive. Inaccurate data that impacts the business—that is the issue of dirty data (as seen in Figure 4-1)!

Figure 4-1 Dirty data cause mistakes.

 REMEMBER

Being incomplete, invalid, or inaccurate, dirty data can cause bad decisions to be made.

Can You Afford Dirty Data?

Dirty data can cause big issues. New research from the Data Warehousing Institute[13] suggests that dirty data cost U.S. businesses an astounding $600 billion a year. A survey of 599 companies showed that one-third of the companies say dirty data caused them to delay or scrap a new system.[25] There's obviously more to dirty data than just duplicating customer listings or incorrectly listing gender designators and default codes. In reality, dirty data can be likened to a time bomb ticking in the dark. Although the floor mat problem mentioned above resulted in lost revenues and impatient customers, the overall outcome was not very serious. Let me give you an example where dirty data could have resulted in a much more tragic outcome.

This incident took place at an organization whose business was the distribution of SKUs throughout the country. One such item was touch-up paint. Sold in little cans, touch-up paint matches the exterior paint of a vehicle and is handy to have around. But, it is a highly flammable hazardous material. Hazardous materials, or hazmats, must follow stringent safety precautions as set out by the Department of Transportation and other federal agencies. Somehow, the data for the touch-up paint were incomplete or invalid and the items were not tagged as hazmats. As a result, they were inadvertently included in an urgent air freight order. As you may be aware, highly flammable materials can explode under pressure on an airplane. Luckily, the mistake was caught in time. The organization was fined hundreds of thousands of dollars. This was a small price to pay compared to the potential loss of human life due to a few small cans of touch-up paint blowing up at 30,000 feet.

As you can see, dirty data cannot be ignored. Inaccurate values can have major impacts on a business. Organizations cannot afford to wait for a time bomb to blow up in their faces before coming to terms with their dirty data. The time to evaluate and fix dirty data is NOW! Get started today and you'll be ahead for the future.

Remember

Dirty data cause major issues costing organizations billions of dollars a year.

What More Can You Lose?

Three little kittens, they lost their mittens,
And they began to cry,
Oh, mother, dear, we sadly fear,
Our mittens we have lost.
The three little kittens, they found their mittens,
And they began to cry,
Oh, mother, dear, see here, see here,
Our mittens we have found.
Three little kittens, put on their mittens,
And soon ate up the pie.
Oh, mother, dear, we sadly fear,
Our mittens we have soiled.
The three little kittens, they washed their mittens,

And hung them out to dry.

Oh, mother, dear, do you not hear,

Our mittens we have washed?

Many organizations have come to realize that having quality or blissful data is key to survival. "Our studies in cost analysis show that between 15% and greater than 20% of a company's operating revenue is spent doing things to get around or fix data quality issues," says Larry English, an internationally recognized speaker, consultant, and author on information quality improvement.[14] That is a significant chunk of change! But the dangers of not fixing dirty data are dire. As you can imagine, dirty data have been the kiss of death for more than a few organizations.

You may be wondering whose responsibility it is to fix the data. And where should data be fixed? The answers are simple. Just like the three little kittens, who lost, found, and dirtied their mittens and eventually took the responsibility to cleanse them as shown in Figure 4-2, business units "own" the data and therefore should assist in cleansing the data. Processes must be implemented to prevent bad data from enering the system as well as propogating to other sytems. That is, dirty data must be intercepted at its source. The operational systems are often the source of informational data; thus dirty data must be fixed at the operational data level. Implementing the right processes to cleanse data is, however, not easy. Just as Paul found, politics, power, and people issues come into play and hinder the process.

Special care must be taken to prevent dirty data from being loaded to a data warehouse. A warehouse consisting of dirty data is useless: Digging through dirty data will only produce more dirt. Dirty data provide bad information. Valid decisions cannot be made based on bad information. Bad decisions result in added cost and lost opportunity. The time it takes to track down, evaluate,

Figure 4-2 Instigators of dirty data must help cleanse the data.

and agree on what the data value should be is often underestimated. From my experience, finding and fixing dirty data at the source of the problem can often take up to 80% of a data warehousing endeavor. Learn from the organizations that have made the mistake of ignoring or only making minor fixes to their dirty data, resulting in data warehouse disasters. It is very important to evaluate and plan adequate time and effort to fix dirty data. Blissful data should be the goal of every data warehouse.

Dirty data can be introduced into a data warehouse when:

1. Bad data already exist in the source system and are copied to a data warehouse.
2. Errors and inconsistencies are created when combining and integrating the source data to load into a data warehouse.

Data warehouses must consist of blissful data to be useful and profitable. Examples of how useless information results in lost customers, lower sales, and less revenue include:

1. Incomplete data – A bank's service manager tells a customer that it is the bank's policy to charge bank fees for minors (the customer's teenagers). He tells her there can be no exceptions to this rule. With an incomplete picture of the customer, the bank was not aware that this customer has had a business account, maintaining very large balances with the bank for more than 10 years. After this unpleasant experience, the customer takes her business and personal accounts to another bank, where they treat her as an important customer.

2. Inaccurate data – An insurance company found that 80% of its claims were for the diagnosis "broken leg." The claims officers, who were paid by the

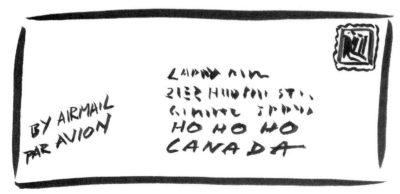

Figure 4-3 H0 H0 H0 are invalid data.

number of claims processed per day, were using "broken leg" as a default diagnosis code as it was faster and easier than looking up the correct code. The shortcut enabled them to process more claims in one day. It worked without a hitch as a broken leg was a valid diagnosis code that passed through the system with no problems. The results were that the claims were paid[15] and the claims officers enjoyed a higher level of pay. However, these garbage data made any claims analysis useless. There was no way to track the types of real diagnosis paid for by the insurance company.

3. Invalid data – A Canadian bank ran a promotional campaign for Christmas loans to customers in certain postal codes. Imagine its surprise when many customers turned up with the postal code H0 H0 H0. Postal codes in Canada allow alphanumeric characters, but H0 H0 H0 is invalid (Figure 4-3). A lack of edits against valid postal codes enabled bank employees to allow dirty data to enter the bank's databases. Without valid postal codes the bank could not determine which areas were good candidates for their marketing campaign. These invalid data prevented the bank from using its demographic data to gain valuable new assets.[14]

As you can see, incomplete, inaccurate, and invalid data can cause problems for an organization. These problems are not only embarrassing and awkward but will also cause the organization to lose customers, new opportunities, and market share.

REMEMBER

Dirty data can cause an organization to lose customers, new opportunities, and market share. At its worst, they can even cause an organization to shut down.

Sitting Among the Cinders?

Little Polly Flinders
Sat among the cinders,
Warming her pretty little toes.
Her mother came and caught her,
And whipped her little daughter
For spoiling her nice new clothes.

Just as Polly Flinders didn't plan on getting her new clothes dirty, no one plans on creating dirty data. It just happens and it happens easily. It's like wearing a white blouse or a light-colored suit to work. Inevitably, coffee will stain your blouse, or that dirty, dusty truck is so close to your car that you can't avoid brushing against it, or you have spaghetti for lunch and it got not just into your mouth but onto your clothes as well. Of course, any of these mishaps could happen on any day of the week, but dirt and stains are more noticeable on white or light-colored clothing. In the same way, dirty data and data quality issues have existed for a long time. But due to the inherent nature of operational data these issues have not been as visible or immense enough to affect the bottom line. Just as dark clothing hides spills and stains, dirty data have been hidden or ignored in operational data for decades.

Organizations need data for their day-to-day business to operate. Just how do data come about? They are gathered, stored, manipulated, and derived by human beings or by operational systems that are designed, built, and run by human beings. Unfortunately, human beings:

1. Make errors.
2. Do workarounds (sometimes known as "taking a shortcut").

We humans make the data dirty. If all organizations have data, and all organizations have people who work with data, then the logical result is that all organizations have

> *Every organization that has data also has dirty data.*

dirty data. Dirty data are so common that I'm going to make this the dirty data rule of thumb: "Every organization that has data also has dirty data." Dirty data are everywhere.

Then, why haven't dirty data raised their ugly heads sooner? Have you heard the term "mission-critical?" When used within an organization, it means that the mission-critical item must be implemented for the organization to succeed. For decades data quality issues in operational data were not visible to senior management. Data quality was not mission critical. The costs of duplicate mailers or missing data were seen as part of doing business. In an operational system, it doesn't matter whether Bill Smith or William T. Smith are the same person. So long as Bill could be billed (yes, the pun is intentional) for his home loan and William for his auto loan, and payments were received on time, there were no issues with the duplicate listing. Often, senior management didn't even realize dirty data problems existed because data for reports were often sanitized and sometimes even manually reworked by employees before being included and distributed.

However, DSS and data warehouses have changed all that. Data warehouses provide clients with microscopes to look at data in every possible way.

The need for consistency made incomplete, inaccurate, or invalid data much more visible. Dirty data gave the wrong picture of the business and had to be fixed.

REMEMBER

Every organization that has data also has dirty data. It is people who create these dirty data.

What's the Dirt on Dirty Data?

"Know the enemy and know yourself; in a hundred battles you will never be in peril."—Sun Tzu, general of an ancient Chinese army.[4, p 101]

An organization needs to know the condition and quality of its data to be more effective in fixing them and making them blissful. Unfortunately, pride, shame, and a fear of looking incompetent all play a part when people are asked to openly discuss dirty data issues. Because data are an asset, some people are unwilling to share their data. They think this gives them control and power over others. The role of politics in the organization is the dirty secret of dirty data.

Gauging the quality of the operational data becomes an important first step in predicting potential dirty data issues for an organization. But many organizations are reluctant to commit the time and expense to assess their data. Some organizations wait until dirty data issues blow up in their faces. The greater the pain being experienced, the bigger the commitment to improving data quality.

Remember my neighbor Paul, who worked at the bank with poor data quality? He was having a difficult time getting people to work together to im-

Figure 4-4 Many organizations won't air their dirty data.

prove data quality. Paul discovered that politics play a major part in preventing the improvement of data quality. Some of the barriers he came across were:

1. Just as no one likes to air their dirty laundry in public, people will not talk about or admit to having dirty data.
2. A mentality of false ownership exists. Paul often heard, "This is our data; we can't share it."
3. It was often "us" against "them." Almost every functional group told Paul, "Our systems work fine, but they keep sending us bad data."

Like I said before, dirty data cause big issues. The commitment and time needed to make data blissful are often underestimated due to the complexities that come into play. Dirty data cannot be fixed by one or two people. It requires the data to be assessed, organizational processes to be evaluated, and a new mentality of ownership to be introduced, rewarded, and accepted. It will involve implementing change (discussed in Chapter 3) . Attaining the goal of blissful data requires a mission-critical mindset where data quality is an extensive and continuous process. Best practices to achieve blissful data are discussed later in this chapter.

REMEMBER

Politics play a major part in preventing the improvement of data quality as people tend to hide their dirty data problems, are reluctant to share data, and are ready to blame others for dirty data issues.

What's the Nitty Gritty on Dirty Data?

Dirty data issues forced a major bank to scrap a $29 million data warehouse that contained nonquality data.[15] A governing organization discarded a $25 million data warehouse that failed to meet expectations.[15] The Montana Department of Corrections nearly lost a $1 million grant as they could not accurately forecast how many of a particular type of offender would be incarcerated in its facility.[14] How can a few people making assumptions, taking short cuts, or making minor mistakes cause so much damage? Well, dirty data can be likened to a virus that starts at the source and, if left unchecked, spreads to epidemic proportions in a data warehouse.

Why does dirty data happen? We already know that people cause dirty data. They make mistakes and take shortcuts when performing encoding and transformation. Operational data are full of codes; the process of converting data into its coded format is known as encoding. This process of encoding introduces dirty data. Let's look at a world-famous example of dirty data caused by encoding.

The world was rudely awakened to the significance and possible impact of dirty data in the 1990s. Remember the dreaded Y2K issue? Corporations spent billions of dollars making sure their systems were ready as the clock ticked over from 1999 to 2000. The first time you heard about Y2K you probably thought, "What a big to-do about nothing; what's so difficult about that?" You were right: As for any other year, by adding one to the previous year you get the next year. Adding one to 1999 gives 2000 (nothing new or difficult here)!

However, if you worked in IT you knew another dirty little secret. IT systems of the 1960s, 1970s, and beyond were set up by people at a time when computer disk space was quite expensive. People in IT were encouraged to make efficient use of computer disk space for files and databases. Therefore, many operational systems were designed to simply store only the two final digits of a year. For example, 1986 was stored as 86 and 1999 as 99. Imagine the enormous memory space savings over billions of dates in millions of operational systems.

The simplification worked well. Whenever the full four-digit year was needed a 19 was prefixed to the two-digit year. Nonetheless, as it got closer to the year 2000 IT people realized the simplification would now lead to trouble. The year 2000 would be simply stored as 00, 00 prefixed with 19 would be 1900, and all types of problems would occur with the difference of 100 years. The simplification would now cause invalid and inaccurate dates and thereby piles of instant dirty data!

Organizations realized they had to make sure their operational systems could handle the year 2000. Fixing the dirty date data became mission-critical; it had to be done for an organization to survive and move into the next century.

The second method of propagating dirty data occurs when source data are combined and integrated for the data warehouse. As you know, operational data from the different functional areas are extracted, integrated, and modified or transformed for inclusion into the data warehouse. This process is known as the extract, transform, and load (ETL) process. Combining or transforming data from many diverse operational systems is often complex. If care is not taken in this transformation stage or the operational data are already dirty, mega amounts of dirty data are loaded into the data warehouse.

The remainder of this chapter deals with the details of encoding and transformation. These examples will show you why dirty data come about so easily and spread so profusely.

 ## REMEMBER

The data encoding and transformation process facilitates the creation and profusion of dirty data.

What's the Scoop on Encoding?

Have you noticed that you are bombarded by codes every day? There are area codes in phone numbers, zip codes in addresses, stock market ticker symbols are codes, abbreviations such as state names can be considered codes, as well as the hundreds of other codes that are so common we don't even think about them. Think about a trip to the airport as seen in Figure 4-5; a boarding pass may contain as many as a dozen codes.

Data consist of many kinds of codes. We all encode or shorten words and messages by coming up with a code that may have a special meaning to us, e.g., acronyms are codes and abbreviations are common computer codes. Data are full of encoded values. Problems begin when ambiguity exists when decoding these values. Thus, the encoding and decoding of data is the root of all evil in creating dirty data. Let's look at some specific types of encoding problems.

Multipurpose Data Values?

Do you have a miscellaneous junk drawer? One day, you decide to clean out that drawer and start sorting through its contents. You find business cards of people you don't remember or haven't seen since the first encounter, plus old

Figure 4-5 Codes are all around us.

keys, pens, paperclips, pictures from cousin Ida's wedding, your grandmother's recipe for banana bread, and directions for programming a VCR you no longer own.

Well, there are data fields just like your miscellaneous drawer. These so-called "kitchen sink" fields hold data that have many meanings or purposes. Codes were thrown in because it was a convenient place to store this miscellaneous data. At one time this provided a quick and easy way to keep track of an infrequently used or special item. For example, you could have a field for customer status called CSTAT, containing the following codes:

1. "1" – customer with checking account.
2. "2" – customer with savings account.
3. "3" – customer with both checking and savings accounts.
4. "4" – loan customer.
5. "A" – business customer.
6. "B" – customer is a minor

You can see that these are cryptic codes. You need to have a conversion table in front of you to translate each of them. Further, some of the values are not mutually exclusive (e.g., a business customer can also have a personal checking account, so should CSTAT contain a "1" or a "4" for a business customer?). If your 8-year-old son, Patrick, had a savings account at this bank the CSTAT field could be coded with a "2" or a "B." Suppose it was coded with a "2." Now when the bank runs a promotion to invite customers to open a credit card any record with CSTAT="2" is extracted and Patrick gets an invitation with pre-approval to get a credit card. The bank doesn't realize he is only 8; all they see is that he has a savings account and therefore is a target for a credit card sales campaign. This is an example of an inaccurate decision based on a field that has multiple and cryptic meanings.

REMEMBER

Multipurpose and cryptic data values are dirty data that can cause bad decisions to be made.

Missing, Invalid, or Dummy Data?

In operational data a missing or invalid code is "bad" but most of the time you can get away with it. The most common example of missing or invalid data is the incorrect gender designator. You'll see a simple example in Table 4-1 where Jose's accounting data where "M" is the code for male and "F" for female. In Mary's sales data, "0" is used to denote male and "1" female. When the accounting and sales data were combined it was decided that an "M" in the accounting data would be converted to a "0" and the "F" would be converted to a "1." What happens when the accounting data contain neither an "M" nor an "F"? Say the gender field was blank or contained something invalid like an "X"; to what would it convert? What if accounting had an invalid "X" as the gender for Jane Doe? Does the "X" get translated to "0"? Or, if the gender field was blank does it default to "0?" In either case, the bad data cause the incorrect designator of Mr. for Jane Doe.

Dummy values are a special case of missing data. For example, say you are filling out an application for a savings account for your daughter, Magdalena, and it asks for her social security number. Because you don't remember it you leave it blank. The bank then assigns it a dummy value of "999-99-9999." Now the bank has trouble differentiating Magdalena from someone who doesn't have a social security number, such as a non-U.S. resident. The nonresident also gets a default value of "999-99-9999."

Care must be taken when assigning dummy values. I have seen an age of "99" or birth dates of "01/01/00" being assigned to people if the age or birth date is not known. You can guess that these dummy values cause inaccurate data for people who are really 99 years old or when January 1, 2000 rolled around.

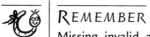 REMEMBER

Missing, invalid, and dummy values cause inaccurate views of data.

Contradictory Data?

One of my first jobs was as a part-time senior coder at the graduate admissions office of a large university. It was at this position that I learned all about encoding and the pitfalls of inconsistent or contradictory values in related fields.

In the admissions office we received hundreds of applications for graduate studies. My job was to enter the applicants into a database and generate reports for the various graduate schools. Naturally, the applicant's mailing address was a key piece of information and had to be correct. But, at times I would find zip codes that did not match the state. For example, the address for applicant Peter Johnson was

1631 Taft Ave,
New York, NY 75219.

The state is New York but 75219 is a Texas zip code. If I were to create reports to show total applicants by state and by zip code, I would have had inconsistent results. Which result would be correct? I wouldn't know. Data with errors cannot be trusted.

REMEMBER

Contradictory data values cause inconsistent and conflicting results.

What About Measurements?

It is funny how sometimes attention to small details can prevent disasters. I once saw dimension fields on a shipping database: the length, width, and height of a particular vehicle accessory. I knew from the description of these fields that these measurements were in inches. Imagine my surprise when by chance I saw a description of these dimension fields sent from a supplier as measured in centimeters.

Different scales for measurements can have serious outcomes. A few years ago, a mission to Mars failed because some distances were coded in kilometers and others in miles. Data with inconsistent units of measure will deliver wrong results.

REMEMBER

Inconsistent measurement units can cause erroneous results.

One Size Fits All?

Size of data values often causes issues. Imagine you buy a house and get a loan for $235,000.25. You obtain a good interest rate and expect to pay about $1,300 per month. Unknown to you, your financial institution had a problem and when you open your monthly statement your loan balance shows as $3,500,025.00. You rub your eyes and look again. Yes, the $3.5 million is still there. At $1300 per month, you're going to be paying off your loan for a long, long, time! After a frantic call to the bank you reach a harried and embarrassed bank manager who stammers an incoherent explanation and assures you that the problem has been fixed and a new statement is in the mail. Fields that are too small can cause problems. If the age field can only hold 2 digits, problems occur for anyone over the age of 99. This could cause your grandmother to receive an invitation to kindergarten on her 104th birthday (the institution would incorrectly think she was 4 years old).

REMEMBER

Inconsistent field size and formats will create inconsistent data.

What's in a Name?

I once worked with a very good analyst named Storm Peters. Incidentally, she told me her sister's name was Gail. I've often wondered why her parents didn't spell her sister's name "Gale." Wouldn't it have matched to have two daughters, one Storm and the other Gale? I also once heard of a girl named "Man." Isn't it peculiar to call a girl "Man?" But similar peculiar naming conventions crop up in the encoding of field names.

Let's take a straightforward value such as order quantity. The field name for such a value could be ORD-QTY, QTY, ORDER-QTY, ON-ORDER, or OO-QTY. Sometimes the field name could get even more cryptic and be encoded as OO or OQ. At other times the field name may not even match the value and could be even more bizarre, such as SENT or MAN. Because field names are encoded by people, they could be anything the person fancied that day. Do not assume you understand the contents of a field from the field name; they can be ambiguous and misleading.

Errors can also result from incorrect supposition of the meaning of a field. For example, does the order-quantity value refer to the number of items on the invoice or the number of items shipped? I wouldn't know and neither would you.

The ambiguous and misleading methods of encoding field names and the misunderstanding of the meanings of data values can cause errors to occur.

REMEMBER

Inconsistent naming conventions cause ambiguity and incorrect results.

How About a Date?

The last but certainly not least encoding category is the many available formats of dates. With the Y2K problem behind us a lot has been said about inconsistent date formats. The media did such a good job of educating the public about how four-character years were stored as two characters to save space; billions of dollars were spent worldwide to make dates consistent to handle the change into the 21st century.

A common difference in date formats is the switch between the month and day in U.S. and European date formats. For example, 05-01-2003 is May 1, 2003, in the United States but Europeans see it as the 5th of January 2003. It is not that one is more correct than the other, but which should it be? If the correct format is not defined, it's up to you to choose. Choose incorrectly and you could be late for that important sales meeting or lose that important contract.

REMEMBER
Inconsistent date formats cause schedules to be missed and loss of opportunity.

In summary, the many facets of encoding can cause uncertainty and confusion about the data. Organizations with a successful data warehouse have found that they need metadata (data about data) to provide details about the data. This metadata are stored in a metadata repository and can be accessed by people who need to find the meaning and location of data values in a warehouse. Metadata are discussed in more detail in Chapter 5.

What About Transformations?

Companies run their day-to-day business with operational systems that are designed around a certain function, such as accounting or sales. These operational systems create large amounts of operational data that become the source or starting point for informational data in the data warehouse.

Imagine Jose designed the accounting application and Mary instigated the sales application in your organization. Jose and Mary are diverse human beings; they designed these applications around their functional groups and processes. There could be some similarities, but there would be hundreds of differences. Now, suppose that Nick, a VP, decides to consolidate the data between the two groups. Let's also suppose that the quality of the data is "good," i.e., there are some missing values and incorrect codes but most of the data values are available and correct. When the operational data are combined, some dirty data could already exist; however, the differences in Jose's and Mary's applications are highly likely to cause more dirty data. Examine the data values* in Table 4-1.

Jose's accounting application codes and values
1. The customer's name is shortened to Bill and contains no middle initial.
2. Customer number is an alphabetic character followed by four numeric characters.
3. Gender is coded as "M" for male (and "F" for female).

---

*Although both groups keep information on the same customer (same social security number) the data look quite different.

■ TABLE 4-1 ■ **Operational Data from Accounting and Sales**

Field	Accounting (Jose) Record 5686	Sales (Mary) Record 9320
Customer Name	Bill Smith	William T. Smith
Customer Number	Y3356	5674-7779
Gender	M	0
Transaction Date	2002033	10-01-99
Social Security Number	123456789	123-45-6789
Balance/Net Balance	$10,040.50	$433.98
Net Purchases	—	$13,399.86

4. Transaction date is coded as a four-digit character year and three-digit character day (the 33rd day of year 2002 is used in our example).
5. Social security number consists of nine numeric characters with no hyphens. All "9s" denotes a social security number that is unavailable or nonexistent.
6. Balance is a seven-digit character field with two decimal places.
7. Net purchases field does not exist in accounting.

Mary's sale application codes and values
1. The customer name is William T. Smith.
2. Customer number is eight-digit characters with a hyphen after the fourth character.
3. Gender is coded "0" for male (and "1" for female).
4. Transaction date is a two-digit character month, a hyphen, two-digit character day, a hyphen, and a two-digit character year, i.e., MM-DD-YY.
5. Social security number contains a hyphen after the third and fifth numeric characters.
6. Balance does not exist in sales, but a field called customer balance does. Customer balance is five numeric characters with two decimal places.
7. Net purchases is a seven-digit character field with two decimal places.

REMEMBER

Operational systems are built around various functions and contain data values and codes that are diverse and unique.

How Does Dirty Data Grow?

Just like weeds in a garden, dirty data grow easily and quickly. Let's look at a simple case where dirty data are propagated into a data warehouse.

By combining the accounting and sales data, both Jose's and Mary's people could "share" the data. Therefore, the operational data from both functional areas must be translated in a way to make it useable for everyone. The method by which the data are combined and translated into a new common structure are known as "transformation rules." Well defined transformation rules are key to producing blissful data.

Velma was hired to work with the two groups to combine their data into a data warehouse. She worked with both Jose and Mary to find out about their functional applications and data. She also discussed their informational data needs and set about designing the customer subject area of the data warehouse. But, Velma created some inconsistent tranformation rules and errors were introduced. The resulting transformed data in the data warehouse could look like the values in Table 4-2.

Record 1
1. Customer number is translated using a number for the leading alphabetic character plus 9900 (e.g., "Y" is the 25th letter of the alphabet, 25 + 9900 = 9925), followed by a hyphen and then the four numeric characters.
2. "M" values are translated to "0" and "F" values become "1."
3. Transaction date is translated to a four-digit year, a two-digit month, and a two-digit day (the 33rd day of year 2002 is February 2).
4. Social security number consists of nine numeric characters with a hyphen between the third and fourth characters and the fifth and sixth characters. (All "9s" is not a valid value and becomes a default value of "000-00-0000.")
5. Net balance is a six-digit field including two decimal places. The most significant digit of $10,040.50 is lost and the resulting amount is $0040.50 or $40.50.
6. Net purchases did not exist in accounting and no transformation rule was applied so it becomes a "null" or missing value.

Record 2*
1. Transaction date is translated to a four-digit year, a two-digit month, and a two-digit day. The transformation rule appended a "20" to the front of the two-digit year.

---

*Customer name, customer number, gender, social security number, and net purchases are simply copied over.

■ TABLE 4-2 ■ **"Transformed" Data in the Data Warehouse**

Field Name	Record 1 (from Accounting)	Record 2 (from Sales)
Customer Name	Bill Smith	William T. Smith
Customer Number	9925-3356	5674-7779
Gender	0	0
Transaction Date	20020202	20991001
Social Security Number	123-45-6789	123-45-6789
Net Balance	$40.50	$433.98
Net Purchases	—	$13,399.86

2. Balance did not exist in sales and this field is set to the net balance value.

Unfortunately, errors were introduced into the data. These errors are discussed in Table 4-3.

I've just shown you a single customer's record being merged from two sources. Multiply these errors by hundreds and thousands of customers over 20 or 30 possible operational systems and you will see why dirty data cause such problems. These problems have to be identified and resolved for proper transformations to be carried out. The amount of time and effort this data transformation requires is often underestimated and at times even bypassed. Learn from people like Paul and save yourself the embarrassment and anguish later. Data transformation rules must be in place to prevent dirty data from happening.

REMEMBER

As operational data are consolidated, many errors can be introduced into the data unless solid transformation rules are in place.

Some Thoughts for Cleansing Dirty Data

The good news is that, just like laundry can be washed and cleaned, so too can dirty data be fixed or "cleansed." Cleansed data are blissful data. They provide accurate, meaningful, and useful information.

Some simple thoughts to keep in mind regarding dirty data are:

- Dirty data issues can be prevented.
- Dirty data can be cleansed.

■ TABLE 4-3 ■ **Summary of Data Errors Resulting from the Transformation**

Data	Problem
Bill Smith William T. Smith	Duplicate records – Bill and William are the same person, but since different variations of his name were used and no matching on address (not shown) or Social Security Number were made, he is now in the data warehouse as two different people, with two different Customer Numbers.
9925-3356	Duplicate keys – Customer number should be unique as it is used as an index or key to search for certain customers. What if Customer Number 992503356 already existed in the Sales data? There would be duplicate customer numbers.
20991001	Date formats – the dreaded year 2000 (Y2K) bug of the twentieth century. When a 2-numeric character year is translated to a 4-numeric character year the dilemma is, should "19" or "20" be the prefix to the 2 character year?
123-45-6789	Missing/default values – Although the Social Security Number translated well for Bill Smith. What about those cases where a Social Security Number is missing? Is this set to spaces? Or does it get a default value such as 000-00-0000?
$40.50	Size of numeric data – the size and format type of numeric data must be consistent and large enough to contain values from all sources to the data warehouse.
—	Field names – are Balance/Net Balance and Net Purchases the same field? Both departments should meet to discuss the *business rules* and the *metadata* for all the fields in the data warehouse.

- It is impossible to clean everything.
- Start with cleansing something.

Cleansing dirty data can be a daunting task and must be taken one step at a time. Steps to improve data quality are:

1. First, evaluate the quality of the data. Take the time to understand the pain being experienced by various groups due to poor data issues. There are commercial tools available to assess data quality, but there are no magical tools to fix the data itself.
2. Establish procedures to prevent dirty data as well as how data should be cleansed.
3. Take the time to go back to the source to fix the poor quality data. The source is usually at the operational data level.

4. Find, assign, or train people as "data stewards" to make sure data are cleansed and stay cleansed.
5. Focus on critical data values first.
6. Establish business rules with internal and external organizations. Make sure external organizations are not polluting your data.
7. Come up with metadata for as much data as possible.
8. Make sure all the right people are involved.
9. Go back to step 2. This is a continuous process.

REMEMBER

Obtaining blissful data is a continuous process with lots of time, people, and effort involved.

REMEMBER THIS!

✔ Being incomplete, invalid, or inaccurate, dirty data can cause bad decisions to be made.

✔ Dirty data cause major issues costing organizations billions of dollars a year.

✔ Dirty data can cause an organization to lose customers, new opportunities, and market share. At its worst, they can even cause an organization to shut down.

✔ Every organization that has data also has dirty data. It is people who create these dirty data.

✔ Politics play a major part in preventing the improvement of data quality as people tend to hide their dirty data problems, are reluctant to share data, and are ready to blame others for dirty data issues.

✔ The data encoding and transformation process facilitates the creation and profusion of dirty data.

✔ Multipurpose and cryptic data values are dirty data that can cause bad decisions to be made.

✔ Missing, invalid, and dummy values cause inaccurate views of data.

✔ Contradictory data values cause inconsistent and conflicting results.

✔ Inconsistent measurement units can cause erroneous results.

✔ Inconsistent field sizes and formats create inconsistent data.

✔ Inconsistent naming conventions cause ambiguity and incorrect results.

✔ Inconsistent date formats cause schedules to be missed and loss of opportunity.

✔ Operational systems are built around various functions and contain data values and codes that are diverse and unique.

✔ As operational data are consolidated, many errors can be introduced into the data unless solid transformation rules are in place.

✔ Obtaining blissful data is a continuous process with lots of time, people, and effort involved.

Politics

Who Owns It Anyway?

CHAPTER 5

AXIOM 5

Build it and they may NOT come!

What is your family culture? I'm not talking about going to the ballet or attending classical symphonies but rather the customs, habits, thoughts, and behaviors shared by members of your household. You may have some house or family rules to support this culture. These rules need not be written down. Because the behaviors are practiced often, the rules are implicit or in general known.

In a house with teenagers, having explicit or written house rules is often a good idea. When rules are written and accessible, they brook no argument. For example, the house rule "If there is school the next day, the evening curfew is 10:00 PM" clearly sets the constraint that on a school night everyone needs to be home by 10:00 PM. Anyone who has lived with teenagers knows that teens will try to bend and test these rules whenever they can. But, when rules are realistic and routinely and consistently applied (you may need to come up with some fitting rewards for obeying the rules or punishment for disobedience) even teenagers will eventually buckle down and follow the accepted family behaviors. You hope that they will then use this knowledge as a basis for making decisions and guiding behavior.

Similarly, organizations have an organizational culture with many implicit rules to support this culture. It is often difficult to fathom the culture until you actually join the organization. Janice was looking forward with great expectations to a rewarding career full of growth and potential when she joined a new organization. However, these expectations never materialized. On her first day, she was thrown into a demanding atmosphere of conflict and high stress. People worked in silos, there was little teamwork, and there was a lot of conflict. Schedules and deadlines were all important, but ironically there were no rewards for quality work. Reworking and revisions were the norm, not the exception. This environment was very different from Janice's initial expectations. After 3 months, Janice could not take it anymore and left the organization.

Although Janice's situation may seem extreme, a culture exists in every organization. Certain cultures work for some people and not for others. In the same way, some cultures are better suited for successful data warehousing environments than others. Data warehousing is all about change and integration. It requires early stakeholder involvement, cross-communication and sharing between groups, and many new and revised processes. A culture that is not ready for a data warehouse will not use it. It will stand empty and unused. An unused data warehouse is a failed data warehouse. Therefore, organizational culture is a key factor in determining data warehouse success. Organizational cultures that are better suited to data warehousing success must have one or more of the following characteristics:

1. A culture that is open and willing to change.
2. Cultures with open upward, downward, and cross-communication.
3. Cultures where people are willing to share ideas, data, and information.
4. Cultures with well-defined structures, goals, and procedures.
5. Cultures with business rules that are well documented and understood.

Data warehouses are about change and integration. Let's see how culture, organizational structure, business rules, roles and responsibilities, and metadata play key roles in affecting data warehousing success.

What Is Culture?

"Culture pervades and radiates meanings into every aspect of the enterprise."[16, p 16]

"Culture hides more than it reveals, and strangely enough what it hides it hides most effectively from its own participants."[17, p 29]

"People cannot act or interact at all in any meaningful way except through the medium of culture."[18, p 188]

"The culture of a people is an ensemble of texts, themselves ensembles . . ."[19, p 452]

Have you noticed that people think, act, and behave differently depending on the group they are with? They may be louder and more talkative than usual, making jokes or poking fun at people, or at the other extreme they could be withdrawn, or even negative and pessimistic. These people are changing their behaviors and thoughts in response to the culture of the people around them at the time. There's nothing wrong with this. I've done it, and I'm sure you have, too. In reality, culture is always around us. It's like breathing: We are so used to taking a breath we don't think about it. Similarly, we shift from one culture to another without thinking about it. At home we think and act according to our family culture, when we go out with friends we respond to the group's culture, and at work we are influenced by the organizational culture. This shift in culture operates at a subconscious level. We are of-

Figure 5-1 Culture of the Village People.

ten not aware of how this culture affects our values, beliefs, ideas, and behavior. We become influenced in the way we think, feel, and make decisions in response to the culture around us.

There are also hundreds of thousands of different cultures. Cultures can be as varied and diverse as the personalities of people. In the late 1970s, a musical group called the Village People became very popular. The group featured men dressed in masculine attire from various occupations and backgrounds (as depicted in Figure 5-1); its catchy tunes became quite popular. The Village People became a symbol for people of diverse cultures being able to work well and get along together.

Therefore, any group of people will develop some sort of a unique culture. Similarly, organizations develop their own unique cultures. The categories of organizational cultures are discussed in the next section.

REMEMBER
Culture is the shared way groups of people think, act, and make decisions.

What Is Organizational Culture?

This is the way we wash our clothes,
Wash our clothes,
Wash our clothes.
This is the way we wash our clothes,
So early Monday morning.

Like the nursery rhyme "All around the mulberry bush," people in organizations have their particular methods of performing work. These actions and behaviors are influenced by the organizational culture. But what are these organizational cultures? A good analogy is to describe an organization's culture as its "personality." Just as an individual has his or her own personality, an organization, too, has its own personality that is often deeply rooted and affects the actions and behavior of the entire organization. As Edward Hall describes in "The Hidden Dimension,"[17] organizational culture is always implicit and hidden, especially from the people it affects the most, the members of the organization. For this reason, it often takes an outsider to pinpoint the culture of an organization. Just as there are millions of personalities, there are millions of different organizational cultures. Most organizational cultures, however, can be grouped into five major categories.

Years ago, I joined a conservative organization with a "club" culture. Employees were made to feel as if they belonged to an association and the organization went as far as calling employees "members." Respect, teamwork, and seniority were valued. Many members had worked their way up the ranks over several years. Some had been in the same position for more than 20 years. They were comfortable, secure, and looking forward to rewarding retirement benefits. As an outsider coming in, I found this club culture stable and dependable. Like the tortoise in Aesop's fable about the tortoise and the hare, the culture plodded along, making steady progress. The strength of this organizational culture is in effectively gaining and securing loyal lifelong customers.

Opposing this club culture is the organization Janice jumped into, where almost everything was done "under the gun," that is, high stress, constant demands, reworking, and deadlines are prevalent and constant. Working in this type of culture is akin to having someone cracking the whip over your head at all times. I call this the "gunshot" culture. Management is dictatorial and task oriented. Task completion, highly specialized skills, and long hours are valued. These organizations undergo frequent reorganization, have high turnover rates, and constantly try to attract new employees. The strength of this organizational culture is in bringing specialized or highly technical products to market.

The third of the organizational cultures is the "r & r" culture. Are you thinking "vacation time?" No, not quite. In this case r & r doesn't stand for "rest and relaxation" but rather for "research and refinement." The r & r culture is similar to the club culture: Employees work in a stable environment, develop new skills, and grow as they work their way up the ranks. The r & r culture differs from the club culture in that the individual is as important as the team. Learning, experimenting, and taking calculated risks are valued. These organizations have usually been around a while; they are solid, well known, and respected in their industry. The strengths of this organizational culture produce innovative, groundbreaking, and inventive products.

The fourth organizational culture is the "project" culture. I would be tempted to call this the "team" culture except employees always have the underlying fear that once the project is over they will be out on their ear. They never feel like they truly belong to a real team. Like the gunshot culture, these organizations are fast paced, use new methods and technologies, and require people with specialized skills. Unlike the gunshot culture, the work is well planned, controlled, and executed. All work is packaged as a project. Therefore, each work unit has a definite start and end. Project management, quality, and benchmarking skills are valued. These organizations are flexible and accept change readily. The strength of this organizational culture is in generating products that are innovative, timely, and quick to market.

Finally, there is the "partnership" culture. This is my favorite. Employees in these organizations work as equal business partners. Each individual contributes his or her own strengths. Problems are brainstormed and the most effective solutions are voted on and selected. Responsibility, growth, ownership, and self-motivation are valued. Leadership shifts from one employee to the next depending on their strengths and the problem to be solved. These organizations are flexible and change frequently. The strength of this organizational culture is in creating products that are unique, responsive to market conditions, and of excellent quality.

Of course, these five culture categories are broad and overlap in a number of areas. But, usually an organization has a dominant culture supported by a variety of subcultures that coexist in harmony or conflict with each other. Global companies have an even greater challenge. They have to ensure that these subcultures tolerate and communicate with each other in a multicultural environment. Therefore, pinpointing the organizational culture is an important aspect of every endeavor not only to minimize conflict and disagreement but also determine the initiation and outcome of an endeavor. For example, an endeavor involving a new unproven technology has a better chance of being started in a culture that encourages risk taking than in an extremely conservative culture. Organizations have found that the project and partnership cultures are better suited for the adaptability to change and integration—key aspects necessary for a successful data warehouse.

REMEMBER

Organizational culture is the personality of an organization. There are five categories of organizational cultures: club, gunshot, r & r, project, and partnership cultures. Project and partnership culture-oriented organizations are more open to change and flexibility.

What Are Artifacts?

Hector Protector was dressed all in green;
Hector Protector was sent to the Queen.
The Queen did not like him,
No more did the King,
So Hector Protector was sent back again.

We have know that first impressions are important. Often, one chance is all you get. Poor Hector Protector in the above nursery rhyme had one chance to make an impression on the queen and chose the wrong color to wear. He would have had a better chance for success by finding out what he could have about the likes and dislikes of the queen. Similarly, a data warehouse has a better chance of success by understanding the organizational culture and making a good first impression. It is crucial to make the warehouse a success the first time or you may not get a second chance. Discover all you can about the organizational culture by looking for clues. Let me illustrate the types of clues to look for with a short story.

One day, a stranger came up to me and introduced herself. This isn't surprising in itself, but her reason for doing so was totally unexpected. Introducing herself as Toni, she said she wanted to meet me because I always wore bright colors, which differed from everyone else in the organization. So she knew I was different. I looked around and realized she was right: Everyone was wearing dark or drab colors, and my pink suit was quite a contrast. The clothing people wear is a visible expression or artifact of the culture of that organization.

Toni, herself, was new to the organization. I noted that she, too, was different from others in the organization. She was more outgoing, friendly, and always ready for a chat. The rest of the staff were reserved, helpful enough if you asked for help, but often busy at their desks or working in small cliques. After that, I started to take note of the other artifacts of the culture. I found rows of cubicles for each of the functional groups, predictive of the silos or boundaries of each group. I saw luxury cars and named parking spots for management, elaborate furniture and corner offices for senior management, and large and impressive conference rooms with highly technical equipment. These artifacts were indicative of the deference given to management hierarchies.

I was concerned not about what I could see but rather what I didn't see. I didn't see people gathering around the water cooler to exchange pleasantries and discuss the latest sports scores. There were no "war" rooms for project teams to gather and brainstorm solutions to problems. I rarely heard peals of laughter from conference rooms or cheers from group meetings where people were recognized for a job well done, nor for the success of a project shared. In fact, group meetings were uncommon. Now I understood why the IT area where I worked was nicknamed "the library." That's certainly what it felt like, a quiet and serious library.

The culture of this organization was short-term goal and task oriented. Change was slow to occur, there was little structure and planning, and rewards seemed to go to those who mindlessly accepted the status quo. There was little trust and teamwork. Management rewarded those who worked to meet the ever-changing scope and schedules with no thought to the quality of the work, that is, quantity of work took precedence over the quality of the work. As you might expect, the quality was so bad that rework was common. There were often numerous "fires" to put out. At times these were serious show-stoppers that had to have first priority, causing high stress and demands on the employees. This organization clearly belonged to the gunshot culture.

After my experience at this organization, I came up with an organizational culture rule of thumb: What management notices and rewards is the best indication of the organization's culture.

> "**W**hat management notices and rewards is the best indication of the organization's culture."

There are visible signs of an organization's culture, but one must learn to notice them. Artifacts can be something as small as a value statement or slogan, as big as the building architecture and furnishings, and as obvious as the clothing people wear, organizational logos and brochures, or the prestigious corner offices. All these artifacts are most obvious to a newcomer or outsider to the organization. Just like that crack in your entryway tile that you step over every morning, sooner rather than later you forget that it is there. Those who have been in an organization for a long time don't notice the artifacts. These artifacts have become part of the general landscape and can be easily ignored.

 REMEMBER

Artifacts are visible expressions of the organizational culture. Artifacts are often more obvious to an outsider of an organization.

How Do Leaders Affect the Organizational Culture?

> Old King Cole was a merry old soul,
> And a merry old soul was he.
> He called for his pipe, and he called for his bowl,
> And he called for his fiddlers three

Leaders affect an organization's culture tremendously. Looking at the rhyme about Old King Cole, you can bet that his kingdom was a merry place. He valued the good life with music and cheer. Thus, leaders set the tone for the cultures and behaviors in their organization. Let me illustrate this with another story from my own experiences.

I had a boss named Barbara who was a super manager. She was intelligent and knowledgeable, cared about people, and was hard working and a great problem solver. Barbara even had a great sense of humor. But, she avoided conflict. Unfortunately, conflict happens in every workplace; when ignored, it doesn't go away: It grows, festers, and eventually manifests itself in different, more problematic forms. Interestingly, I realized one day that I had begun to avoid conflict, too. Subconsciously, my behavior was being influenced by Barbara's actions. And I wasn't the only one influenced: Other managers in the group seemed to be burying their heads in the sand as well. Needless to say, there were many problems in that organization.

How could this happen? Easily. Our thoughts and behaviors are affected by the culture around us, and the behavior modeled by the leaders of the organization sets the tone for the cultures and behaviors of the organization. Is this good news? You bet! A strong leader can change and transform the organizational culture. She can set the direction and the organization will follow.

REMEMBER

Leaders set the tone for the culture of an organization; therefore, it is possible for the culture of an organization to be transformed by a strong leader.

Why Do You Need to Understand Your Organizational Culture?

Interestingly, if you ask someone about the culture in their organization they'll tell you about its vision and mission statements. Vision and mis-

A caterpillar's mission: Be a butterfly.

sion statements are important, but they are not an organization's culture; they are its goals. A vision is the ideal they are striving to achieve. There may be a huge gap between the ideal and the current state of actions and behaviors. Just like a caterpillar must go through a series of changes before it becomes a butterfly, "change" is always necessary to reach goals.

Many organizations have tried to implement change and failed. Others have wasted a lot of money setting goals they could never reach as they failed to first assess where they originally stood. Therefore, to be successful at reaching goals you must determine the size of the gap between the goal and the current position. If the gap between the ideal and existing situations is too large, it is doubtful that the goal will be achieved. Organizations must know and understand the current organizational culture to be successful at implementing change. We know that it is the organization's culture that drives its people to action; therefore, management must understand what motivates their people to attain goals and objectives. Only by understanding the current organizational culture will it be possible to begin to try and change it.

We know a leader sets the tone for the organizational culture. What, then, does it take for this leader to transform the culture? It is similar to implementing change. The leadership skills of the CEO or other senior management play a key role in influencing people to change. Kotter[10] defines leading change as involving:

- Establishing direction - developing both a vision of the future and strategies for producing the changes needed to achieve the vision.
- Aligning people – communicating the vision by words and deeds to all those whose cooperation may be needed to achieve the vision.
- Motivating and inspiring – helping people energize themselves to overcome political, bureaucratic, and resource barriers to change.

In other words, a leader needs to set the direction, align the right people to assist in implementing the change, and provide incentives to change in the desired direction. What a coincidence! These are the same steps needed to establish a data warehouse. Creating a successful data warehouse needs a leader to set the direction, find and establish the right people to assist, and provide the motivation for people to change in the direction of the data warehouse. Where should this leader come from? We need to look at organizational structures that have worked for many organizations.

Remember

Organizational change can be implemented by a leader who sets the direction, aligns the right people to assist, and provides incentives to change in the desired direction.

What Role Does the Sponsor Play?

Change must come from the top. You've heard that often, I'm sure. In the last section we found that leaders set the tone for the organizational culture. Therefore, if the senior managers embrace change the rest of the organization will accept change more readily.

I remember a VP's particularly memorable speech. She was addressing an organization that was a cross between a gunshot and club culture, that is, a lot of reworking was carried out by people who'd been in the same jobs for a long time. Both these cultures are slow to accept change. Fiona, the VP, was brought in to implement change. She shook the audience up with her speech. "We are going to change, and once we finish changing we are going to change again," she said. "So, if you don't like change get out now because you won't like what we are going to do." A lot of people nervously waited for the changes to happen. Others (a minority) eagerly anticipated and even looked for these changes. In the next few months, Fiona set the direction and the goals to be achieved, aligned change agents to help her lead the change, and started a reward and recognition program for those willing to march in tune to this new growth and opportunity. Fiona had set the wheels of organizational change in motion.

A data warehouse is all about change and integration. The decision for achieving a successful data warehouse cannot be made by a first-line or middle manager. It should be a strategic direction that comes from the CEO and senior management team and filtered down through all levels of the organization. But how does this happen? With the help of change agents, naturally. Middle management must function as change agents to help integrate the change and provide the fitting rewards to the people to motivate them to accept and embrace the change. These change agents get their direction from a person who is focused and committed to the vision. This person is the data warehouse sponsor. Thus, the data warehouse sponsor manages the expectations and motivation of the data warehouse change agents. It is a critical role for data warehousing success.

Many projects contain a project sponsor. A project sponsor is the individual or group that provides the funds for creating and maintaining a project. The sponsor for any project is important but the data warehouse sponsor has an even more crucial role. Because the decision to build a data warehouse must come from the top, the data warehouse sponsor must also come from the top. Some of the important responsibilities of a data warehouse sponsor include:

- To promote the data warehouse – without the right data warehouse sponsor to promote it, a data warehouse could be built but the business units may not come to use it.
- To implement change – if the sponsor does not have the influence to enable change or there is misaligned direction, then it is not worth the effort to even try to build a data warehouse.
- To bring the business units together – data warehouses require the involvement of many of the organizations' cross-functional units; hence, the data warehouse sponsor must have the legitimate power and the influence to bring these people together to carry out the process changes and cross-functional integration necessary for a successful data warehouse.
- To set the direction and resolve conflicts – the data warehouse sponsor must set the strategy for the data warehouse and make decisions when conflicting views arise.

- To implement the processes to ensure blissful data – the data warehouse sponsor must have the communication skills and authority to overcome political issues that will come up when functional groups must share and transform data.

The data warehouse sponsor is a leader who shares the vision, implements change, integrates the business units, overcomes resistance, makes decisions to support the goals, ensures blissful data, and provides the leadership and leverage needed to reach the warehouse goal.

REMEMBER
The data warehouse sponsor provides the leadership and leverage needed to reach the goal of a successful data warehouse for the organization.

What About Organizational Structure?

Let's look at some common organizational structures to see which structure lends itself to the culture of change needed for data warehousing success.

The business organizational structure shown in Figure 5-2 is the most prevalent for data warehouse implementation. All data warehouse administration (DWA) is centralized in the information technology (IT) organization. Either the manager of the DWA group or the CIO becomes the data warehouse sponsor. That makes sense, you say: A data warehouse is very technical and belongs in IT. Unfortunately, not! Remember that a data warehouse is an entire environment. The environment belongs to the business. Thus, the sponsorship of the data warehouse also belongs to the business.

Although this type of organizational structure may get a data warehouse up and running, there is the risk that a majority of the business units won't

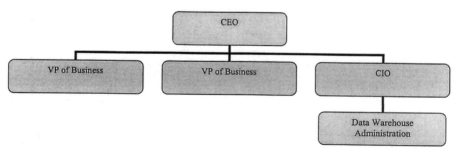

Figure 5-2 Data warehouse administration centralized in information technology.

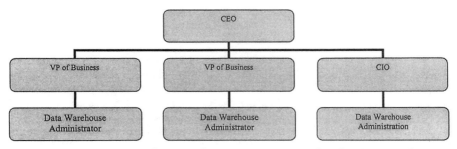

Figure 5-3 Data warehouse administration spread to business units.

use it, or will use it only sparingly. The DWA manager does not have the power or influence to produce the change for the data warehouse to succeed. Middle managers from the business units see no reason to act as change agents for yet another tool from IT. A CIO does not have the time or focus to be a dedicated data warehouse sponsor. Too many organizations have tried this structure and failed. Be wary of the pitfalls of such an organizational structure.

Will the organizational structure presented in Figure 5-3 work? It has the DWA centralized in IT, but there are also administrators within each of the business units. This is more like it, you say, at least the DWA has moved into the business sector. But, look closer. Can you see why this organizational structure will not work? Who is the data warehouse sponsor? Is it each of the VPs? It could very well be. Each VP or his/her delegate could be a data warehouse sponsor for the business unit. Each business unit can do "its own thing" and the DWA group in IT simply handles the technical and operational aspects for each of the business units.

Actually, this type of organizational structure is common. It usually occurs when the goal of achieving a data warehouse does not come from the top of the organization and each business unit goes ahead in its own direction. At other times, the business unit does not want to go through the standards and procedures of the DWA group and builds a functional data mart according to its own specific needs. There is no integration of data or requirements between the business units to give an overall view of the organization. The ownership of the data is also unclear. This type of organizational structure runs the risk of creating multiple independent data marts and having multiple versions of the "truth." Which data mart is correct? Which version should you believe? I don't know the answer and neither would you. We've already seen many of the long-term problems caused by multiple independent data marts in one organization.

Last and certainly not least is the organizational structure shown in Figure 5-4. This organizational structure contains a dedicated branch for data warehousing. All data warehouse sponsorship and administration comes from

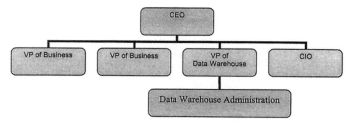

Figure 5-4 Data warehouse administration within its own division.

this branch. It clearly shows that senior management supports and is committed to data warehousing. I recommend this type of organizational structure for data warehousing success. Benefits of this structure are:

1. The VP of the data warehouse is clearly defined as the sponsor.
2. The sponsor is able to work with the business units and IT as an equal partner.
3. There is a centralized group of data quality stewards to work with knowledge workers across the organization to ensure blissful data.
4. The data warehouse is viewed as an "investment" and does not have to be constantly justified or restricted.
5. Data sharing is more visible and rewarding.
6. Cross-communication is facilitated.
7. Resistance to change is more easily overcome.

A dedicated division in the organization for data warehousing has the benefits of a clearly defined data warehouse sponsor, centralized data quality support and ownership, facilitated data sharing, communication, and cross-functional integration.

 REMEMBER

Organizational structure plays an important role in the success of a data warehouse. A recommended structure places a division dedicated to the data warehouse with a sponsor as an equal partner with the CIO and VPs of business.

What Are Business Rules?

I was once asked, "What are business rules?" My simple answer was, "The simple truth." To expand upon that, I'll say, "A business rule is any

Business rules are the truth, the whole truth, and nothing but the truth.

rule on the who, what, when, where, why, and how of an organization." Basically, business rules are the lifeblood of an organization. They are why the organization exists. Luckily, many functional groups have some subset of their business rules defined. They may call these rules something else, such as operating procedures, standards, or process documentation, but within these documents the business rules are defined.

So business rules are just like house rules. They are policies of an organization and contain one or more assertions that define or constrain some aspect of the business. Their purpose is to provide a structure and guideline to control or influence the behavior of the organization. Further, business rules represent the business and guide the decisions that are made by the people in the organization.

Hold on a minute! I've already said that organizational culture absolutely influences the thoughts, actions, and decisions made by people in an organization. Business rules, in turn, are the written and visible expressions or artifacts of the organizational culture. Amazing, isn't it? Before I began writing this book, I never realized what a strong relationship exists between organizational culture and business rules.

REMEMBER

Business rules are the policies of an organization and represent what the business does. Explicit business rules are artifacts of the organizational culture.

Where Do Business Rules Originate?

Business rules come from many sources. They could come from organizational policies, industry policies, standards, regulations, general rules-of-thumb, heuristics, and/or experiences. They can come from all over an organization and are closely tied to the organizational culture. Therefore, a primary area to obtain business rules is from the other artifacts and ideals of the organizational culture. Slogans, policies, vision and mission statements, objectives, and goals are all indicative of the organization and its culture.

Business rules are related to the organizational culture in other ways, as well. The mere existence of documented business rules is an indication of the culture. Have you ever been in an organization where nothing was written down? There were a few key people who knew how everything worked but all this knowledge was in their heads. These subject matter experts (SMEs) are invaluable to the organization; without them, daily operations could grind to a halt. These organizations live in constant fear that should these SMEs become unwell or—heaven forbid—be hit by a bus, their knowledge will be gone with them. Therefore, it is crucial for these SMEs to unload all that knowledge in their heads. Unfortunately, this is a catch-22: The SMEs are often too busy to stop what they are doing, and until they do the knowledge remains locked in their brains. With the right rewards, assistance, and incentives from management, it can be done. And, it needs to be done sooner rather than later. Remember the organizational culture rule of thumb? What management notices and rewards is the best indication of the organization's culture.

I've also been in organizations that use reverse engineering to obtain their business rules. What is reverse engineering? According to the Taxonomy Project of the IEEE-CS Technical Council on Software Engineering (TCSE),* it is the process of analyzing a subject system with two goals in mind:

1. To identify the system's components and their interrelationships.
2. To create representations of the system in another form or at a higher level of abstraction.

In plain English, it means to acquire the logic and relationships of how things work from the systems that are already in place. In my case the system was an operational computer system, but a system could be any type of procedure or process. So instead of starting with business rules and creating a system around the rules, we went backward and extracted business rules from the system: hence the name reverse engineering.

Therefore, there are many ways to obtain business rules. A recommended method for creating business rules is to ask the customer, i.e., ask the people actually doing the work to document their knowledge. The next section discusses some guidelines for generating business rules.

 REMEMBER

Sources of business rules include existing documentation, the organizational culture, the people who do the work, SMEs, and reverse engineering.

What Are the Guidelines for Generating Business Rules?

There are many types and forms of business rules, some of which are complex and confusing. But, the best guideline for generating business rules is to "keep it super simple" (my definition of the KISS rule). A business rule can be a single fact, a simple truth, or a group policy. The next primary guideline for generating business rules is right in its name, i.e., business rules are de-

---

*www.tcse.org/revengr.

fined and owned by the business' people. With these two guidelines in mind, you'll be able to recognize good, bad, and really ugly business rules. Further guidelines with examples of good, bad, and ugly business rules follow.

Business rules should be:

Declarative

Declarative statements do not care about how the rules are enforced. They represent a fact or a definition. Business rules simply state "what is true."

Good

A customer can have one or more savings accounts.

Bad

A customer can have one or more savings accounts as long as each has a different account number.

Ugly

A customer can have one or more savings accounts, each with a different account number, and each account may have multiple names associated with it.

Indivisible

Indivisible statements cannot be broken down into smaller statements. Keep it simple and have one rule per statement. Yet, each rule must be inclusive enough to be a complete thought.

Good

A customer must be 18 years or older to open a checking account.

Bad

A customer with a savings account can also open a checking account unless the customer is a minor.

Ugly

A customer who is a minor can have a checking account as long as it is shared with someone else who is over age 18.

Expressed in Clear, Concise Language

A business rule is written in plain English and should not contain any cryptic codes.

Good

A customer must have a savings account to obtain a loan.

Bad

For each loan a customer must be valid with account = "1" and tot-days > 90.

Ugly

For loan = valid, check account code = "F16925" or "Q67291" and write to error report; otherwise, set MDT = "Y" and send message T21.

Business Oriented

A business rule does not contain conditional statements, lists, loops, or database updates, typically found in program logic.

Good

A preferred customer has a combined account balance greater than $49,999.

Bad

If SUM(Accounts) > $49,999, move "Y" to customer status and send letter X291.

Ugly

L1: If ACCT-TOT < than $50,000 and more accounts then add next account balance to ACCT-TOT, and go back to L1; otherwise, move "Y" to customer status and send letter X291.

To reiterate, business rules are simply stated facts or policies that are developed and defined by the business. The IT group may assist the business to develop these business rules and then incorporate them into the technical systems.

 REMEMBER

Business rules should be simple and owned and defined by the business; they are declarative, indivisible, expressed in clear, concise language, and business oriented.

What Are Metadata?

Jeff, a VP, once said he wanted to have a "world-class" organization but didn't go on to describe his definition of "world class." He left his vision open to misinterpretation and a host of assumptions. Now, Jeff could have meant that he wanted his organization to reach a high level of standards achieved by only a few elite organizations in the world. But, Ed could think that by "world class" Jeff meant he wanted his organization to make new advances in technology. And, Susan may think that by "world class" Jeff wanted to reach additional international markets and increase global sales in the next fiscal year. In other words, to make sure everyone has the same understanding Jeff needed to define what he meant by "world class." In the same way, organizations must define their data. They need to have common definitions about the data used by the business, how they are created, when they are changed, and where they are stored. Organizations need metadata.

What are metadata? Metadata are a data dictionary. For example, a library catalog is metadata of the publications data and a sales catalog is a metadata of the merchandise. Any data about data become metadata. The key purpose of metadata is to facilitate the retrieval and understanding of the data. Metadata ensure that blissful data are meaningful and useful to all business clients in the organization.

If you consider my previous analogy that business rules are the who, what, when, where, why, and how of an organization and the lifeblood of the enterprise, then metadata are the who, what, when, where, why, and how of the data and the arteries and veins that carry the lifeblood to all groups within the enterprise. Thus, metadata are necessary to augment and enhance business rules.

Let's look at some business rules from the previous section and see what metadata are needed. Recall the sample business rules:

- A customer can have one or more savings accounts.
- A customer must be 18 older to open a checking account.
- A customer must have a savings account to obtain a loan.
- A preferred customer has a combined account balance greater than $49,999.

Each of these business rules contains one or more key terms. Terms such as customer, savings account, checking account, loan, and account balance must be defined in the metadata repository. A metadata repository is the database where the definitions of the data elements are kept. This repository is useful to anyone in an organization who needs to know what a certain data item really means. Metadata for that data element will tell you the definition of the item, where it came from, as well as where it exists. There are three main types of metadata.

1. Business metadata or the definition of data elements in the data warehouse, such as: Customer – A person with an active or inactive account. Active customers must have a current billing address. Each customer has a unique customer code. All customer information exists in the customer table.

2. Database metadata or the definition of the various databases and tables of the data warehouse, such as: Customer Table – A database that contains all data elements pertaining to customers. Customer data originate from the new accounts system and are updated daily with changes from the customer billing system and the customer loan system.

3. Application metadata or the definition of terms and functions specific to various functional groups, such as: Customer Delinquency Report (CU2951) – A daily report that shows customers with late loan payments. The number of late payments per customer is shown annually and over the life of the loan. This report is used by the accounting department to determine customers in good standing.

As you can see from these examples, metadata can be extremely comprehensive. Metadata are crucial for a data warehouse as this information provides a common, integrated understanding of the data. Everyone in an organization needs this common understanding to perform cross-functional analysis. I read that Albert Einstein never bothered to remember his phone number. Instead of cluttering his mind with an item of data he knew he could look up, he kept his mind free for other pieces of information. He was, in effect, using the principle of the metadata repository. Metadata allow people to look up the meaning of any data item instead of trying to memorize everything about the data.

However, metadata come with a caveat. How much metadata is enough? Some data warehouses never got off the ground because they *Keep enough metadata to provide value.* drown in metadata. Others were built and used successfully without any metadata. The rule of thumb is to "keep enough metadata to provide value." It is more important to keep a molehill of metadata up-to-date and useable than to have mountains of outdated metadata that no one uses.

Metadata make a data warehouse easier to use and the data more readily understood. Just like cleansing dirty data and explicitly stating business rules, starting a metadata repository and keeping it updated should be incorporated into the organizational culture. As the organization and data warehouse grow, such artifacts only increase in value.

Remember

Metadata are any data information about data. There are business, database, and application metadata. Keep enough metadata to provide value.

What About People, Power, and Politics?

"Never insult an alligator until after you have crossed the river."—African proverb

Business rules and metadata are so innocent in their own right yet devilish when combined across an organization. Business groups may make excuses to avoid spending time and effort to pull their business rules and metadata together. But business rules and metadata belong to the business groups, therefore, they are the authority on their business rules and metadata. In addition, building a data warehouse involves many people across many functional areas. What happens when you get these people together to combine their business rules and metadata? Just ask anyone who has asked three or more business groups to define "customer." Not a single group's definition will match another group's definition. No wonder some organizations become buried in metadata. They spend hours going around in circles without ever arriving at a solution.

Figure 5-5 Conflicts arise when combining business rules and metadata.

It's inevitable that people will develop conflicting business rules and differing metadata. Various functional areas may think that their rules and definitions are superior to others. As depicted in Figure 5-5, there will be power plays, power struggles, heated meetings, and long arguments. Some functional groups may not want to share their rules and definitions and will try to separate or distance themselves from the process. Others will withdraw completely. How will these conflicts be resolved? How do you get people to agree? This is where the data warehouse sponsor comes in. I've previously mentioned that this important person is the magnet who brings the business together, making decisions to support the goals and providing the leadership and leverage for growth. The data warehouse sponsor arbitrates when conflicts arise, makes decisions when conflicting views occur, and makes sure all functional groups stay involved. Hence, it is clear to see why the data warehouse sponsor must have the focus, power, and influence to produce the change and the integration skills needed for keeping the goal of the data warehouse in sight.

REMEMBER

The process of integrating business rules and metadata between functional groups will result in conflict, differences of opinion, and abandonment. The data warehouse sponsor is the key influence to keeping the goal of the data warehouse in sight.

REMEMBER THIS!

✔ Culture is the shared way groups of people think, act, and make decisions.

✔ Organizational culture is the personality of the organization. There are five categories of organizational cultures: club, gunshot, r & r, project, and partnership cultures. Project and partnership culture-oriented organizations are more open to change and flexibility.

✔ Artifacts are visible expressions of the organizational culture. Artifacts are often more obvious to an outsider of an organization.

✔ Leaders set the tone for the culture of an organization; therefore, it is possible for the culture of an organization to be transformed by a strong leader.

✔ Organizational change can be implemented by a leader who sets the direction, aligns the right people to assist, and provides incentives to change in the desired direction.

✔ The data warehouse sponsor provides the leadership and leverage needed to reach the goal of a successful data warehouse for the organization.

✔ Organizational structure plays an important part in the success of a data warehouse. A recommended structure places a division dedicated to the data warehouse with a sponsor as an equal partner with the CIO and the VPs of business.

✔ Business rules are the policies of an organization and represent what the business does. Explicit business rules are artifacts of the organizational culture.

✔ Sources of business rules include existing documentation, the organizational culture, the people who do the work, SMEs, and reverse engineering.

✔ Business rules should be simple and owned and defined by the business; they are declarative, indivisible, expressed in clear, concise language, and business oriented.

✔ Metadata are any data information about data. There are business, database, and application metadata. Keep enough metadata to provide value.

✔ The process of integrating business rules and metadata between functional groups will result in conflict, differences of opinion, and abandonment. The data warehouse sponsor is the key influence to keeping the goal of the data warehouse in sight.

Politics

Who's Going to Pay?

CHAPTER 6

AXIOM 6

The right data
warehouse investment
can bring significant
business value!

Have you ever experienced that "project from hell" where anything and everything that can go wrong does? If you have, you know that these terrible experiences can happen anytime, in any place. They can occur not only in your professional life but can also take place in your personal life. But, projects from hell don't sour overnight; there are warning signs along the way. The problems begin when we ignore these red flags.

We've seen some pretty hilarious movies or sitcoms about terrible vacation ordeals, weddings that went totally wrong, and home improvement plans that turned into a nightmare. Believe me, though, it's no laughing matter when you're the one involved. At such times, only a clear vision of the end goal can pull you through and help you turn the project around.

Unfortunately, data warehousing endeavors can easily become projects from hell. My friend Randy knows what such a project is like. He was the project manager of a data warehousing initiative that more than tripled its original budget and was over 1 year overdue. After 18 months, Randy's boss decided "enough was enough" and cancelled the project.

The idea started at a business lunch between a CEO and a software vendor. "Oh yes," said the vendor. "We can help you set up a state-of-the-art data warehouse in just 4 months." The CEO was intrigued by the promise of the "fast" technology change and the integration of the company's many disparate systems. He wanted to believe that a data warehouse was the answer to all his problems and was attracted by the thought of all the right information available at the touch of a button. "Let's go for it," he declared, setting up the directive and a generous budget (or so he thought) of $400,000, with a target completion date of 6 months.

As you know the project was cancelled 18 months later. There was little to show for the additional $1 million spent over the initial budget of $400,000. Almost $1.5 million later, together with wasted time, extensive shouting and finger pointing, and many voluntary as well as involuntary resignations, it was finally over. Only the costly lessons learned, bad feelings, ruined careers, and the pain of failure remained.

In retrospect, Randy said, the red flags indicating the project didn't have a chance were there all along; they were just ignored. These are some of the warning signs he saw but thought could be overcome:

1. The budget and deadlines were set before the project was even evaluated (no one wanted to tell the CEO that his estimates were insufficient).
2. There was no clearly defined business objective other than making a "fast" technology change.
3. Vendor consultants were hired to share knowledge with the development team, but the overburdened project team had little time to spend learning new methods and tools and very little knowledge transfer took place.
4. There was a lack of involvement from the business managers.
5. Business sponsorship was missing, resulting in little commitment from the business divisions.
6. The benefits of a data warehouse were never shared. Business analysts were never asked what they needed from the data warehouse, nor were they told how a data warehouse could help them in their work.
7. There was no time to capture business rules and metadata.
8. There was no preliminary assessment of the quality of the data, resulting in thousands of hours spent tracking and chasing dirty data issues.
9. The project team had a turnover rate of over 50%.

The lesson learned is that when a project fails everyone pays. Not only does the organization get less than expected, but reputations are tarnished, profits are not realized, and hoped-for market share is lost. The project team literally pays in sweat and tears. No one likes to be associated with a failure. Randy himself had never been associated with a failed project before and quit the company soon after the project cancellation. He left with no new job or prospects; he just had to put the entire situation behind him.

What Randy didn't realize is that many organizations have data warehousing project failures. Pride, politics, shame, and fear of looking incompetent prevent organizations from discussing such failures. The failures are quickly swept under the carpet and it becomes politically incorrect to even raise the specter of these projects from hell. There is the false mentality that if the failure isn't discussed it never happened.

Data warehousing is a proven technology and success has been achieved many times by many different organizations. Suppose, for an instant, that Randy's project was successful. Imagine if all the benefits the CEO wanted had been realized. The organization would have achieved blissful data, meaningful and useful information would be retrievable at the touch of a button, disparate systems would be integrated, and the organization would be equipped with the technology and tools to face the future. Wouldn't the organization and the lives of its employees be enriched by these new capabilities? Definitely! With a full view of the organization's data and the right information, everyone from the CEO to the newest college intern could learn so much more about the organization and be able to enhance their decision making while enriching themselves in the process.

I've already mentioned that a data warehouse is all about change and integration. I'd like to add now that a data warehouse also brings enrichment. Enrichment leads to success. As you know success begins with a goal, a plan on how to reach this goal, and the proper execution of the plan to achieve victory. In this chapter, we look at important elements of the plan—costs, risks, and people—and see how these elements come together to play significant roles in the battle toward change, enrichment, and growth afforded by a data warehouse.

Where Does It All Begin?

"A journey of a thousand miles begins with a single step."—Chinese proverb

Life is often like a business. We spend our time and energy pursuing our most important goals. We strive to reach these goals within our limits of time and cost. Similarly, business organizations pursue goals that help them

1. Increase profits.
2. Decrease costs.

Organizations that succeed in making a profit are the ones that survive. But, highly successful organizations don't just survive; they aspire to new levels of excellence. They know the importance of constantly exploiting new opportunities that can bring significant business value. These organizations are always looking for new discoveries like the two scientists depicted in Figure 6-1. They embrace endeavors that not only bring value with increased profits and decreased costs but also merit opportunities where the organization can leap ahead of the game and beat the competition. These are the innovative organizations that look to the future, dare to go forward, take calculated risks, and plan for success.

What does it take for an idea to become reality? Every project or idea begins somewhere. Ideas can begin on a golf course, at a baseball game, or at a conference where someone hears a success story or sees an impressive demo. But, ideas become reality only if the vision is shared, a sponsor is obtained, plans are laid, and people get involved. According to PMI (16), there are six main reasons for an endeavor to come about:

1. A market demand, e.g., the growing popularity of sports utility vehicles (SUVs) required car companies to quickly design and produce SUV models to compete in the market.

Figure 6-1 Looking closely for new discoveries.

2. A business need, e.g., a market downturn forces a large retailer to analyze sales data to determine its least profitable stores; these stores are closed for the retailer to survive.
3. A business client request, e.g., a request for an automated warranty claims system to replace an outdated manual process that was inaccurate and labor intensive.
4. A technological advance, e.g., the economics of storing large amounts of data on a single computer platform with relatively quick access has made it possible for organizations to set up data warehousing environments.
5. A legal requirement, e.g., the mandatory inclusion of air bags in newer-model vehicles led to the distribution and sale of air bags.
6. A social need, e.g., a rise in the aging population requires additional healthcare products and services.

Often, an endeavor may be the result of a combination of two or more of the above reasons. However, the single most important reason for an endeavor to begin is the expected value it will bring to the organization. For a business, this translates into how the endeavor or its product will help increase profits, decrease costs, or provide opportunities to leap over the competition. At times the problems solved by the endeavor are crucial for survival. Thus, the higher the benefit value, the higher the importance of the endeavor.

REMEMBER

The primary reason for an endeavor to begin is the prospective value it will bring to the organization. The value can be in the form of survival, increased profits, decreased costs, or an investment toward the future.

What's a Business Case?

At one time, a business manager's request was authority enough for an endeavor to begin. I remember a customer manager with a loud voice and demanding manner who always got what she wanted. The managers with less strident manners often lost out even though their requests may have brought more value and benefit to the organization.

Fortunately, those days are over. Today, many organizations require every endeavor or large project to go through some sort of needs assessment to justify its necessity. Needs assessments, feasibility studies, preliminary plans, statements of requirements, business cases, and proposals are all preliminary requests for work to begin. To be consistent, let's call any such request a business case. A business case defines the "need" or problem to be solved and proposes a justifiable solution. Sometimes, the endeavor can be mandatory, as in the case of a legal requirement. However, every endeavor must contain an analysis of the value or benefits to be realized versus the effort and cost to be expended. This comparison is often made in the form of a return on investment (ROI) analysis (more on ROI later in this chapter). A high ROI value makes a strong case for the endeavor's approval.

Many organizations require a business case to contain the following items:

1. The product description or the required characteristics of the results of the endeavor.
2. The strategic plan or how this endeavor supports the strategic goals of the organization.
3. The justification for and benefits of the endeavor. Any preliminary ROI analysis results available should be included. In addition, any identified risks or consequences of not following through with the endeavor should be stated.
4. Background or research material, including market studies, case histories, readiness of the organization, and metrics to be met for success.

A business case is a preliminary document. It states a "need" and provides the benefits and justification for fulfilling this need; it may define various strategies, potential risks, and other relevant background information. This document provides a starting point for the expansion of the idea as it makes its way to reality.

Business cases are collected, reviewed, evaluated, and compared for value by strategic decision makers in the organization. The business case is either selected or rejected depending on the value it brings and how well it will support the goals of the organization. Once a business case is selected, the endeavor is formally initiated. Its charter then needs to be defined and resources assigned to implement the endeavor.

REMEMBER
A business case defines the "business need" or problem to be solved and justifies a solution. A business case should contain the results of a preliminary ROI analysis.

What's the Formula for Success?

"The great mistake that most people make is not realizing one key point: The failure to commit to excellence, to victory, leads by default to the subconscious acceptance of mediocrity and eventual defeat."—Brian Tracy[4, p 7]

Have you found how much easier it is to start an endeavor than to finish it? I certainly have. Some efforts go smoothly and wrap up easily, others are full of delays, while yet others never get completed or are only partially completed. For every experience, good or bad, there comes a time where it should be completed or cut off and closed. At that point, it's always helpful to look back and ask two questions:

1. What went right?
2. What could have been done better?

Let's apply these two questions to Randy's disastrous project. First, let's see what was done right. To be fair to the CEO and the information technology (IT) group, they did what they could to make the data warehouse a reality. The CEO cleared the path, put up the money, and set the directive for the warehouse. The IT group provided a technically savvy, seasoned, and well-proven project manager, some very good technical staff, and a reputable software vendor. With the company's r & r culture (the research and refinement culture is defined in Chapter 5), there was lots of optimism and a high can-do attitude. Initiatives had always succeeded in the past and the company had grown quickly and successfully. Last, but certainly not least, the data warehouse sponsor, Brian, was director of the IT department. Brian was filled with boundless energy and a passion for innovation. With such strength and energy, the project team believed they could move mountains. Unfortunately, this time the mountain came crashing down on top of them.

What could have been done better? Hindsight always consists of 20-20 vision. It's easy to say, "Randy and his team should have heeded all those red flags when they happened." This is true, but what could the team have done to take the necessary precautions to prevent these events from happening in the first place? They could have been more proactive in thinking about what needed to be done, what could go wrong, and what they would do if difficult or unpleasant events did occur. In other words, they needed a game plan. Randy knows the importance of a good game plan, but because the schedule was so tight he figured they could get by and skip many of the planning steps. Like the mountain hiker in Figure 6-2 who ignores the signs for falling rocks, thinking he could get by before the next rock slide, disaster occurs. Randy, of course, now regrets his decision. He knows they couldn't have prevented all the negative events from happening, but with a plan they could have had better control from the start. A good game plan would have provided the strategies to assure triumph and avoid defeat.

In "Victory," Brian Tracy[4] likens life and work to a series of battles. In a battle, there is constant competition against uncertain forces in a turbulent

Figure 6-2 It's dangerous to ignore red flags.

environment. There is a never-ending succession of problems and crises. Sounds familiar, wouldn't you say? High paced endeavors are a battle. However, Tracy continues to add that men and women who achieve great things are those who take their responsibilities and situations seriously. By leaving nothing to chance, they are ready to perform consistently well in the critical battles and key moments both in life and at work.

I like taking the approach that life and work are similar to facing a series of battles. Some battles are won and some are lost. But, have you noticed that while certain people seem to win more battles than they lose others seem to lose consistently? What's the difference between those who often win and those who lose? Over the years I've studied a lot of projects and people. The people who win are prepared to face a battle with some sort of a plan; they fare better than those who give no thought to what actions or goals need to be achieved. Successful people not only survive but reach beyond their goals, enriching themselves in the process. They find the right sponsors to assist by supporting the goals and influencing others to implement the plan. And they get the right people to take action to reach these goals. People who win are the ones who set goals with a plan to achieve the goals. Their game plan is their key to success.

These observations led me to devise a formula for success – success is a combination of a good game plan, the right sponsors to support the plan, and the right people to implement the plan, i.e.:

"Success = a good game plan + the right sponsors + the right people."

"Success = a good game plan + the right sponsors + the right people."

Let's think about this formula for a moment and apply it to an endeavor. The game plan contains the goals and objectives of the endeavor and the strategy to achieve these goals. With clear goalposts and the right sponsorship, everyone involved in the endeavor moves in the direction of the goals. The right people have the skills and knowledge to take action and implement the plan. The formula works!

What about personal success? Does the formula still work? Yes, it certainly does. When it comes to your own personal success, you are the best sponsor and the best person for the job, so the formula simplifies to:

Personal success = a good game plan + you.

"Your personal success = a good game plan + you."

People who achieve personal success are the ones who set goals, decide how to reach those goals, and take action. Successful people take responsibility for their own actions. They execute their plans to the best of their ability and strive to meet or beat their goals. The formula works again!

Finally, let's apply this formula to a data warehousing endeavor. Data warehouses involve significant amounts of change and integration. They also impact on a lot of people in the organization. But, with a game plan

"Data warehouse success = a good game plan + the right sponsors + the right people."

to clearly set the goals and objectives; the right sponsorship to lead and encourage people to move toward the goals; and the right people who believe in the data warehouse, are open to change, and ready to battle the endeavor will succeed.

R EMEMBER

Successful people set goals and use a well-thought-out game plan as their commitment to success. A formula that works for personal or data warehousing success is:

Success = a good game plan + the right sponsors + the right people.

What's a Good Game Plan?

"Live life as if you were going to die tomorrow and plan life as if you will live forever"—Chinese proverb

While evaluating a vendor's software solution to supply and distribute product orders, I called various other companies already using the software. I'll never forget the advice I got from Keith, whose company had implemented the software. His comments were, "Make sure you have pots of money, lots of free time, and a head of dark hair . . . because I have none of that anymore." Keith had obviously fought a tough battle with enough stress and worry to turn him prematurely gray as depicted in Figure 6-3. Happily enough, Keith still retained his sense of humor.

My simple story illustrates the importance of a good game plan. A game plan determines how the battle will be fought. It is the plan of attack and the

Figure 6-3 Keith with a head of white hair.

strategies with which to achieve the goals. A well-thought-out game plan leaves "nothing to chance" and has no room for ad hoc assumptions. A game plan forces us to think of possible risks and contingencies early and be prepared to battle these risks if and when they happen. Of course, it is impossible to predict the future, but by planning for as many risks and opportunities as possible responses can be swift and effective. In other words, a game plan contains the who, what, when, why, and how the endeavor will be accomplished. A game plan shows that you are ready to do battle and WIN.

The Project Management Institute (PMI) uses a project plan as its main document to set a baseline and guide a project. This document contains many of the planning documents and decisions; it is used to guide project execution, facilitate communication, identify risks, provide a baseline for progress measurement and project control, and determine when success has been met. Therefore, a project plan is used to keep all the key details of the project so that anyone who reads it can obtain a clear understanding of the work that is going to be done to accomplish the goals. This sounds very much like a game plan. Therefore, a project plan is similar to a game plan and the terms are sometimes used interchangeably.

There is another major advantage of a game plan: It fosters open communication, which is critical to the success of any project but crucial for a data warehouse endeavor. A data warehouse impacts on a lot of people in the organization. They must be informed of the who, what, when, why, and how the endeavor will be accomplished. Stakeholders need to know and understand the game plan.

REMEMBER

A game plan contains the who, what, when, why, and how the endeavor will be accomplished. Stakeholders need to know and understand the game plan.

What Should a Good Game Plan Contain?

Jack and Jill
Went up the hill
To fetch a pail of water.
Jack fell down
And broke his crown
And Jill came tumbling after.
Up Jack got

And home did trot
As fast as he could caper
Went to bed
And plastered his head
With vinegar and brown paper

Although it would be ridiculous to think that a game plan is needed for something as simple as fetching a pail of water, we can use the nursery rhyme about Jack and Jill to illustrate the characteristics of a good game plan. Such a game plan would contain the reason or goals to be attained (a pail of water), the environment (a hill with a well where water could be drawn), the resources, such as the people (Jack and Jill), equipment (the pail, a well with a rope), time, and effort that would be needed, and the risks (Jack or Jill could fall, the pail could have a hole, or the water could be muddy) that could occur. Last, but not least, the game plan must contain the final acceptance criteria, i.e., what would make Jack and Jill's effort a success? Is success defined as their safe return with a bucket three-quarters full with clean, clear water? This criterion is used to recognize when goals have been achieved and the endeavor is complete.

It is important to note that a game plan guides the work of the endeavor. Therefore, as the amount or scope of work increases so does the need for a well-thought-out game plan. In addition, as work progresses changes will come about (you can count on this) and plans will need to change. There is a constant cycle of plan work, do work, examine work, go back and replan, do, and examine, until finally the acceptance criteria are met and the effort is complete. In the meantime, the status and progress of work must also be measured and reported to management and stakeholders. Therefore, a game plan contains a variety of elements. Some of the key elements are:

1. The charter – formal authority for the endeavor and the business needs the effort seeks to solve. Lists the name of the executive sponsor or sponsoring department.
2. The goals and objectives – a description of what is to be accomplished and the benefits to be realized. Include specific results from the ROI analysis.
3. The approach or strategy – a brief description of how the endeavor will be accomplished. The assumptions of the commitment and involvement of the various groups are addressed.
4. The risks – an evaluation of opportunities or events that can take place. List any constraints and assumptions for the endeavor.

5. The scope baseline – a breakdown of the work that needs to be done into smaller, more manageable pieces, sometimes called a task list or a work breakdown structure (WBS).
6. The schedule baseline – the time estimates for each of the tasks in the WBS. Each task rolls up to a total timeline for the endeavor.
7. The cost baseline – the cost estimates for each of the tasks in the WBS. Each cost rolls up to a total cost for the endeavor.
8. The milestone chart – a timeline showing target dates for important outcomes of the endeavor.
9. People, organization, and communication plans – the skills, environment, structure, and internal and external communication methods to be utilized for the endeavor.
10. Criteria for recognizing success – who and what will determine the endeavor as accepted and complete.

As you can see, a game plan can be a large and detailed document. I have sometimes found it prudent to keep the game plan to two levels: a high-level game plan for executives and management and a more detailed version for the development and core business support teams. A data warehouse game plan should always be created with the involvement of key players from the various business areas. It broadens ownership of the project, getting people to work together from its earliest stages to contribute toward a more successful data warehouse.

In the next few sections, we'll look at some of the more important elements of a game plan in greater detail.

Remember

A game plan contains the charter, goals and objectives, approach, risks, scope, schedule, and cost baselines, milestone chart, people, organization, and communication plans, and criteria for success.

What Needs to Be Done?

Every endeavor needs one or more goals, where a goal is a desired result or a purpose. I've already mentioned that life is a series of battles. A slightly more friendly analogy is comparing an endeavor to a sporting event. Every sports game has a goal to be reached to win. For example, in an ice hockey game one team's objective is to propel the puck into the net (or goal) and score while keeping the opposing team from scoring. Every member of the team knows this and they work together to score and prevent the other team from putting the puck into their net. The objective of the game is clear and simple: "Score more goals than the other team in three periods of play and win."

General Dwight D. Eisenhower[4, p 13] led the Allied forces in World War II with the clear orders to: "Proceed to London. Invade Europe. Defeat the Germans." During the Gulf War of 1991,[4, p 13]

> "*S*mart Objectives are SMART: Specific, Measurable, Assignable, Realistic, and Time-based."

U.S. Air Force pilots were given the directive with regard to the Iraqi air force: "If it flies, it dies." These goals are clear and concise and leave no room for ambiguity.

Objectives are often defined to support the goals. Objectives give more detail about what is to be achieved. It is often said that objectives must be SMART, which stands for: Specific, Measurable, Assignable, Realistic, and Time-based.

The qualities of a SMART objective are therefore:

1. Specific: The objectives must be clear and simple and leave no room for ambiguity or confusion.
2. Measurable: The objectives must have some unit of control to determine their status; this status may vary from partial to full completion.
3. Assignable: The objectives should be meaningful and self-contained as a unit so that a person or group can take responsibility for their completion.
4. Realistic: The objectives must be reasonable and achievable within the allotted timeframe.
5. Time-based: The objectives should have a specific duration with an expected delivery date for performance to be tracked.

As you can see, objectives that are SMART are clear and precise. Clear objectives, together with detailed plans, will contribute significantly to success.

Unclear objectives are the number one reason for data warehouse failures. Hence, it is crucial that data warehousing endeavors have clear goals and objectives that are specific, measurable, assignable, realistic, and time-based to win the game and succeed. The path to data warehouse success is never a straight path; there will be many dips and valleys. But, data warehouse success can be like a pot of gold on a mountain top: Getting there may not be easy, but as shown in Figure 6-4 by keeping a picture of the pot of gold in sight the dips and valleys can be navigated until success is achieved. Keep in mind that data warehouse endeavors involve the efforts of many people, each of whom must have a clear understanding of the goals to be achieved. These goals and objectives create the focused vision for which the organization must strive to reach. If there is no vision or unclear goals, people wander around as if in a fog, confused and disoriented. Beware the pitfalls of vague or ambiguous goals.

Figure 6-4 Keep a clear picture of the end goal in sight.

A specific business goal may be to be a dominant player in the large-screen TV sales and maintenance industry. The objectives to support this goal could be:

1. Sign up 3000 new customers per month by setting up a new advertising campaign by mid-February.
2. Respond to customer service requests in 2 days (a 50% quicker response than current levels) by hiring and training 25 technicians in the next 6 months.
3. Develop customer appreciation program to obtain 80% repeat customers by the third quarter of the fiscal year.

Note how the goal is clear and the objectives specific; they each have some unit of measurement, can be assigned to certain groups for ownership, and can be realistically completed in the specified time period.

REMEMBER

Goals for an endeavor must be clear and simple. Objectives must be SMART: Specific, Measurable, Assignable, Realistic, and Time-based.

What's the Approach?

"Theirs not to make reply,
Theirs not to reason why,
Theirs but to do and die,
Into the valley of death
Rode the six hundred.
—Alfred Lord Tennyson (1809–1892)[20, p 401]

Luckily, we do not have to be like the soldiers of the Light Brigade, immortalized by Alfred Lord Tennyson in his famous poem, "The Charge of the Light Brigade at Balaklava." Not many of us would go charging to our deaths without knowing why or for what. Early on, we are trained to ask the reason why. We learn to evaluate "What do I have to invest to get the results I want?" The investment does not necessarily have to be money; it could involve time, effort, or some other form of sacrifice. But, the greater the investment or bigger the sacrifice the more cautious we become in making sure we get value for our investment. First, we wonder, "Is it worth it?" Then, we think about methods to increase the payback or lessen the investment. In other words, we start thinking about strategy, or more efficient methods to get to the same goal. This is the basis for ROI. We analyze the payback for the investment.

Return on investment pops up everywhere. It is a commonly used term to describe the financial measurement of the payback of an investment. It contains an element of time. Let's look at a simple case of ROI analysis.

$$ROI = benefits\ realized/cost\ or\ investment.$$

Mario and his wife Hazel invested $10,000 in a kitchen improvement project. Mario had read somewhere that a major kitchen remodeling pays 71% back on the homeowner's investment,* so they hoped to someday get a substantial portion back of their $10,000 investment. Unexpectedly, 1 year later Mario and Hazel had to move to another state so they put their house on the market. After a couple of weeks, their home sold for $14,000 more than their neighbor Fred's house (which had the same floor plan and

---

*www.homestore.com/HomeGarden/Decorate/Features/ByRoom/KitchenApps.asp.

lot size but no kitchen upgrade). Assuming that the windfall of $14,000 was due to the kitchen upgrade, Mario happily calculated that the ROI for his kitchen improvement actually came to 140% ($14,000/$10,000) × 100). Not a bad return on their investment in the period of 1 year! This 140% is considered the tangible or hard ROI.

Mario and Hazel loved cooking and had created many gourmet meals in their upgraded kitchen in the 12 months before they moved. Therefore, they had already received some benefit on their investment. This benefit was intangible and it's difficult to attach a dollar value to it. This is known as soft ROI. Because the hard ROI had already been calculated to be 140%, the combination of the tangible and intangible, the hard and soft ROI, was worth even more than 140% for the year in question. Their total ROI could therefore have easily been more like 180 or 200% for the year! (I'll talk more on soft ROI later in the chapter.)

Mario and Hazel obviously made the right decision to upgrade their kitchen. By analyzing ROI before the endeavor began, they also obtained a tool for determining if the payoff could meet or beat their expectations. In this case, the 140% was a lot higher than the original 71% ROI they had expected to achieve. Last, but not least, Mario and Hazel learned something they could apply to their future endeavors: A thorough up-front ROI analysis is an effective tool in making decisions.

Similarly, organizations know that to stay competitive they need to invest in projects and solutions that provide strategic and financial benefits. These organizations insist on ROI analysis for proof that there is measurable payback for the investment before any endeavor is approved. ROI analysis reveals the financial impact of a project and permits an assessment of its value. A preliminary ROI analysis is often required when presenting the business case for an endeavor. A second, more thorough ROI analysis should also be completed as part of the game plan.

What is the ROI for a data warehouse? This is one of the most important questions to be asked by anyone in the organization. The main advantage of a detailed ROI analysis is the evaluation and definition of all the benefits that will be realized. These benefits should then become the slogans to be shouted from the rooftops by everyone involved in the project. Everyone from the CEO to the newest analyst in the organization should know these benefits. Only when every stakeholder understands the benefits of the data warehouse will he or she be committed to contributing toward its success.

Therefore, the successful approach in building a data warehouse is first to perform an effective ROI analysis. Share the benefits of the warehouse with every individual who will be affected, whatever his or her level in the organization.

REMEMBER

ROI analysis reveals the financial impact of an endeavor and permits an assessment of its value. The main advantage of a detailed data warehouse ROI analysis is the definition of all the benefits that can be realized.

What's the Triple Constraint?

Once the benefits of an endeavor are determined, the next important element in ROI analysis is determining the amount of work involved; this is called the "scope" or "scope of work." An endeavor with a large scope will usually require more effort and incur greater cost. In addition to higher costs, the larger the scope the longer the endeavor will take to complete.

Therefore, another key element of ROI analysis is the payback period or length of time it takes for the costs of the investment to be recovered. As we saw from Mario and Hazel's case, payback of the endeavor is determined by the additional savings, increased revenues, and attainment of soft benefits. Because the present value of money is always greater than the same amount of money in the future, the longer the payback period the less effective the investment. Note that "cost" has been mentioned with regard to both scope and time. Therefore, scope, cost, and time are clearly interrelated and together they are known as the "triple constraint."

If you consider scope, time, and cost as sides to a triangle as in Figure 6-5, you can see that whenever you change one of the sides it will impact one or more of the other sides. For example:

1. If you add more work to the endeavor the scope increases and either time or cost or both will have to increase, that is, more work will take

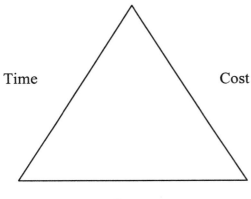

Figure 6-5 Triple constraint.

more time to complete or more people need to be hired to do the work, resulting in a higher cost.

2. If you want to decrease the time on the endeavor, you must either decrease the work or bring in more people to do the work, resulting in a higher cost.

3. If you need to decrease the cost of the endeavor, you either decrease the work or increase the time for the existing people to do the work.

Scope, time, and cost are crucial to every endeavor; they each have corresponding baseline plans that must be integrated into the overall game plan. These baselines are very important in controlling and tracking progress throughout the endeavor and are often known as performance measurement baselines.

REMEMBER

Scope, time, and cost are interrelated in every endeavor and are known as the triple constraint.

Was It the Lack of a Nail That Caused the Kingdom to Be Lost?

For want of a nail the shoe was lost,
For want of a shoe the horse was lost,
For want of a horse the rider was lost,
For want of a rider the battle was lost,
For want of a battle the kingdom was lost,
And all for the want of a horseshoe nail.

A key element in the calculation of the ROI is cost or investment. The cost of an endeavor is always a consideration. Many endeavors have failed on the side of conservatism, where benefits are not realized due to the fear or reluctance in making the investment and paying the costs. These organizations lost the kingdom for the want of a nail as in the above rhyme. Naturally, high costs are always tied to high risk. The higher the cost the more there is to lose if the endeavor fails. But, often high risks also have high payoffs. Highly successful organizations are those that have dared to move forward, taking calculated risks in doing so. Looking back in history, battles are not necessarily won by those with the most resources but by those who are bold, act quickly, and have a good game plan and determination to win.

Getting an entire organization to support a goal is not easy. Getting the right sponsors for a data warehouse is often a challenge. Frequently, the question asked will be, "Can we afford a data warehouse?" Perhaps the more important question is to ask, "Can we afford to not have a data warehouse?" Without a doubt, a mind-boggling question to ask is, "Where will we be if our competitors have a data warehouse?" An analysis should be accomplished to answer these questions. With the results of this analysis the right sponsors will come forward.

Business clients and management must realize that a data warehouse creates an environment of enrichment where intelligent decision making and insight become the normal day-to-day activity with no constraints to the imagination. Every stakeholder from the CEO to the newest business analyst must understand the limitless possibilities of a successful data warehouse. Once they understand the data warehouse will give them not only what they want but also what they "need," they'll be more willing to commit and invest in its creation and expansion. Once they begin to see the warehouse as an investment and not just a cost, they will become the right sponsors for the data warehouse.

Let's review the benefits of a data warehouse: A data warehouse provides the capabilities to:

1. Predict new trends and respond quickly to them.
2. Understand and better serve the customer.
3. Understand the total business of the organization.
4. Increase productivity per employee, resulting in increased profitability for the organization.

According to a 2002 study,[21] organizations that have successfully implemented and utilized analytic applications (such as data warehousing) have realized returns ranging from 17% to more than 2000%, with an average ROI of 431% over 6 years. More than half (63%) of the organizations in the study had a payback period of 2 years or less.

A data warehouse is expensive; this is a fact. Once all the expenses are added up it can cause quite a shock as depicted in Figure 6-6. Where does all the money go? There are three main areas where money is spent. These are:

1. People resources – consultants, project management and support, business analyst support, training and facilitation, policies, processes, and business rules definition, as well as consulting and knowledge transfer resources.

Figure 6-6 It costs HOW MUCH?

2. Software resources – applications software including access tools, development tools, data extraction and data quality assessment tools, as well as annual license fees, support, and upgrades.
3. Hardware resources – servers, computer memory, PC upgrades, and storage media.

People resources form by far the largest cost in a data warehouse environment, but success can be achieved only with the right people. They are the lifeblood of an organization! Keep in mind that you get only one chance to provide a first impression; it is best to perform a detailed ROI analysis and determine the realistic cost to build the data warehouse right the first time.

Over the years, I've found that the cost, time, and effort in certain key areas are often grossly underestimated. These include:

- Dirty data investigation and correction – tracking down, evaluating, and fixing dirty data issues can take huge chunks of time.
- Validation of data – extensive training needs to take place so that business analysts and managers can become familiar with the access tools needed to validate data, and prove its trustworthiness.
- Business rules and metadata integration and agreement – business rules from the different functional groups must be combined and metadata defined. More time may be needed for the people involved to reach agreement.
- Knowledge transfer from consultants – in the rush to bring new products to market, consultants come in, work wonders, and leave. When consult-

ants are used, time and money must be allocated for them to transfer knowledge to in-house staff.

- Warehouse growth and maintenance fees – once the data warehouse is established it can't remain stagnant. A successful warehouse will grow by leaps and bounds. A good rule of thumb is to plan for it to grow significantly—as much as 10 times its original size in the first 3 years.

Investigating, fixing, and validating data, integrating business rules, obtaining agreement on metadata, training and development of staff, and significant warehouse growth are all areas that could require substantial resources that could drive up costs. Be extra careful when evaluating the time and effort needed for these activities. They can make the difference between the successful outcome and the unmet expectations or failure of a data warehouse.

REMEMBER

Data warehouses have brought lucrative ROI averaging over 400% to organizations. But organizations must be ready to make considerable investments in people resources, software, and hardware for the data warehouse to succeed.

Who Are the Right Sponsors?

"The strength of the wolf is the pack, and the strength of the pack is the wolf."—Rudyard Kipling

Previously, I mentioned that once key stakeholders see the data warehouse as an investment and not just a cost they become the right sponsors for the project.

Figure 6-7 The strength of wolves.

A truly successful data warehouse comes about with help from many people within each area and every level of the organization; it always requires a team effort. These people work as change agents and get others to share in the vision and be energized to participate in the data warehouse. These change agents form a pack of wolves with the strength to push the endeavor forward. They are the sponsors of the endeavor. Thus, sponsors must be involved early and understand their roles and contribution toward the success of the warehouse. Some important sponsors and their roles are:

1. Chief executive and senior managers – these are the champions of the data warehouse. Without their support, the project won't fly. As leaders and visionaries they set the tone for the cultures and behaviors of the organization. If they embrace the environment of change, integration, and enrichment brought about by a data warehouse, so will the rest of the organization.

2. IT staff – they provide the leadership for a data warehouse. Technology is the medium used to deliver the data warehouse; therefore, IT people are often the key instigators of a data warehouse. Remember, though, that the data warehouse belongs to the business, but IT provides the environment that brings the business together. IT provides the knowledge and skills for the selection of the hardware platforms, the software tools, and the network to connect all the pieces. In addition, IT, working hand-in-hand with the business, provides the cleansed, integrated, blissful data that supports all areas of the organization.

3. Business clients – they have the final word on the success of the data warehouse. As they use the data warehouse and get answers to their business problems, further energy is unleashed to ask more and more questions. Once they understand the possibilities, responsibilities, opportunities, and challenges that they hold in their hands, they realize that they can unlock the mysteries of the business and reach a potential higher than ever imagined.

Simply stated, a data warehouse is built with the combined contributions of a team of sponsors from every level and area within the organization. They act as change agents to influence other members of the organization. Look on the people involved in the warehouse as members of a sports team. Senior management, as the coaching staff, sets the strategy for the game plan, IT provides the equipment and playing field, and the business clients are the players who block the opposition and score the goals. These key players energize and invigorate the audience. Just as it takes team effort to win a hockey game, it takes involvement from every change agent in the organization to promote data warehousing success. The right sponsors are an important factor in the formula for data warehousing success.

REMEMBER

Senior executives and managers, IT staff, and business clients all come together as the right sponsors for the data warehouse.

What About the Big Bad Wolves of Politically Motivated Decisions?

Unfortunately, we've already seen that data warehouse endeavors are fraught with politics. In Chapter 1, I mentioned that the big bad wolf is everywhere. These bad wolves are people who have a hidden agenda, i.e. they have secret schemes for their own glory. They make decisions to support these schemes instead of decisions to support the organization. Such decisions are politically motivated decisions. Data warehouse endeavors already face challenges from people who put up resistance, power struggles, withdrawal, and unwillingness to share data, but politically motivated decisions are more dangerous than all other types of resistance combined. Politically motivated decisions can lead to data warehouse disaster.

I've already mentioned that the lack of a clear business objective is the primary reason projects fail. The next reason for failure is when politically motivated decisions affect the endeavor. These are decisions that don't support the project goals; rather, they are made for short-sighted reasons or personal advancement and glorification. Let me explain with a short story.

I once worked on a project where a software solution was to be purchased from a vendor. Five "best in class vendors" were selected and invited to present their products. The evaluation was progressing and had been narrowed down to two finalists. However, I realized that one of the finalists didn't have a chance: not because it was the weaker product but because all the decision makers were being influenced to choose the other product. The influencer was Harry, a business manager who was in deep pockets with the salesman of product "xyz."

Harry was new to the organization and had worked with product "xyz" at his previous organization and had some knowledge of its complexities. It was a good product in many ways but included complexities that would require special support and maintenance that could cause problems in the long term. Harry wasn't interested in the long term. He wanted a quick fix that would also make him look good. With product "xyz" he could display his knowledge and satisfy his need to be "a hero" to his business unit.

Harry's decision was purely for self-advancement and self-glorification, not necessarily for the achievement of the project's goals and objectives. Be on the lookout for people like Harry. They are poison to the endeavor. Such politically motivated decision makers are not the right sponsors for a data warehouse.

Beware of politically motivated decisions such as:

- Overly complex procedures and processes that require many resources – this may be an attempt to build an empire.
- Using complex or proprietary technology because that was the only way to get the project funded – this will cause costs to stack up in the long term.
- Using consulting firms or vendors based on high promises or a cheaper price tag with no real alignment or relationship to the project goals – failure, reworking, or purchasing additional products or services will be expensive.
- Favoring a single vendor although no evaluation or credibility of the vendor's capabilities has been established – time, money, and resources are lost.
- Business units creating independent data marts with the assistance of outside vendors and bypassing IT – this short-sighted fix to obtain a quick solution will result in problems and additional costs down the road.
- Using hardware or software already purchased – saving costs in the short run could result in more costs in the long run.
- Not providing training because the tools are intuitive – training is still necessary for business clients to understand and validate the data.

Many politically motivated decisions are short-sighted views of saving money in the short term, with no thought of the long term. Because data warehousing endeavors have high costs, they are fraught with political pitfalls. In the previous chapter I mentioned that change must come from the top and so must the data warehouse sponsor. The data warehouse sponsor must also be politically savvy, able to recognize and stifle any such politically motivated decisions.

R EMEMBER

Beware of people who make politically motivated decisions for short-term solutions with long-term problems or for personal glorification. They are not the right sponsors for a data warehouse and can cause the endeavor to fail.

What Are Little Bangs?

Once upon a time, the "Big Bang" was the way to go. What's the Big Bang? It's where a new capability was made available all at once. Let's say the IT group was implementing a new accounting system on Tuesday evening. When you left work on Tuesday, everything was as it had been for the last 5 years. But, on Wednesday all the accounting applications you knew had changed. Even though everything might be working well and you now have more capabilities than before, you probably feel annoyed at being moved out of your comfort zone so abruptly.

As endeavors got bigger and more complex, it became increasingly apparent that the Big Bang method was not the right way to go. Big Bangs are full of risk. Too many things can go wrong. Endeavors run late, large amounts of money have to be invested, and for a long time little value is seen for the effort expended. More and more organizations began using a milestone chart that contains a number of little bangs or milestones. A milestone, as you know, is a significant event, such as a 21st birthday. Similarly, in an endeavor a milestone is a significant event that marks the achievement or completion of a major deliverable. This major deliverable could be a project objective. The milestone chart or schedule provides a timeline, identifying the entire project's major deliverables as seen in Figure 6-8.

A milestone chart is an important tool for a data warehouse endeavor. Little bangs or milestones must be planned every 45 to 60 days throughout the project's implementation. These little bangs highlight the progress being made and the additional value being delivered. These little bangs also provide the ideal occasions to celebrate and advertise your successes. Of course, these milestones must be both real and effective to keep stakeholders interested and involved. Use these occasions to promote the data warehouse. Make sure you also publicize any expense reductions, revenue increases, or gains derived from each milestone's tactical or strategic benefits.

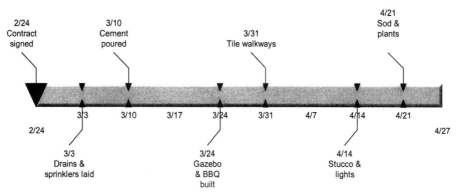

Figure 6-8 Milestone chart.

A milestone chart has another advantage: It can be used as a payment schedule for vendors. Payments along the way can be tied to the completion of a deliverable. Any risk of the deliverable not being made on time is then shared between the vendor and the purchasing organization. Let me tell you a story about Greg and Jan and how their landscaping project went wrong.

A few months ago, Greg and Jan began a large landscaping project. They thought they had done everything correctly. They had come up with the scope and main features of the endeavor and interviewed many landscaping vendors. Eventually, they selected a professional landscaping company and signed a contract after they had finalized the cost, discussed the payment schedule, and set the targeted completion date.

Despite their efforts, the project didn't go well. Somehow the landscaper poured the cement before the pipes for the sprinklers were laid down. This meant they had to burrow under the cement to place these pipes, causing additional work and delay. Rain, sporadic workdays, and other mishaps caused the schedule to slip even further. Greg's 50th birthday party, their original completion date, came and went and still the landscapers were dragging their feet.

Greg had been patiently making payments according to the schedule, but then he started to notice that the amount and value of the work performed was significantly less than the sum of dollar amounts paid over the weeks. He started getting nervous and informed the landscaping firm that they had to catch up with the work before he would make any more payments. Unfortunately, once Greg stopped paying the landscaper completely stopped work. Greg and Jan were left with open trenches, piles of rubble, broken tiles, and half-built walls in their front and back yards. Four months later, they are still no closer to a completed yard than 2 months ago. There was not much Greg and Jan could do but try to convince the landscaping firm to complete the job.

What could Greg and Jan have done to ensure the performance of the landscape contractor? Think about the risks of the project. Who carried the bigger burden of risk? I would say it was Greg and Jan. They paid money up front for materials and labor that never materialized. How could they have shared some of the risk with the landscaper? Perhaps they could have tied each payment to a feature or deliverable of the overall landscape plan. The payment schedule could have looked like Table 6-1.

Note in Table 6-1 the fifth week payment of $2000 was not made because the schedule had slipped and work was delayed and incomplete. The landscaper would then be forced to complete the seating wall and tiled walkways before he would receive further payment. Greg and Jan would be in a better position to negotiate the completion of the work over the next couple of weeks.

■ TABLE 6-1 ■ **Landscaping Deliverable/Payment Schedule**

	Deliverable	Payment Amount	Status
Start	Deposit	$1000	Paid
Week 1	Drains and sprinkler pipes laid	$2000	Paid
Week 2	Cement patio and walkways poured	$3500	Paid
Week 4	Gazebo and BBQ	$3500	Paid
Week 5	Seating wall and tiled walkways	$2000	Not paid (partially complete)
Week 7	Stucco, brickwork, and lights	$2000	Not paid (late)
Complete	Sod and plants	$2000	Not paid

R E M E M B E R

Little bangs or completed deliverables in a milestones chart highlight the progress being made and value delivered. Little bangs provide ideal occasions to celebrate and promote the benefits and successes of the data warehouse.

Who Are the Right People?

"He who gains victory over other men is strong, but he who gains victory over himself is all-powerful."—Lao Tse, a wise Chinese philosopher

Over the years I've worked with many different types of people. Each individual had a different personality and varied interests and opinions, yet everyone also had a strong desire to be needed and make a difference. In their own individual ways, they all want to bring value to their jobs and make meaningful contributions. With the right empowerment, people will expand their horizons and produce astonishing results. Not only are these people more productive in making larger contributions to the organization, but they themselves are also enriched in the process.

A data warehouse can provide such empowerment. It allows people to be able to access the information they need to support their decision making. A data warehouse has near limitless possibilities. A well-designed data warehouse allows all kinds of creative questions to be asked, bringing the possibility of wildly lucrative answers in return. Companies with successful data

Figure 6-9 Risk takers enjoy taking risks and risk avoiders hate taking risks.

warehouses have found profits from areas that were not even considered in their initial ROI calculations.

In Chapter 5, I discussed organizational culture and how it impacts on the thoughts and behaviors of the people within an organization. We know that leaders have a tremendous affect on the organizational culture and that cultures that accept change more readily have a better chance of data warehousing success.

People make decisions every day, many of which are based on their tolerance of risk. There are people who love living life in the fast lane; they are risk seekers, or risk takers. They will tend to be aggressive in their investment strategy, betting on the higher payoff. On the other hand, there are those who want to play it safe all the time. Risk avoiders or risk-averse people are conservative in their speculation. It is clear who is the risk taker and who was forced to go along on the mountain climbing expedition in Figure 6-9.

Ironically, a lot about tolerance for risk can be learned by observing people at the racetrack. Basically, people fall into three categories when betting on horses:

1. My friend Gene enjoys going to the horse races. When he goes, he often does well. It's not that he is an avid gambler; but he likes the challenge of calculating the possibility of the risk of losing his money or gaining a large payoff. He is willing to take the risk, i.e., he is a risk taker. Risk takers like Gene may place their money on a horse that is a "long shot," the unknown or unproven horse that has a slight chance of winning. But, they place their bet based on some preference, instinct, or knowledge about the horse's lineage or heritage. Because the probability of the horse winning is low, should the horse win the payoff is high. Betting on a long shot contains a higher risk but can deliver high ROI.

2. Jim sometimes goes with Gene to the racetrack. Jim likes to play it safe. He bets on horses with "short odds," i.e., he likes to bet on the horses that have high potential to run a good race. Some people like to play it safe and bet on proven horses because the probability of winning is high. Although the payoff is medium, the bettor doesn't often lose. Jim belongs among the people who are risk neutral. Betting on a horse with short odds contains a medium risk; there is a chance to make some money without the danger of losing too much money.

3. Last, some people don't go to the horse races; on the rare occasion that they do, they don't place any bets or bet only small amounts on one or two races. These people are risk avoiders or risk averse. This behavior contains little risk; these people don't have much chance of either winning or losing.

This tolerance for risk is very much a part of the organizational culture (discussed in Chapter 5). If people feel they will be penalized for trying something new and failing, management is sending the message that risk taking is not acceptable. The culture then becomes risk averse. A risk-averse culture does not accept change easily as change brings uncertainty and fear of failure.

On the other hand, if the organizational culture embraces change then people would be willing to try new innovations and overcome barriers as they arise. People would be willing to take risks. Significant change, such as that introduced with a data warehouse, is a lot easier to implement in a culture of risk taking and flexibility. Consequently, an organizational culture that encourages risk takers will have a better chance of succeeding in the environment of change and integration brought about by a data warehouse.

REMEMBER

People want to be empowered and bring value to their organization. The right people for a data warehouse are those who are willing to take risks, become more productive, and gain enrichment in the process.

WIIFM?

I once asked a management executive and a couple of business analysts two questions:

1. If you had the right information, what is it worth?
2. How will you use this information to bring value to your organization?

I was amazed at the answers I got. These people had dozens of ideas on methods to increase profits and reduce costs for their organization. In addition, they said having the right information to perform their job would increase their job satisfaction and performance considerably. One analyst even confided that she was considering leaving, as she was not gaining any enjoyment from the contributions she was making. She fervently wished for better information, which would enable her to make a difference to the organization.

Have you heard of WIIFM (pronounced, "whiff-em")? WIIFM stands for "What's In It For Me?" I'm sure this thought has often crossed your mind. From our youngest days, we learn to perform or repeat behaviors that produce some type of reward. As an infant taking your first step, you were rewarded by cheers, smiles, and applause. So, you take another step and get the same positive rewards. Soon you are running all over the place and learning other behaviors that produce positive rewards. As you grow, you learn to negotiate or bargain for bigger rewards. By the time you are 8, you may be negotiating for an increase in your allowance for tidying up your room. With adulthood, you automatically think of WIIFM whenever you are asked to do something. A WIIFM is just another form of ROI. It's an evaluation of what you will get in return for your effort or investment.

The WIIFM type of benefit is often tied to "soft" or intangible ROI. Soft ROIs are a lot more difficult to measure than hard ROIs. Let's go back to Mario and Hazel's kitchen improvement scheme. The hard ROI is indisputable: The kitchen improvement increased the value of their home by $14,000. The lucky couple got a 140% return on their investment of $10,000 in the short period of 1 year. But, how do you place a dollar value on the pleasure they took in cooking in their upgraded kitchen? Their lives were enriched by the new kitchen. It is a lot more difficult to measure this enrichment in terms of dollars. The value of soft ROI is subjective. The upgraded kitchen is worth a lot more to a gourmet cook such as Mario than to his cousin Janet, whose idea of cooking is to heat TV dinners in the microwave.

However, soft ROI can be measured. How? Suppose Mario and Hazel cooked about 300 meals in the span of 1 year in their upgraded kitchen. They assigned a value of $50 for each of these meals. This value includes the pleasure and costs saved for staying in (rather than going out) to enjoy their new kitchen. This gives them a value of $4500 (300 × $50) in benefits. The combined payback from their investment would therefore be 185% [($14,000 + $4500)/$10,000) × 100]: a remarkable return on their investment.

Having the right information can result in employees making decisions that bring in thousands or even millions of dollars in revenue, and even more in direct cost savings. Use these answers to estimate the value of the benefits that a data warehouse can bring to your organization.

I've already mentioned that building a data warehouse first requires an effective ROI analysis. Share the benefits to be realized with others in your organization, and you'll be able to get their full involvement in preparing the goals and objectives.

REMEMBER

We all look for WIIFM in our personal and business lives. A data warehouse provides both enrichment and increased job satisfaction WIIFM to both individuals and the organization.

What Are the Aspects of Hard ROI?

In calculating ROI for a data warehouse endeavor consider all aspects of hard ROI. These include:

- Direct cost savings from reduced inventories, increased production, quicker distribution, and more efficient use of staff, resources, and assets.
- Increased profits by retaining existing customers and obtaining new customers and ability to cross-sell and respond quickly to changing market conditions.

REMEMBER

Hard ROI comes from direct cost savings or increased profits.

What Are the Aspects of Soft ROI?

All aspects of soft ROI for a data warehouse endeavor can be considered with the help of the organization's specialists, who can assign a dollar value to soft ROI. These include:

- Improved customer satisfaction due to quicker response and an improved knowledge of customers' needs.

- Increased productivity from improved data quality.
- Enhanced decision-making capabilities by management and analysts due to clean and consistent data.
- Improved analysis capabilities for the entire organization with the availability of integrated and pertinent information.
- Establishing a reputation in the industry as an innovative leader instead of a follower.
- With organizational culture change, employees are empowered to widen their horizons, obtain additional information, try new queries, and find new data relationships.
- Given higher levels of job satisfaction, employees obtain a stronger sense of ownership of their job performance and capabilities.

These soft ROIs are difficult to measure but often have critical and widespread impact. They are important benefits in the ROI analysis calculation.

REMEMBER

Soft ROI or intangible benefits such as greater levels of customer satisfaction and higher levels of employee job satisfaction. Soft ROI cannot be ignored as they provide important benefits with a wide impact on the organization.

What's Plan A . . . or Plan B . . . or Plan C?

Do you watch cartoons? The characters in a cartoon often have an objective. In a cartoon I used to watch, the hero and mouse leader, Herman, always came up with a plan to gain the objectives. Let's call this plan A. More often than not, barriers get in the way and plan A goes haywire. The mice then switch to plan B. If that fails, not to worry, Herman has plans C, D, E, and F up his sleeve. With each plan, the various mice are assigned clear tasks and responsibilities, with Herman always taking the most dangerous role. The mice work together to overcome the barriers along the way to gaining their objectives. You may laugh and say, "It's just a cartoon," but Herman and his mice friends summarize the characteristics needed for a successful data warehouse.

These are some lessons Herman and his mice friends enforced or taught me:

- The clarity of the goal is essential.
- There is always more than one way to go from point A to point B. By thinking of a number of strategies on how to reach these goals, the mice increased their chances to meet or beat their goals.
- The best-laid plans can go awry, so always have a back-up plan or two.

Figure 6-10 Success = a game plan + the right sponsors + the right people.

- Assign clear roles and responsibilities; every person must understand the importance of his or her contribution to the overall plan.
- Teamwork is essential.
- Herman and his troops made split-second changes when things went wrong. Speed, flexibility, and the ability to change are important characteristics for success.
- Risk is always lurking and assumptions can be totally wrong. There are many uncertain events or conditions that, once triggered, will have certain consequences.
- Risks are not always negative; unexpected events can have a positive effect on the goals and objectives. Seize these opportunities as they arise.

Like the team in Figure 6-10, Herman and his friends were successful as they worked together with a game plan, the right sponsorship, and the right mice to get the job done. To reiterate, they knew the formula for success is:

Success = a game plan + the right sponsors + the right people.

REMEMBER

Clear goals, multiple strategies, clear roles and responsibilities, boldness, teamwork, speed, flexibility, the ability to change, managing risk, and seizing opportunities when they arise are important characteristics in gaining objectives. The formula for success is:

Success = a game plan + the right sponsors + the right people.

REMEMBER THIS!

✔ The primary reason for an endeavor to begin is the prospective value it will bring to the organization. The value can be in the form of survival, increased profits, decreased costs, or an investment toward the future.

✔ A business case defines the "business need" or problem to be solved and justifies a solution. A business case should contain the results of a preliminary ROI analysis.

✔ Successful people set goals and use a well-thought-out game plan as their commitment to success. A formula that works for personal or data warehousing success is:

Success = a good game plan + the right sponsors + the right people.

✔ A game plan contains the who, what, when, why, and how the endeavor will be accomplished. Stakeholders need to know and understand the game plan.

✔ A game plan contains the charter, goals and objectives, approach, risks, scope, schedule, cost baselines, milestone chart, people, organization, communication plans, and criteria for success.

✔ Goals of an endeavor must be clear and simple. Objectives must be SMART: Specific, Measurable, Assignable, Realistic, and Time-based.

✔ ROI analysis reveals the financial impacts of an endeavor and permits an assessment of its value. The main advantage of a detailed data warehouse ROI analysis is the definition of all the benefits that can be realized.

✔ Scope, time, and cost are interrelated in every endeavor and are known as the triple constraint.

✔ Data warehouses have brought lucrative ROI averaging over 400% to organizations. But organizations must be prepared to make considerable investments in people resources, software, and hardware for the data warehouse to succeed.

✔ Senior executives and managers, IT staff, and business clients all come together as the right sponsors for the data warehouse.

✔ Beware of people who make politically motivated decisions for short-term solutions with long-term problems or for personal glorification. They are not the right sponsors for a data warehouse and can cause the endeavor to fail.

✔ Little bangs or completed deliverables in a milestone chart highlight the progress being made and value delivered. Little bangs provide ideal occasions to celebrate and promote the benefits and successes of the data warehouse.

✔ People want to be empowered and bring value to their organization. The right people for a data warehouse are those who are willing to take risks, become more productive, and gain enrichment in the process.

✔ We all look for WIIFM in our personal and business lives. A data warehouse provides both enrichment and increased job satisfaction WIIFM to both individuals and the organization.

✔ Hard ROI comes from direct cost savings or increase profits.

✔ Soft ROI or intangible benefits such as greater levels of customer satisfaction and higher levels of employee job satisfaction. Soft ROI cannot be ignored as they provide important benefits with a wide impact on the organization.

✔ Clear goals, multiple strategies, clear roles and responsibilities, boldness, teamwork, speed, flexibility, the ability to change, managing risks, and seizing opportunities when they arise are important characteristics in gaining objectives. The formula for success is:
Success = a game plan + the right sponsors + the right people.

CHAPTER 7

Project Management

Is It the Silver Bullet?

AXIOM 7

The three Rs of data warehouse project management: recommunicate, recommunicate, recommunicate.

Have you noticed that when you tell a story about that "vacation ordeal" or your "terrible 2-year-old" or even your "home improvement project from hell" someone has to tell a story that tops yours? Are you guilty? I certainly am! I've even butted in and not let the other person finish her story. But now that I know I'm guilty I've become a better listener. Good listening skills play a major part in effective communication skills.

My friend Kim is a project manager with prime responsibility for one or more projects at a time. She has to communicate with the project sponsors, project customers, business clients, technical teams, and core and extended teams. In fact, every stakeholder of each of her projects has to be kept informed and updated about schedules, costs, milestones, and deliverables. Problems have to be solved, conflicts have to be dealt with, and requests for modifications must be evaluated and accepted or rejected. Kim spends more than 90% of her time communicating; she is a very busy lady.

Kim has a repertoire of knowledge and skills. In addition to her communication skills, Kim has many other skills needed for the strong management of projects. She can take a large project and break it up into smaller, more manageable, pieces; she then estimates schedules and budgets, assigns resources, identifies potential risks, procures outside services when necessary, and utilizes a process to control change. She listens attentively to her customers' needs, gets people to perform the work, and delivers quality products on time and within budget. With such outstanding discipline, Kim's projects are often successful and result in high levels of customer satisfaction.

You already know that a data warehouse is about change, integration, and enrichment. But, how do you bring all these qualities together and track and control all aspects of the endeavor? A proven method is by using the skills and knowledge of project management. The field of project management utilizes the concept of work being handled as a project with an emphasis placed on certain skills and knowledge to begin, plan, execute, control, and finish the project. A project manager is assigned to make certain the correct skills and knowledge are being applied. A project management methodology provides the step-by-step processes to define the work, plan and track schedules and costs, emphasize quality, motivate people, handle risks, obtain services and resources, and perform the communication and integration to incorporate all aspects of the project.

Success, as you know, is based on securing a good game plan with the right sponsors and people to carry out the plan. Data warehouse projects require high levels of change and integration, many units of work, wide and varied costs, many risks, and the involvement of many people; therefore constant communication and integration are mandatory in such projects. The disciplines of project management are perfectly suited for warehouse projects and can increase the chances of its success. In this chapter, we look at important elements of project management – scope, time, cost, people, quality, risk, communication, integration, and procurement—and see how these elements come together to play significant roles in the battle toward data warehouse success.

What's a Project?

We all work. I used to think that any work was part of a project but found this to be untrue. All projects involve work but not all work belongs to a project. I now define a project as:

> *A project is the concerted effort of work performed in a specific amount of time to create a unique end result.*

"... the concerted effort of work performed in a specific amount of time to create a unique end result."

There are projects of all shapes and sizes. They can be small, medium, large, or humongous. The size of the project is usually determined by the amount of work that needs to be done. Something as simple as packing up the contents of a desk could be a small project, a kitchen improvement would be a midsized project (although it could quickly escalate into a larger endeavor), and landing a rocket on the moon would be a large project. But, what makes these endeavors projects instead of just plain work? Let's see what they have in common. First, each of these efforts involves one or more individuals doing some focused work. Second, each had a finite beginning and an end. Last, but not least, a unique end result was produced as an outcome of the work that was done. For example, various boxes with different contents are produced from the desk packing effort, a new distinctive kitchen results from the remodeling, and the rocket that was built is like none ever flown and landed on the moon before. Hence, all three of these efforts fit the definition of a project and can be labeled as such.

When is work just plain ordinary work then and not project work? Think about work that is ongoing, repetitive, or does not create a unique product or service. For instance, day-to-day work to keep an organization running is neither unique nor temporary; therefore, repetitive operational work is not project work. Or, the assembly of 1000 cars at a factory does not produce a unique product; therefore, it is ordinary work. However, the design, development, and production of a new car model are temporary, with a unique end result, and thus qualifies for project work.

The end result of a project doesn't have to be a product; it could also be a service. Therefore, the work performed by a consulting firm to assist an organization in creating a data warehouse is in itself a project. This means that there can be subprojects within a larger project. Many subprojects often exist within large projects.

In addition to the final end result of a project or a subproject, there can be many interim products or services within the project, called deliverables. Some of the deliverables from the aforementioned projects could be: a kitchen design and layout plan, the contract, new flooring, finished cabinets, painted walls, schematics for the rocket, the rocket model, training the astronauts, the flight plan, the landing plan, the re-entry plan, test results, execution results, pictures, and samples from the moon. As you can see, the larger the project the more documents and deliverables are produced. These interim deliverables are necessary as stepping stones or milestones to deliver the successful end result of the project.

Thus, projects involve work to be performed in a specific amount of time to create a unique end result. This means every project involves people who do the work; the communication and integration necessary to orchestrate these people within the constraints of time, costs, and other resources; handling the risk that occurs; and the measurement of project quality and performance needed to produce the interim deliverables and the final end result.

R EMEMBER
A project is the concerted effort of work performed in a specific amount of time to produce a unique end result.

Why Use Project Management?

Now that we know that projects involve work for a specific amount of time and produce a unique product or a service, we can better understand the need for project management. First, let's look at what constitutes project management.

> *Project management is the utilization of certain knowledge, skills, tools, and techniques to ensure project work gets done.*

You know projects need people to do the work. These people must be able to handle the work that needs to be done to create the product and deliver the project. They use certain tools and techniques to help them define the quickest, most efficient methods to create the deliverables that are required. There may be a game plan or strategy on how to proceed. They may use a tracking or control method to measure progress. And, they may have to change strategies or rethink their game plan should unexpected events occur. In other words, these people are using principles of project management to help them ensure their projects will be successful. Hence, project management can be defined as:

> "... the utilization of certain knowledge, skills, tools, and techniques to ensure project work gets done."

As the number of deliverables in a project increases, the number of people needed to complete these deliverables also increases. As the number of people on a project increases, cost and schedules typically increase and projects become more complex. Complex projects require a higher level of communication and integration. A complex project also contains greater risks and becomes more difficult to control. As the percentage of project failures increased, organizations came to realize that a strategy was needed for handling and controlling project complexities to ensure the end result could be delivered. They recognized the importance of defining their project management methodology.

In Chapter 6, the formula for success was defined as the sum of the game plan, the right sponsors, and the right people. A project management methodology carries this formula to the next level: How should these crucial ingredients be integrated to make them work well with each other? What documents and deliverables must be produced to ensure that the work of the project is being accomplished within the triple constraints? Are the right people doing the work they are best fitted to do? Thus, project management is a tool. It is used to increase the chances of project success.

REMEMBER

Project management is the utilization of certain knowledge, skills, tools, and techniques to ensure project work gets done. It becomes a tool to ensure that the end results of the project will be delivered successfully.

The Wall Was Pastry and Piecrust, Is That All?

> *Little King Boggen, he built a fine hall;*
> *Pastry and piecrust, that was the wall;*
> *The windows were made of black pudding and white,*
> *Roofed with pancakes—you never saw the like*

A couple of years ago I visited the Great Wall of China. If you've been there, or as you can see in Figure 7-1, this is the wall of walls. Just like King Boggen's

Figure 7-1 Great Wall of China.

fine hall in the nursery rhyme, there's nothing like it. This great wall is impressive; at one time it stretched on for more than 4000 miles. It is wide, about 10 feet across, with many steps that go up and down from the many watchtowers, dipping and curving with the rough terrain. It is old, with some sections built before the Qin Dynasty (221 to 206 BC). But, most of all, the Great Wall is amazing! How was such a feat accomplished with the lack of machines and modern technology? What was used to cut and lift the heavy stones into place? What was used to hold the stones together? Where did the stones come from?

I don't know the answers to these questions about the Great Wall, although a tour guide did tell me that sticky rice flour was used to make a paste to hold the stones together. (Inconceivable!) I can surmise that the Great Wall was a large project with many subprojects that involved the efforts of hundreds of thousands of people over many years. It was built without modern project management skills and knowledge; yet, a unique end product was produced, delivered by people doing work for a temporary amount of time. How was it all accomplished? To understand the enormous effort and sacrifice behind this large project, let me tell you an old story about Meng Jaignu, a young Chinese bride whose husband was assigned to work on the Great Wall.

The Great Wall is located in North China, where it is often cold. Meng Jaignu worried about her husband working in the cold weather, so she made him a warm padded cotton jacket. When it was finished she hurried to make the journey toward the portion of the wall being built by the men of her village. However, by the time she got there she found that her husband was dead. Devastated at her loss, Meng Jaignu wept so many tears that a portion of the wall collapsed. By some strange chance, at the center of the pit that was created lay the body of her husband. The distraught young bride then threw herself into the sea and drowned.

It really doesn't matter whether this story is true or not. What it does highlight is that every project has constraints and risks. You already know about the triple constraints of scope, time, and cost from Chapter 6. Apparently, the Great Wall was accomplished with an unconstrained number of resources and little consideration to risk. Projects today always have the constraint of resources, such as people, costs, time, equipment, and materials. Project risks and safety are also primary concerns. We can no longer assign thousands of human resources to a project with little regard for their safety. How many lives did it take to build the Great Wall of China? Even if Meng Jaignu's husband was the only life lost, the answer is still simply, "too many." Project management is needed to limit and control the people, the time, and the cost of a project while still completing the objectives of the project.

RЕМЕМBER

Project management is needed to limit and control the resources on a project while meeting the project requirements for success.

Who Are the Lucky Project Managers?

"There is no such thing as a good project manager—some project managers are just plain lucky."

"The more a project manager plans, the luckier he/she gets."—Project Management proverbs[22]

Every project needs a person with project management skills and knowledge to be the key person to make sure the project work gets done. This per-

Figure 7-2 Project managers clear the way.

son clears the way for others to get their work done, just like the woman in Figure 7-2. This person is known as the project manager. Some large projects have subprojects with subproject managers to help the project manager clear the path as shown by the man in Figure 7-2.

Recall Kim, my project manager friend at the beginning of this chapter. Kim is always busy making sure the project work gets done. She does a lot of planning, which in turn helps her accomplish successful projects; she is a lucky project manager.

Kim knows there are special knowledge, skills, and tools that help her manage projects. Like a conductor of a symphony she must orchestrate different groups of people to work well together. She uses project management principles and methodologies to ensure the project work is done in the allotted time and within specified costs to the satisfaction of customers. Kim also knows that projects need people to do the work. Leading, communicating, integrating, and motivating people on a project are very important project management skills. A project is only as good as the people doing the work. Her job as the project manager is to clear the path for these people to do their work. Kim is a resource for her projects.

Lucky project managers like Kim know the formula for project success. This formula is the same for the success of any endeavor, including a data warehouse success. Thus, keep in mind that proj-

Project success = a good game plan + the right sponsors + the right people!

ect success and data warehouse success are entwined. Project management skills and knowledge are essential for data warehouse project success. The project manager must create a good game plan, make sure the right sponsors are in place to promote and support the plan, and get the right people with the skills and knowledge to implement the work as detailed in the plan. Project managers use skills of managing communication, scope, time, cost, people, quality, risk, procurement, and integration to obtain the involvement and expectations of project stakeholders. These project managers increase their possibilities of "happy" customers and accomplishing successful projects.

Let's look at some outcomes where project management skills worked and others where these skills were lacking:

The Lucky

The Trojan Reactor Vessel and Internals Removal Project in Oregon was awarded the PMI 2002 International Project of the Year Award.[23] It successfully removed and disposed of a commercial nuclear reactor. This 42-month project was completed on time and cost $4.2 million less than the original estimate of $26.1 million. It involved many Portland General Electric employees and about 12 subcontractor firms to do the work.

The Not So Lucky

The development of the Diplomat Resort in Hollywood, Florida, faced many challenges with missed schedules and escalating costs. This $600 million project was more than 1 year behind schedule and plagued with conflict as well as technical and legal issues.[23]

The Unlucky

The National Ignition Facility at the Lawrence Livermore National Laboratory began a project to develop the world's most powerful laser with the technology advances to achieve atomic fusion. After some time, it was expected to overrun its estimated budget of $2 billion by another $2 billion and be 4 to 6 years behind schedule. Included in the overrun of $2 billion is $50 million for additional project management efforts.[23]

The Trojan Reactor Vessel, Diplomat Resort, and National Ignition Facility are all large, complex projects, yet the Trojan Reactor was able to come in on time and under budget whereas the other two projects could not. Although there are hundreds of factors and reasons for project failure, I would suspect that the not so lucky projects needed project managers with stronger project management skills and knowledge. Let's take a closer look at the field of project management and its processes and knowledge areas as they pertain to successful projects.

 REMEMBER

Lucky project managers know the formula for successful projects:
Project success = a game plan + the right sponsors + the right people.

What Project Management Knowledge Do You Need?

Although projects have existed forever, the field of project management is still very young. However, as projects become more and more complex the need for project management becomes more apparent. Just like data warehousing, project management is growing rapidly in strength and popularity. You will begin to notice requirements for good project management; let's see what it entails.

According to the Project Management Institute (PMI), the field of project management can be subdivided into six broad categories of performance called performance domains.[24] Each performance domain contains specific actions or tasks that require certain knowledge and skills. The six performance domains are:

1. Initiating the project – authorizing the project and getting it started.
2. Planning the project – defining the project objectives and the courses of action to meet these objectives to deliver the unique product or service of the project by creating a plan.

3. Executing the project – coordinating the people and resources to carry out the work of the plan.

4. Controlling the project – regular monitoring and measuring of progress to identify any variances from the plan, and taking the necessary action to correct the variance.

5. Closing the project – formal acceptance and close-out of the project or phase.

6. Professional responsibility – the legal, ethical, and professional behaviors expected of the project team.

The first five performance domains of initiating, planning, executing, controlling, and closing the project are where the actual work of the project is performed. These domains overlap with groupings of processes and are sometimes referred to as process groups. Therefore, there are also the process groups of initiating, planning, executing, controlling, and closing. The sixth performance domain of professional responsibility is applied throughout the life of the project.

Remember

Project management can be delineated by the six performance domains: initiating, planning, executing, controlling, and closing the project, and professional responsibility.

Is Project Management the Silver Bullet?

Consider the boats in Figure 7-3. They were designed, built, and delivered on time and within budget to the customer. But, was the project a success? This project would be a success only if these strange boats were what the customer ordered. If the customer had ordered rowboats, then these boats with huge sails and large fans are not what the customer wanted. Although the project was done on time, it did not give the customer what he was expecting and therefore cannot be called a success.

It is important to keep in mind that it is the customer who classifies a project as a success or failure. Open communication with the customer to identify the customer's implied and stated needs is mandatory for success. Project management defines the processes and describes the tools and techniques for this open communication. But, whether the communication is handled effectively often depends on the skills, experience, and capabilities of the project manager. Thus, utilizing project management principles and processes may dramatically increase the chances of project success but does not guarantee it. Success still depends on having the right people on the project. In

Figure 7-3 The customer ordered rowboats.

other words, project management can be the silver bullet to success but in the end is only a technique. To reiterate, it is people who make the difference between project success and failure.

I've already mentioned that the work of the project is completed in the five process groups: initiating, planning, executing, controlling, and closing. These process groups interact closely with each other, that is, a project or phase is initiated in the initiating process group and then various elements of the project are defined and planned in the planning process group. Once planning is done, the work is executed and measured in the executing and controlling process groups. By evaluating the work, it may be found that more planning needs to be done or that all the work of the project is complete and so the project is closed in the closing process group. The work of the project loops between planning, executing, and controlling as many times as needed until all the project work has been completed and accepted. These three process groups must also work hand in hand, that is, with only planning nothing will be produced, carrying out the work of the project with no previous planning or control will result in rework, and with no control you may as well throw your plans out of the window.

Each of these process groups contains one or more processes. Each process produces one or more tangible results or deliverables, which can become the input to another process, until the final end result is obtained and approved.

In summary, project management provides the processes and techniques for projects to succeed but it is not the silver bullet. It is not going to magically make every project a success, nor will it turn every ill-fated project around; but it can and has been used to increase the chances for success. The customer ultimately classifies a project as a success or failure.

REMEMBER

The five process groups—initiating, planning, executing, controlling, and closing—all work together to provide the processes and techniques that can deliver successful projects, but the right people are still required to make it all work.

How Is Project Work Orchestrated?

Project management involves integrating and orchestrating all project work to ensure that all parts of the project integrate well together and the project goals are achieved. I think of a project manager as an orchestra conductor like the one shown in Figure 7-4. This conductor has to make sure each rhythm section performs its part at the right time, right sequence, pitch, and tone to make sounds that are well integrated into a musical whole. Like a symphony performance, where a piece of music has an introduction, some sections of music are produced in sequence, some melodies are repeated, until a finale or close, a project also contains phases where it moves from the initiating process

Figure 7-4 Orchestrating project work.

to planning, executing, and controlling, back to planning, more executing, and controlling, until all work had been accepted and the phase is closed. The same process groups are repeated for the next phase until all the work of the project is complete and accepted and the project is closed. Note that the planning, executing, and controlling process groups can loop or work can move back and forth between executing and controlling processes multiple times depending on the needs of the project. To see a simple example of this sequence and looping, let's look at a sample project.

Have you ever coordinated an office move? If not, have you ever moved house? Moving is definitely a project. It has a beginning and an end; it is always unique, and the result is that you end up in a different location with hopefully all your belongings intact. Some of the many steps you may go through as they relate to the process groups could be as follows:

1. Like every other project a "move" begins with a business case of why you need to move. Perhaps you've outgrown your current residence or your daughter is learning to play the clarinet and you need a soundproof music room. You perform a preliminary return on investment (ROI) analysis by checking houses for sale in your neighborhood and prices for houses you may want to purchase.

2. Once the decision is made to move you may have a family meeting to authorize the actual start of the project. Perhaps you'll go out to dinner to celebrate this decision. This is the kickoff party of the initiating process group.

3. Now it's time to set up your game plan. You come up with some goals and objectives, such as the characteristics of your dream house, the price range you can afford, and the target selling price of your current home. You begin research by looking at houses for sale. You may call some banks to discuss loan rates and points. You also start talking to real estate agents about putting your current house up for sale, speculate on what types of offers you may get, and consider what needs to be done to "stage" your current house for a quick sale that could maximize your asking price. As one of your objectives is to move in June, you set up a baseline schedule, budget, and milestone chart of key deliverables. You evaluate some of the risks, such as not being able to sell your home in a timely manner; can you handle double house payments? And, for how long? You work through all aspects of your game plan.

4. Next, you are ready to begin executing your plan. You find your dream house by pure luck and make an offer. In the meantime, you pack or discard some of your clutter to make your current house more presentable. Two weeks later you receive an offer on your current house.

5. Is this the offer you are looking for? Evaluating the offer is part of the controlling process group. You decide to respond with a counteroffer. In the meantime you find that two other potential buyers have sent in offers on your dream house, so you increase your offer and make adjustments to the game plan. You continue to pack items you know you won't use for a while.

6. A few days later, your counteroffer is accepted on your current home and your dream house owners accept your increased offer. The timing is incredible! You open escrow on both the sale of your old home and the purchase of your new home.

7. Now comes the heavy planning for the actual move. You create a packing schedule. Next, you start executing this plan, packing the items in every closet, drawer, cupboard, and every nook and corner of the garage. You may find you need to purchase more boxes, have a garage sale, or throw many items away.

8. In about 2 months, you get the keys to your new home. The big day of the move arrives. All your planning and packing come together. Your move is hectic but well organized. The right boxes and furniture are all in their appropriate rooms because they were so well labeled. The game plan worked!

9. Can you relax yet? No, not quite. There is still more work to be done. Now comes the unpacking and figuring out where everything goes. Eventually, all the boxes are unpacked and the house surpasses all the expectations you've been envisioning over the last 4 months.

10. Your family throws a housewarming party to close out the successful move project. It was well planned, managed, and executed.

As you can see, the project moved from the initiating process to planning, executing, and controlling, back to planning, more executing, and controlling, until all work had been accepted and the phase is closed. These process groups provide a sequence of events that take place and are repeated until all the goals and objectives of the project are achieved. In addition, large projects can be broken down into multiple phases; each of the five processes and their iterations can be repeated for each phase.

Remember

A project moves through the five process groups, looping within the planning, executing, and controlling process groups for as many times as necessary until the project end result is approved and the project phase or the entire project is closed.

What Are the Knowledge Areas?

PMI defines one more dimension of project management. This dimension consists of nine bodies of knowledge and practices, defined in terms of the processes. These bodies of knowledge are called the knowledge areas. Familiarity with these knowledge areas and application of these practices are crucial to project success. These nine knowledge areas are defined in "A Guide to the Project Management Body of Knowledge" (PMBOK Guide)[25] as the knowledge areas in:

1. Project integration management.
2. Project scope management.
3. Project time management.
4. Project cost management.
5. Project quality management.
6. Project human resource management.
7. Project communications management.
8. Project risk management.
9. Project procurement management.

You already know that each of the five process groups contain one or more processes. The PMBOK Guide[25] describes 39 processes in all. These processes in turn are arranged into the nine knowledge areas. An understanding of the specifics of the knowledge areas provide better chances for completing the work of the project, leading to success. The nine knowledge areas with their corresponding descriptions are shown in Figure 7-5. In the next few sections, we'll go into more detail on each of the nine knowledge areas.

A data warehouse project is about change, integration, and enrichment. All these knowledge areas come into play in every project, but depending on the project certain knowledge areas need more emphasis than others. Because change and integration are key aspects of data warehouse projects, the knowledge areas of emphasis for data warehouse project success are project communications, risk, and integration management.

Remember

The field of project management encompasses nine knowledge areas: project integration management, project scope management, project time management, project cost management, project quality management, project human resource management, project communications management, project risk management, and project procurement management. The knowledge areas of emphasis for data warehousing project success are communications, risk, and integration management.

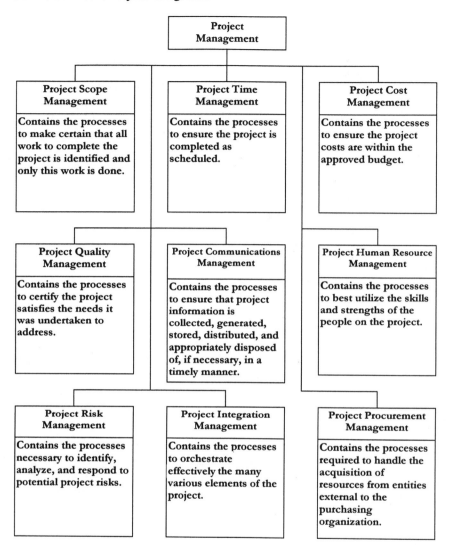

Figure 7-5 Knowledge areas.

Thinking Scope

Everyone on the project must think scope. Scope can be defined as "the work of the project." Without scope the project does not exist. Project scope management contains the processes to make certain that all work to complete the project is identified and only this work is done.

Figure 7-6 Manage expectations.

Keep in mind that people often have varying expectations as depicted by the couple in Figure 7-6. Even if these expectations are well managed, project scope tends to grow. Everyone from the company president to every client thinks they are entitled to add a few bits and pieces to the project scope. This is known as scope creep. Many project managers are optimists and allow project scope to increase, but learn from a seasoned project manager—the best word a project manager needs to repeat is NO. Saying no isn't easy but it has to be done for the project to succeed. Don't get me wrong: Changes in the project are inevitable, but every change should be evaluated, approved, or declined. Here are some guidelines for scope management:

1. Have a clear picture of the project goals.
2. Create objectives to be achieved to support the goals. These objectives must be Specific, Measurable, Assignable, Realistic, and Time based (SMART).
3. Create a work breakdown structure (WBS) by taking the major project deliverables and breaking them into smaller and smaller components until adequate budget (costs) and time estimates can be developed. Each bottom level component of the WBS should have a manageable deliverable.

4. Verify that all work on the project is covered by the WBS; review objectives and deliverables with the customer and get a sign-off.
5. Create a list of project objectives and deliverables.
6. Review the objectives and deliverables with the customer to obtain acceptance and sign-off.
7. Set up a change control and evaluation procedure. Make sure it is followed.
8. Establish the close-out details. Define the key factors that must be met for the project to be considered a success. Specify the expected means of inspection to determine whether results that conform to requirements must be defined and accepted by the customer.
9. Put it all in writing (you'll thank yourself later).

REMEMBER

Project scope management contains the processes to make certain that all work to complete the project is identified and only this work is done.

Thinking Time

Time is a precious resource. By breaking up the work of a project into smaller pieces, your estimates of the time it takes to finish the work becomes more accurate. Accurate estimates can make the difference between a good project and a bad one. With realistic estimates and a solid schedule you have a better chance of avoiding those 90-hour work weeks, degraded team morale, and sacrificing quality "just" to meet the schedule. Project time management contains the processes to ensure the project is completed as scheduled.

Project schedules are often the weakest link in a project. Schedules are fraught with difficulty and risk as hundreds of unexpected glitches can cause delays. Schedules also have another strange trait: I've found that if a completion date is ever mentioned, come hell or high water, someone will remember the date and try to hold you to it. Do not mention any dates until proper planning of schedules has been completed. Here are some guidelines for project time management:

1. Take each of the deliverables identified in the WBS and identify the specific activities to produce the deliverable.
2. Sequence these activities in the order in which they must be performed. For example, the pipes for sprinklers and drains must be laid in the soil before cement is poured in a landscaping project.

3. Estimate the duration or time it will take to complete each of the activities. To increase the accuracy of her guesses, my friend Kim would:

   - Ask the people who would actually carry out the activity.
   - Look at previous similar projects.
   - Ask an expert in the field.
   - Utilize a scheduling model or tool from the industry.

4. Create a project schedule baseline with start and end dates for each activity. Review this and get a sign-off from the customer.

5. Create a milestone chart to show the scheduled start or completion dates of key deliverables (identified during scope management processes). Get another sign-off.

6. Determine all activities on the critical path. This is the path of activities that must take place for the project to be completed within the schedule. Therefore, it is the longest path of project work. Any delays in the critical path will delay the project.

7. Focus on the critical activities. Watch for other activities that may lag or fall behind and change the critical path.

8. As changes get approved or work actually gets done, the project schedule will change. Manage the actual changes when they occur.

9. Chart the final schedule and post it on a common wall. Keep it updated with actuals so everyone can measure progress.

10. Use a project management software tool to help keep all the schedules straight and document the project schedule.

REMEMBER

Project time management contains the processes to ensure the project is completed as scheduled.

Thinking Cost

Ahhhh! Yes, money. Sooner or later it always comes down to money. Money is the lifeblood of the project. Funding or budgeting in a project is always tied to the cost of resources. If the project has no money to pay the people to do the work and buy the supplies or equipment needed, the project grinds to a halt.

My friend Frank is a long-time project manager. He trained his daughter Cheryl in many aspects of project management. Cheryl proved her project management mettle a few months ago when she planned her wedding. Cheryl's parents gave her a sum of money to use for the wedding, and any excess dollars were hers to keep. The full amount became the project budget. Cheryl created a game plan, estimated and controlled costs, and carried out her plan for a wonderful wedding.

Not only did Cheryl meet her goal to have a great wedding, but the wedding expenses came in under budget. With the extra money, Cheryl and her new husband were able to upgrade the cabin on their honeymoon cruise. Therefore, project cost management contains the processes to ensure the project costs are within the approved budget. Here are some guidelines for project cost management:

1. Identify the resource requirements and the quantities needed to complete the deliverables of the WBS and the time duration estimates. Resource requirements include the people, money, facilities, equipment, supplies, and knowledge.

2. Determine where resources will come from and their rates. For example, will the people doing the work come from the organization or will they have to be contracted through project procurement management? Special skills may require higher consulting rates.

3. Remember the project objectives in determining project budget. If you are remodeling your kitchen and your objective is to have a top-of-the-line, state-of-the-art kitchen, you will have to pay a lot more than for a simple functional kitchen. A good rule of thumb to remember is that you get what you pay for.

4. Costs and schedules are tightly linked. Anytime you want something sooner, you must be prepared to pay more by adding more people to the project or paying for people to work longer.

5. Get help in estimating costs for each activity. To increase the accuracy of her cost guesses, my friend Kim would:

   - Ask the people who would actually do the work.
   - Look at a previous similar project.
   - Ask an expert in the field.
   - Use a cost model or prototype from the industry.

6. Create a cost baseline. Review this and get a sign-off from the customer.

7. If and when variances to the cost baseline occur, focus on the critical path activities. You may want to put more resources onto these activities. Watch out for other activities that may lag or fall behind and change the critical path.

8. As changes get approved or work actually gets done, cost estimates will change. Manage the actual changes when they occur and take immediate corrective action.

9. Put it all in writing. Include the "whys" of both positive and negative cost variances as lessons learned for future projects.

REMEMBER

Project cost management contains the processes to ensure the project costs are within the approved budget.

Thinking Quality

I once joined an information technology (IT) organization that had a customer manager named Ron. Ron had a 30-50 rule. The first time I heard it I fell into his trap and asked, "What is a 30-50 rule?" He informed me with relish that it means he gets only 30% of what he asked for from IT and of that only 50% would work. Doing the quick math in my head, I said, "That's only 15% project quality." "Yes," said Ron, "Pretty dismal isn't it?" I was appalled at such a low number and wondered about the organization I had just joined.

Project quality is one of the easiest areas to ignore. Ignore project quality and be prepared for product and performance problems as illustrated in Figure 7-7 Bypassing quality planning or cutting out quality inspections are seemingly shortcuts to time and budget constraints. But, sooner rather than later, these shortcuts always come back to haunt you. Beware of the negative consequences when errors go undetected and costly rework must be applied. Just as Ron implied, dismal project quality leads to customer dissatisfaction. This could lead to cancelled projects and lost revenues.

Project quality is a combination of producing what the project set out to do and the service or product created satisfying the expressed and implied needs of the customer. Poor project quality is therefore always tied to poor product quality. Product quality is the totality of characteristics of the product and its ability to satisfy its fitness for use. In Ron's case, the projects completed for him produced only 30% of what they set out to do, and only 50% of that met his needs. Therefore, the project quality is one-half of 30% or 15%. The product quality is even less than 15% as partial features cannot be brought to market and are often worthless.

Project quality management contains the processes to certify the project satisfies the needs it was undertaken to address. Here are some guidelines for project quality management:

1. Identify the quality standards for the project and how they will be satisfied.

Figure 7-7 Low-quality construction results in an unacceptable product.

2. Meet with project stakeholders and customers and ask them for their expectations of the project objectives, goals, schedules, costs, and deliverables.
3. Create a "cost of quality" document. This document should include three types of quality costs. These are inspection/prevention costs, evaluation costs, and failure/rework costs.
4. Perform quality audits on work results. This is a structured review of quality management activities.
5. As a result of the quality audit, create quality improvements to improve the effectiveness and efficiency of the project
6. Continuously monitor and control project quality.
7. Put it all in writing.

Note: Quality is also often confused with grade. Grade is a category or rank given to items that serve the same functional use but has different levels of technical characteristics. For example, a low-grade carpet serves as a floor covering just as well as a high-grade carpet but after a short while it can show wear, the color may fade, or stains are difficult to remove, whereas better performance is expected of the high-grade carpet.

| R EMEMBER
| Project quality management contains the processes to certify that the
| project satisfies the needs it was undertaken to address.

Thinking Human Resources

I've found that projects are always unique because of the mix of people working on them. Their diversity, complexity of interaction, relationships, responses, and conflicts provide constant challenge and interest. People make or break a project. Always choose the right people.

Choosing the right people is easier said than done, of course. A good trick is to focus on the critical tasks in the WBS. First, find people to match closely the skills required by the critical tasks. At times you may have to compromise. Budget constraints may point to a lesser-skilled resource. I've found that a person with a positive attitude, plus a willingness to learn, may at times be a better option than a highly skilled resource with a bad attitude. In addition, working with positive attitude people such as those shown in Figure 7-8 is a lot more fun! Project human resource management contains the processes to

Figure 7-8 Choose people with positive attitudes.

best utilize the skills and strengths of the people on the project. Here are some guidelines for human resource management:

1. Build a diverse team. Choose people with different strengths, specialties, knowledge, and temperaments. In this way, they can learn from each other, have varied and creative solutions to problems, and overcome their weaknesses by building on the strengths of each other.
2. Use the people requirements identified in cost management. Refine these requirements to determine the skills and competencies needed to get the work done.
3. Define all project roles and responsibilities for individuals and/or groups. Each role should have a clear list of responsibilities.
4. Obtain a skills inventory for all the people who may be used on the project. If external resources are to be used, ask for their skills, too. If a skills inventory for an internal candidate isn't available, ask for assessments and build one.
5. Create a project organization chart. This chart is intended to show clear reporting relationships.
6. Match the skills to the work that needs to be done and build the best team with the options you have.
7. Interview each potential team member and listen to his or her goals, interests, and expectations. You will have better luck going with your second choice if your first choice has no interest or enthusiasm for the project.
8. Start team building practices right away.
9. Plan for some small, and some not so small, success and recognition celebrations along the way. This will keep interest, enthusiasm, and teamwork going.
10. Put it all in writing.

REMEMBER

Project human resource management contains the processes to best utilize the skills and strengths of the people on the project.

Thinking Communications

A rule of thumb for the amount of time a project manager spends in communication during a project is upward of 75%. For a project manager of a data warehouse, I would recommend at least 90%! Communicate well and often or

Figure 7-9 Lack of communication results in useless products.

the data warehouse could be a useless piece of architecture as shown in Figure 7-9.

Project communications management contains the processes to ensure that project information is collected, generated, stored, distributed, and appropriately disposed of, if necessary, in a timely manner. Here are some guidelines for communications management:

1. There is no such thing as too much communication in projects – use face-to-face meetings, e-mails, voicemails, one-on-one meetings, team meetings, breakfasts and lunches, written and verbal status reports, group reviews, audits, and social get-togethers.
2. Use colocation with a "war" room whenever possible. Colocation is where as many team members as possible are in the same physical location to enhance their performance as a team. A war room is where the team can congregate easily for brainstorming sessions, problem solving, or reviews. Project material can be posted for easy reference.
3. Interview stakeholders to obtain their expectations of project reports and results.

4. Create a communications management plan to detail the method for how information will be collected, to whom it will be distributed, the schedule of when and how it will be delivered, where project information can be accessed, and how and when it will be updated.
5. Distribute project information and results in a timely manner. Negative project results must be shared as well as positive results, with plans for getting back on track. Project information needs to contain any possible impacts to the schedule and budget.
6. Make many project presentations. Team members can share in this experience.
7. Hold performance reviews to access project status and progress with team members and stakeholders. Use variance and trend analysis to look ahead and predict project status and progress.
8. Document lessons learned as they happen. Keep project records up-to-date and archive for future project reference.
9. Practice project closure to confirm that the project completed what it set out to do and the product or service has been formally accepted by the customer.
10. Put it all in writing.

REMEMBER

Project communications management contains the processes to ensure that project information is collected, generated, stored, distributed, and appropriately disposed of, if necessary, in a timely manner.

Thinking Risk

Teenagers think risk all the time. They fear the risk of not fitting in, the risk of rejection, the risk of parents embarrassing them, and a few dozen other negative consequences from their peers. They take steps to mitigate these risks by dressing alike, hanging out with the "in" crowd, and trying to look "cool." In their minds they come up with "what-if" scenarios and do what they can to keep their friends away from their parents and vice versa. I've found that project managers need to do the same (no, not keep their friends away from their parents, but rather plan for uncertainty).

Risks are inherent in projects. Unexpected events will come up as depicted in Figure 7-10; you can count on it. The successful project managers are the ones who think risk all the time. They are constantly looking ahead and thinking of uncertain events that could happen. They play "what-if" scenarios in their heads to mitigate problems that could happen. When uncertain or un-predicted events do happen, they measure the impact and minimize the con-

Figure 7-10 Unexpected events will occur.

sequences of negative events while maximizing the probability and consequences of positive events.

According to the PMBOK Guide,[25] project risk is an uncertain event or condition that, if it occurs, has a positive or a negative effect on a project objective. While not often a consideration, positive risk events do occur. Where negative events pose a threat to the project's objectives, positive events afford an opportunity to improve on an objective. Project risk management contains the processes necessary to identify, analyze, and respond to potential project risks. Here are some guidelines for project risk management:

1. Spend time to plan the handling of risk events in the project. Some risks are known—these are the ones that can be identified and analyzed. Other risks are unknown. Although it is impossible to plan for every

unknown, build some contingencies into the project based upon past experience and knowledge. Document the risk approach and methods in a risk management plan.

2. Identify all the risk events that could happen.
3. For each risk event identified, assess the impact if it does happen by assigning numerical values to quantify impact. The more severe the impact, the higher the numerical value. This step is often difficult; nevertheless, it is important and cannot be ignored. Gather as much information as you can about these risk events and document the causes or triggers that could cause these events to occur. For example, a project using a new technology contains the risk of certain features not working at all or not working as well as expected. Prototypes must be created to test important features or extra resources must be allocated to circumvent project delays if and when a critical feature fails to deliver.
4. For each of the risks identified, compute the risk score (i.e., the probability times the impact). Come up with a list of risk priorities using this score.
5. Determine the probability of achieving each of the project objectives. Given the identified risk scores, are the scope, schedule, and cost objectives realistic?
6. Come up with a plan for what should be done if any of the identified risks come about.
7. Continually and consistently monitor the project to see if any risk triggers have occurred, if responses are adequate, and if any known or unknown risk events occurred.
8. As risk events do occur take immediate corrective action, come up with workaround plans, and use brainstorming meetings to solve problems.
9. Put it all in writing.

REMEMBER

Project risk management contains the processes necessary to identify, analyze, and respond to potential project risks.

Thinking Procurement

Sometimes an organization has too much work. If necessary services from other organizations can be bought. These procured services are usually for a limited amount of time. The activities involved with procuring and controlling these services are known as procurement. Because procuring and managing the people is for a specific amount of time, procurement management itself can be classified as a project.

I once worked in an organization that did not procure any outside services. Phillip, the CIO, believed that project demands could be handled by resources working more overtime. Needless to say, morale was low, turnover was high, and Phillip is no longer at this organization.

Procurement has been around for a long time. Farmers hired extra farm hands at harvest time to deal with the extra work. Or, items of machinery were leased just for the period of time they were needed. Procurement for projects mainly deals with the acquisition of human resources. Projects require people to do the work. Project demands may require high levels of effort for certain periods of time. Instead of hiring and firing internal resources, resources are procured from an external organization for the time they are needed. Two primary reasons for procuring external resources to achieve project scope are for the knowledge these resources contain and to meet project resource demands.

Special skills are needed to handle the acquisition of project resources. Project procurement management contains the processes required to handle the acquisition of resources from entities external to the purchasing organization. Following the assumption put forth by the PMBOK Guide,[25] project procurement management uses the term buyer as the purchasing organization and seller as the organization providing the goods or services. The seller is an external organization. Here are some guidelines for project procurement management:

1. Using the project goals and objectives, determine if project requirements can be met by procuring products or services externally. This step also contains research into what may be available commercially. The decision to procure externally is also tied to the project objectives. For example, a complex, secretive new technology with highly customized modules should be completed in-house for security reasons and a lack of qualifying packages on the market.
2. If it is decided to procure externally, continue with the following steps.
3. Create a statement of work (SOW) to detail the work that needs to be done. Each SOW must be written in enough detail for the seller to understand:
   a. The scope of work that needs to be performed.
   b. The deliverables that must be produced.
   c. The type of contract the buyer is considering.

4. Create other procurement documents needed to solicit bids from prospective sellers. Any special requirements such as various technical skills, knowledge, or methodologies must be present. The criteria used to select from the various buyers should also be included.

5. Obtain sellers' proposals and evaluate them. It is best to narrow down the sellers to the two or three top contenders and evaluate each in further detail. Preliminary negotiation can take place with these semi-finalists before selecting the finalist.

6. Once the finalist is selected a contract between the buyer and seller is signed. Just as milestones are identified in project time management, milestones should be identified for the delivery of various deliverables by the seller. A payment schedule based on the acceptance of these deliverables should be part of the contract. In this way, both the buyer and seller share the project risk.

7. Administer the contract. This includes keeping track of work results and distributing status and progress in a timely manner. Using input from the seller, verify work results (accept or reject) and handle change requests, claims or disputes, and seller payments.

8. Hold performance reviews to access project status and progress with team and stakeholders. Use variance and trend analysis to look ahead and predict project status and progress.

9. Document lessons learned as they happen. Keep project records up-to-date and archive written material for future project reference.

10. Once all deliverables are accepted or if the contract is terminated early (due to contract disputes or breech), close out the contract. Confirm that the seller completed what they had been contracted to do and validate that the deliverables have been formally accepted by the buyer. Inform the seller in writing that the contract is completed.

11. Put it all in writing.

REMEMBER

Project procurement management contains the processes required to handle the acquisition of resources from entities external to the project organization.

How Do You Integrate It All?

I recently moved to a new housing tract that upon completion will contain 91 homes. The construction and rollout of the homes were divided into six phases. My house was in the third phase, so with three more phases to go the tract is a hive of activity. I see carpenters, roofers, dry-wallers, cabinet people, carpet layers, landscapers, masons, electricians, phone-company employees, painters, and other workmen. Watching the foreman, Dave, darting from activity to activity I realized that a foreman is just like a project manager. His main job is to integrate the work of all the people on the tract.

Building a tract of homes is a project. Therefore, the first thing Dave needs is a project plan. The purpose of a project plan was discussed in Chapter 6. This plan defines all the work that needs to be done for the goals and objectives of the project to be met. Dave must then execute activities according to the plan. The plan should be detailed enough so that Dave knows when he is deviating from the plan. Dave also controls any changes that come up and makes adjustments as necessary to the plan. Project integration management contains the processes to orchestrate effectively the many various elements of the project. Here are some guidelines for project integration management:

1. Create a project plan. This important document is a collection of the many planning documents from the other eight knowledge areas already discussed. It will change over the life of the project as more information comes about.

2. The project plan should include:

   - The business need - why the project exists.
   - The goals, objectives, and project deliverables.
   - The WBS.
   - The milestone chart.
   - Baselines for project scope, cost, and schedule.
   - All subsidiary plans such as the scope, staffing, quality, risk, communication, and procurement management plans.
   - Project constraints and assumptions.
   - Key issues to resolve or anything else that could help or deter the project.

3. Many skills come into play in getting the work done. The most important skill is that of communication, which includes presentation, negotiation, listening, conflict resolution, leading meetings, and motivating skills.

4. Control changes as they come about. Use a change control process where change requests are collected, evaluated, and accepted or rejected.

5. Major change may require rebaselining of scope, cost, and schedule baselines.

6. Reiterate these steps for the entire life of the project.

7. All this has to be in writing.

REMEMBER THIS!

✔ A project is the concerted effort of work performed in a specific amount of time to produce a unique end result.

✔ Project management is the utilization of certain knowledge, skills, tools, and techniques to ensure project work gets done. It becomes a tool to ensure that the end results of the project will be delivered successfully.

✔ Project management is needed to limit and control the resources on a project while meeting the project requirements for success.

✔ Lucky project managers know the formula for successful projects: Project success = a game plan + the right sponsors + the right people.

✔ Project management can be delineated by the six performance domains: initiating, planning, executing, controlling, and closing the project, and professional responsibility.

✔ The five process groups—initiating, planning, executing, controlling, and closing—all work together to provide the processes and techniques that can deliver successful projects, but the right people are still required to make it all work.

✔ A project moves through the five process groups, looping within the planning, executing, and controlling process groups for as many times as necessary until the project end result is approved and the project phase or entire project is closed.

✔ The field of project management encompasses nine knowledge areas: project integration management, project scope management, project time management, project cost management, project quality management, project human resource management, project communications management, project risk management, and project procurement management. The knowledge areas of emphasis for data warehousing project success are communications, risk, and integration management.

✔ Project scope management contains the processes to make certain that all work to complete the project is identified and only this work is done.

✔ Project time management contains the processes to ensure the project is completed as scheduled.

✔ Project cost management contains the processes to ensure the project costs are within the approved budget.

✔ Project quality management contains the processes to certify the project satisfies the needs it was undertaken to address.

✔ Project human resource management contains the processes to best utilize the skills and strengths of the people on the project.

✔ Project communications management contains the processes to ensure that project information is collected, generated, stored, distributed, and appropriately disposed of, if necessary, in a timely manner.

✔ Project risk management contains the processes necessary to identify, analyze, and respond to potential project risks.

✔ Project procurement management contains the processes required to handle the acquisition of resources from entities external to the project organization.

✔ Project integration management contains the processes to orchestrate effectively the many different elements of the project.

Data Modeling

Why Model the Data?

Have you ever won something? It needn't have been a million dollar jackpot (although that would be nice), just something that made you feel good and put a smile on your face. It could have been a successful weekend at the slot machines in Las Vegas, winning a bingo game, or having the right numbers in the football pool at work. Money or material items don't even have to be involved; winning could be a landscaping project that came out beyond your expectations, giving a flawless speech in front of a large crowd, or getting recognition for a job well done. All of these events are successes and when they happen they make you happy.

So, how would you define success for a data warehouse? I would say when the business clients are "happy." Satisfied clients are those who are happy with the performance of their data warehouse. They feel that the goals, objectives, and milestones they were expecting were met or even exceeded. Happy business clients embrace the capabilities that have come their way with the data warehouse. They busily start to dream up new questions to ask and find new areas to explore to bring value to their organizations.

Ted is a business manager at a retail chain that uses three channels for sales: brick-and-mortar stores, the Internet, and catalogs. Ted's company keeps detailed information about its 25 million customers in a data warehouse. Customer data from all three channels of sales are integrated into this data warehouse. Having all these data in one place, Ted is able to gain a comprehensive view of all customer interactions and perform predictive modeling and analysis on various markets. His analysis gives him interesting results. It showed him that customers who bought from all three channels spent three to five times more than customers who just bought from one channel.

Armed with this knowledge and other information from the data warehouse, Ted identified 86,000 customers for a mailing campaign, inviting them to come into a store and sample a new line of fragrances. The marketing campaign was a huge success. By targeting customers who fit into a certain profile, the rate of return from the direct mailing was more than 40%, i.e., about 35,000 customers responded to the invitation and visited a store. More than 60% of these customers then purchased one or more items at the store. What a difference from the old method of bombarding all 25 million customers with expensive mailings for products most customers were not even slightly interested in seeing, let alone buying!

Data warehouses are all about change, integration, enrichment, and flexibility. Business clients need to be able to ask any questions they can dream up. A data warehouse should be able to handle questions that no one has even thought of yet. One way of making sure the warehouse will be flexible is first to model the business with the help of a data model.

Modeling the business ensures that all the business rules of an organization are satisfied within the data warehouse. The model must also be flexible enough to adapt quickly to new or modified business rules within the organization. As the organization grows and evolves in response to market demands, so must the data model.

Let's find out more about data models and how they relate to data warehouse capabilities, performance, and response times.

What Is a Data Model?

The technology sector is full of strange terms. One of the strangest I've come across in a technical context is "quiesce point." I'm not going to try and explain what a quiesce point is, but a quick look in my dictionary has the closest match as "quiescent – inactive, still; dormant." Believe me when I say a quiesce point is an appropriate term for checking a database when it is inactive or dormant. Why someone came up with a term that only the French can pronounce is another story.

After "quiesce point," the term "data model" doesn't seem that strange. A data model is a schematic showing all the data in the warehouse, how the data relate to other data, and how the data should be structured. Remember the plastic or metal models of planes, cars, or ships you may have had as a child? These models were small but technically accurate representations of the real object. Such models are commonly used in organizations. By assembling a design on a smaller scale, the model can be tested and adjusted without the expense of diving into the creation of the full-scale product and modifying it when it doesn't work.

Airplane manufactures often model airplanes in a wind tunnel such as the one depicted in Figure 8-1 to simulate aircraft in flight. I once heard that chicken carcasses were thrown at the windshields of these model planes to replicate birds in flight. During one such test the windshield shattered, much

Figure 8-1 Models allow a "test" of the end result.

to the horror of the test simulators and observers. It was discovered that the chicken bodies were still frozen in their bags. From this experiment, the test simulators found that the glass of the windshield would not stand up to the force of a frozen bird at a high speed. Although a real airplane has little chance of hitting a frozen chicken in flight, some birds could have a large force of impact at high altitudes. Learning from this model simulation, the airplane manufacturer adjusted the strength of the glass to safeguard against such an incident in real flight.

In the same way, a data model built to fit the business can be used to test if the warehouse will stand up to the rigorous demands made of it. A data model is easier to view and understand and cheaper to modify and adjust than the finished product. A data model provides a "test" of what is to come. The more thoroughly a model is tested, the stronger and more robust is the resulting end product. Thus a data warehouse data model is used to test if the warehouse can handle all aspects of the organization's business and adjustments are made before the actual warehouse build begins.

REMEMBER

A data model is a schematic showing the data in the warehouse, how the data relate to other data, and how the data should be structured. It is used to ensure that the data warehouse can substantiate all business requirements.

Why Do Data Need to Be Modeled?

What a concept! Starting a design by identifying the data elements that are needed, how these elements relate to each other, and the most efficient method of arranging these data to facilitate their use. This practice of manipulating and organizing data is known as data modeling. Actually, the practice of data modeling has existed for decades. But, because functional databases have only a few departmental users and performance could be fine-tuned by systems people, data modeling was often bypassed or ignored. This is no longer the case: A data warehouse has hundreds of databases and thousands of data elements, compounded by many users accessing the data in multiple ways. Proper data modeling is crucial for data warehouse performance and success.

How does a good data model enhance data warehouse performance? To answer this question, let's go back to my analogy of your memory being a data warehouse. Human memories are amazing! They can store large amounts of data and the ability to access this information rapidly. The central nervous system provides the brain and the network of sophisticated nerve cells that send synapses to process data in nanoseconds. Even as you read this text, your brain could be thinking three or more other thoughts. Information is processed quickly, retrieving and discarding or retrieving and selecting data from hidden cells of your memory. In a matter of split seconds, you make decisions based on these data. These capabilities are provided so naturally and easily that you hardly realize the effort. Data warehouses must provide the same sort of capability, not just to a single person, but to all the people who access the data warehouse at the same time.

We all know data warehouses contain tons of data. A data model actually patterns how the data should be structured into the database or data warehouse. It organizes the data so that related data exist together as one entity. Each entity is then linked to other entities by special relationships. These relationships are used to find and access data in response to queries. The speed at which the data are found depends on the existence of links between the data. The more precise the relationship, the quicker the access. Although it is impossible to define all data relationships, frequently accessed relationships can be defined. By arranging the data in these patterns of most frequent use, the performance of the warehouse is raised for a larger percent of queries. Eureka! Modeling the data speeds data access. Data modeling goes hand-in-hand with data warehouse performance.

The absence of a data model or even a bad data model will bring a warehouse to its knees, i.e., response times will be slow or nonexistent (the query gets no response). Slow performance will generate unhappy clients quickly.

According to Jill Dyche[12, p 270] a bad data model will result in

- Slower response times.
- More complex queries.
- Heavier reliance on metadata.
- Reworking of the data model.

Frequent slow response times, bad performance, or complex queries will drive people away from using a data warehouse. Complicated queries are a double whammy as they require more time to formulate the query and a slower response time. Heavy reliance on metadata will slow analysis. Once people find the warehouse cumbersome to use and walk away, it will take a larger effort to bring them back.

The data model actually makes an excellent communication tool. It must model the business and stand up to the business rules. Therefore, business clients must participate in the creation and approval process of the data model. Use these discussion sessions to determine what they would like to see from the data warehouse and their expectations on response times. Keep in mind that their expectations on performance are a critical aspect of acceptance criteria in determining project success.

Some people try to make the business fit the data model. They create a data model without much input or approval from the business units and then ask the business groups to change their processes to fit the patterns of the data warehouse. This constitutes data warehouse suicide! Why? The first obvious reason is that the data will not reflect the true nature of the business. Without the utilization of the business rules, there are bound to be ambiguity, contradictions, and response time delays. I can guarantee countless data quality issues. Thus a data mausoleum will be built from the model instead of a data warehouse of blissful data. With difficult access and poor data quality clients will quickly avoid the data warehouse. A second reason why a data model that doesn't fit the business won't work is that a data warehouse already encompasses significant amounts of change; business units already have numerous changes to deal with in utilizing the capabilities afforded by the data warehouse. Asking them to make more changes for no other reason than to fit the data model would be unwise. It will drive the business units away from the data warehouse before they even had a chance to reap the benefits. Always keep in mind that the model should fit the business rather than have the business try to fit the data model.

REMEMBER

Modeling the data correctly enhances data warehouse performance. A bad data model will result in slow response times, more complex queries, and unhappy customers.

What Does a Data Model Look Like?

Simple Simon met a pie-man

Going to the fair.

Said Simple Simon to the pie-man,

"Let me taste your ware"

Like Simon in Figure 8-2, you may find that you have to try something first before you find whether it works for you. The same applies for data modeling; modeling the data allows a sample of the end result. There are also quite a few different types of data models, such as star schemas, snowflake schemas, fact constellation schemas, etc. Data modelers have argued for years about the best practices for modeling data. They advocate one method over another for one compelling reason or another. It's not necessary to expand upon the technical advantages or disadvantages of one method over another, technical experts in IT are available for this purpose. My only recommendation is to go with the

Figure 8-2 Simon finds he likes the pie.

type of model that provides the greatest flexibility, i.e., the model that can adapt quickly to new or modified business rules of your organization and grow and evolve as the organization grows and evolves. Your organization cannot afford a data warehouse that cannot grow or change to meet changing market demands.

In Chapter 1, I mentioned that a database is like a file cabinet with folders arranged in different drawers. Imagine each drawer of folders to be like a table of rows and columns (like a spreadsheet). Each table contains data that are somehow related to data in the tables of one or more of the other drawers. Because a relationship exists between the tables, the database is then said to be a relational database. A data warehouse can contain a few to hundreds of relational tables, collected into many relational databases.

Let's see what the data model in Figure 8-43 entails. Each box, known as an entity, represents a table of data within the data warehouse. Each entity contains a collection of data pertaining to a particular subject area of the business. The subject areas in Figure 8-3 are customer, product, component, sales, and manufacturing. Each entity contains an identifying value or key field, such as CUST ID, PRODUCT KEY, and SALES KEY, so that unique occurrences of the data can be found. The key field plus other characteristics of the subject area make up the attributes of each of the subject areas. Connectors between entities illustrate relationships that exist between the attributes of the entities. Examples of relationships that could exist between the entities of the data model in Figure 8-3 could be:

- A customer buys a product.
- A product belongs to a component.

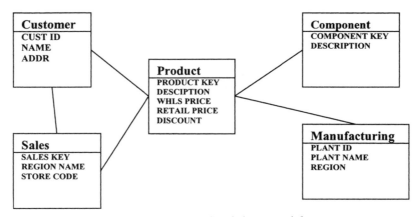

Figure 8-3 High-level data model.

- Sales are made to a customer.
- A product is created at manufacturing.

As you can see, a data model gives a graphical representation of the structure of the data and its relationships between the components of the business. The major components or subject areas of the business are represented by entities. A data model consists of entities of an organization's business, attributes of these entities, and the relationships between the entities.

It is important that the data model is created with contributions and participation of the business. The data model ensures the business rules of an organization are satisfied. Who knows these business rules better than the business units? Once the data model is complete, it must be reviewed and understood by the business clients as they need to test the data model and ensure that it stands up to their requirements. Finally, once the model is actually built into a data warehouse it should be able to handle queries and any other analysis that business clients may demand from it.

REMEMBER
A data model consists of entities of an organization's business, the attributes of these entities, and the relationships between these entities.

Why Care About Capabilities and Performance?

Response times are often used as the benchmark for measuring data warehouse performance. Queries are submitted frequently by many people in an organization. Therefore, the response time for queries is the most visible and

Figure 8-4 Response time is used to measure performance.

prevalent standard of performance seen by everyone who uses the data warehouse. It is important that response time requirements are obtained early in the data warehouse endeavor and the design of the warehouse supports response time needs. Slow or unacceptable response times will generate unhappy business clients very quickly. Long waiting periods will quickly discourage people from using the data warehouse. Bad performance will drive business clients like the one in Figure 8-4 away from using the data warehouse.

Response times are often driven by the nature of the query. There are two types of queries:

1. Canned queries – predefined queries that are used frequently by one or more persons. These queries are standard and shared. They can be used to produce a report that is monthly, weekly, daily, hourly, or on request. A department may have a library of canned queries for everyone to use so that the query need not be rewritten every time. The resulting data can change but the question remains the same. Business clients often use canned queries to get the information to perform analyses for their jobs. Canned queries can range from simple to highly complex. Decisions made from canned queries are usually tactical in nature. Because these queries are planned, their response times can be fine-tuned to be quick and predictable.

2. Ad hoc queries – original or unplanned queries. These queries occur on the spur of the moment or in response to uncommon customer inquiries. They are usually unique and submitted by a single requestor who is running some type of analysis or trying to solve a problem. Ad hoc queries can lead to startling discoveries that can result in new and exciting opportunities. They can also range from the simple to the very complex. The response time from complex ad hoc queries can be long, sometimes hours or days, but the results can be tremendous. Decisions made from ad hoc queries are usually strategic in nature, that is, ad hoc queries can open doors to new business opportunities and may just be the silver bullet an organization needs.

Queries are used to provide a goldmine of information. Business clients use queries to get answers in minutes instead of the days, if not weeks, it used to take to gather and analyze data from multiple sources. With the quicker turnaround times, employees have more time to act on the information and make more knowledgeable decisions, bringing better value to their organizations and increasing job satisfaction.

REMEMBER

A query to a database or data warehouse provides the basis for analyses in understanding data. Response times to canned queries are quick and predictable, but response times to ad hoc queries can be in minutes and hours.

Are You Like the White Rabbit?

"Oh dear! Oh dear! I shall be too late!"—The White Rabbit[26, p 1]

Sometimes, it seems like we are all like the White Rabbit in "Alice in Wonderland," scurrying from one destination to another, worried about being late, yet not sure where we are headed.

In every business, vast amounts of time and staff resources are spent gathering data from multiple sources, wading through day-to-day data by-products, and analyzing and interpreting data to make decisions on how to move forward. More often than not, getting the right information takes so long that there is little or no time to evaluate the best plan of action. We know that data alone do not bring profits; it is the resulting action based on the right information that brings in the returns.

We saw in Chapter 3 that various types of on-line analytic processing (OLAP) came about to provide quicker access to the data for analysis and informed decision making. Data warehousing capabilities came along with the ability to store and access large amounts of data, opening the door to business intelligence. Let's see what additional capabilities are provided by a data warehouse.

Suppose a PC magically appeared on your desk one day with a note taped to it, saying, "I can provide access to a new data warehouse. Try me!" Well, because this is make-believe, you were magically familiar with the access tool and savvy enough to use the tool like a pro. You knew exactly what to do. Here are some application examples of what you might have done.

Querying

First, you already know about queries, so you type, "Show me the stores with annual revenues greater than $500,000." You press the button to submit the query and then hold your breath to see what happens. In less than 1 minute, a report comes back that displays store names, locations, sales, expenses, and the years where the revenue amounts exceeded $500,000 over the last 10 years. Wow! You're impressed. Previously, to get the same information you had to look up three operational reports, a file cabinet in the corner of the accounting department, the sales department's database, and one or two spreadsheets. Then you had to do some manual manipulation of all the numbers you gathered. This usually took 2 weeks, sometimes more. Now the same information is at your fingertips in less than 1 minute.

You quickly think up some other queries just to get the feel of the application and the data warehouse. As you get answers, you become more excited about the new capabilities available to you.

Simple queries are the most common access method used by the largest number of employees in an organization's data warehouse. This data access and faster turnaround (1 minute instead of 2 weeks) facilitates the decision making process.

REMEMBER
Quick and easy access to data provided by queries enables employees of an organization to obtain information for analysis and decision making support.

Slicing and Dicing

Now you're ready for more powerful analysis. You're going to do research by delving into some specific data. You may not know it, but you are going to perform some multidimensional analysis. Multidimensional analysis is an intimidating term, but all it means is that you're going to look at data from different perspectives or angles. Each of these vantage points is called a dimension, thus the term multidimensional.

Think about what you see when you enter a classroom. If you use a door at the front of the room you get a different perspective than if you come in from a door on the side. It's the same classroom, with the same chairs, desks, shelves, posters, and so on, but depending on your perspective you may see the same items slightly differently. From the

> *Multidimensional analysis allows viewing data from different perspectives or dimensions.*

door at the front of the room, the chairs and desks are arranged in vertical rows facing a larger desk to your left. From the side, the chairs and desks are arranged in horizontal rows facing a larger desk to your right. From each perspective you see details you don't see from the other. Multidimensional analysis follows the same process. By looking at data from different dimensions, various details or relationships about the data that went unnoticed before are suddenly visible.

Multidimensional analysis uses a "multidimensional database (MDDB)" (what else did you expect?), the kind of database contained in a data warehouse. When I think of a multidimensional database I always think of a Rubik's Cube. This puzzle from the early 1980s had nine colored squares on each side of the cube. Each set of nine squares could be twisted clockwise or counterclockwise. The goal of the puzzle was to start with a multicolor-sided cube and rotate the sets of squares until each of the six sides of the cube was a single color, i.e., one side showed the set of nine blue squares, another side showed only red, the next green, and so on. I spent hours trying to solve the puzzle with no success.

Fortunately, multidimensional analysis provides answers more easily than the Rubik's Cube puzzle. In multidimensional analysis the data are arranged in a block (like a Rubik's Cube) with three or more dimensions. You can obtain different views of the data by specifying what data to retrieve based on a dimension. Just like the Rubik's Cube, you can twist and turn or slice and dice the MDDB to view the data using the different dimensions.

Some common dimensions of MDDBs are "time," "product," and "geography." You can drill down or go from summarized data to more detailed data on any dimension. Because you are drilling down into the data, many people confuse multidimensional analysis with data mining. However, data mining represents the next step beyond multidimensional analysis and is discussed in the next section.

Let's look at a simple example of multidimensional analysis. Say you needed to analyze the revenues of a retail chain over a period of 3 years. You could submit a query such as, "Show me the revenue for the North, East, South, and West regions for 2001, 2002, and 2003." The results can be seen in Table 8-1.

■ TABLE 8-1 ■ **Revenue for the North, East, South, West Regions**

	2001 (millions)	2002 (millions)	2003 (millions)
NORTH	1.4	1.9	2.1
EAST	1.9	3.2	3.0
SOUTH	.7	.9	1.2
WEST	3.5	3.6	3.5

Next, you may want to look at the year 2003 in more detail, so you drill down (simply double click on the appropriate column) and get the revenue for each quarter, as seen in Table 8-2.

Note the unexpected low revenue for the Southern region in quarter 4 of 2003 (shaded in Table 8-2). You may want to drill down again and display the totals by region. In doing so, you recall a tornado that caused the closure of eight stores in the South during the fourth quarter of 2003. Now you understand why revenues were so low for those regions. The ability to drill down into detailed data enables you to understand the data, analyze the situation, and compare information.

Complete understanding of the data brings you closer to the next level of analysis, advanced analysis, which is covered in the next section.

REMEMBER

Slice-and-dice or multidimensional analysis enables viewing data from different points of perspective or to gain insights or discover data details that were previously unnoticed.

■ TABLE 8-2 ■ **Drilling Down to Quarterly Revenues for 2003**

	2001 (millions)	2002 (millions)	2003 (millions)			
			Q1	Q2	Q3	Q4
NORTH	1.4	1.9	.4	.5	.5	.7
EAST	1.9	3.2	.3	.6	.6	1.5
SOUTH	.7	.9	.3	.4	.4	.1
WEST	3.5	3.6	.5	.5	.5	2.

Advanced Analysis

"Sometimes luck comes as the result of your persisting with what you are doing until the tables finally turn and you get your chance."[4, p 283]

Advanced analysis is perhaps the most exciting type of analysis available simply because you are going where no man or woman has gone before. I like to call it persistence analysis because it involves intelligently trying as many options as you can until you finally break through and uncover something new. Therefore, let me define advanced analysis as:

> *Advanced analysis is the detection of patterns, behaviors, and relationships in data that were previously only partially known or at times totally unknown.*

". . . the detection of patterns, behaviors, and relationships in data that were previously only partially known or at times totally unknown."

This means advanced analysis involves getting to the answer without even knowing the question. Sounds far out? It's not as far-fetched as it seems. By having the right data integrated, organized, and structured in a data warehouse, people have found the answer to the "unknown question." These answers provide huge payoffs in terms of new and lucrative increases in revenue for the lucky organization.

However, I'd like to add a word of caution at this point. Advanced analysis is just what it is labeled, i.e., "advanced." Just as a baby must learn to walk before he or she can run, organizations must first learn the basics of querying and slicing and dicing before its analysts are ready for advanced analysis. Think about a high-performance car such as a Ferrari F2003-GA, the new Ferrari F1 car. It has taken over 50 years for the Italian car maker to evolve its cars into this superb machine. Similarly, organizations new to the world of data warehousing cannot jump straight into advanced analysis and expect miracles to happen. They need to take these capabilities one step at a time and evolve to new levels of performance. They must learn to walk before they can run.

I've already mentioned the next term used in a data warehousing context, data mining. This is a form of analysis of detailed data. Like a miner who digs deep into the ground for diamonds and precious stones, the analyst digs deeper and deeper into data to find relationships, patterns, or associations between data values. The analyst is mining the data, hoping to find the "diamond in the rough" or the relationship between data that can provide the huge payoff for the organization. Therefore, data mining is an advanced analysis activity that is often used interchangeably with the term advanced analysis.

Advanced analysis itself can then be split into two areas:

1. Known unknowns – where some of the factors or relationships are known but others are unknown. Sampling, forecasting, or predictive modeling methods can be used to foresee certain trends and lifecycles and are used in known unknown types of advanced analysis. For example, you know that a bad snowstorm will increase the demand for picks, shovels, bottled water, and other emergency goods. You also know that the probability of a bad snowstorm occurring is higher during the winter months in the northern region. But, you don't know when, where, for how long, or how badly a snowstorm may affect specific areas of the northern region so you may use a calculated statistical factor in your analysis. As a result of your analysis, a large quantity of crucial supplies could be shipped to the central station of the northern region in November to prepare for a quick, flexible response to any snow or ice storms that may occur.

2. Unknown unknowns – this is called "zero hypothesis" analysis. In theory there is no premise to go by but in reality some sort of a relationship is suspected. It entails looking for answers based on an educated guess or an instinct. For this reason, this type of analysis is sometimes called knowledge discovery. You don't know what answers there are because you don't know the questions yet. But, you do know patterns and associations are hidden in the data. Trying every combination and permutation is beyond the possibility of the human mind, but there are knowledge discovery tools that can hit on every combination; as tools get more refined more and more new discoveries will be made. This is where the next frontiers lie. What discoveries lay hidden in the data? It may be something as exciting as cars that produce water instead of carbon monoxide or jet fuel that burns in outer space. As Buzz Lightyear in the movie "Toy Story" would say, "To infinity and beyond!"

 REMEMBER

Advanced analysis or data mining is the analysis of detailed data to detect patterns, behaviors, and relationships in data that were previously only partially known or at times totally unknown.

Care to Compare the Analysis Methods?

As you can see, a data warehouse must be built to provide a wide range of analysis capabilities. Queries present the quick, optimum data that empowers the employee to make decisions and take swift action. Slice and dice or multidimensional analysis offers different perspectives to view the data. By using

■ TABLE 8-3 ■ A Comparison of Analysis Methods

Query	Slice & Dice	Advanced Analysis
Provides answers to "What happened?"	Provides answers to "What happened and why did it happen?"	Provides answers to "What could happen?" and "Tell me something I may need to know . . ."
Used by many people in the organization	Used by knowledge workers and super business clients	Used by statisticians, data analysts, and business strategists
Very frequent use	Frequent use	Moderate or rare use
Response generally in seconds	Response generally in minutes	Response could be in hours
Activities: Query and Reporting	Activities: OLAP	Activities: Data Mining and Knowledge Discovery

the ability to drill down to more specific data, the analyst is able to investigate and compare information and decide the best course of action. Advanced analysis provides the most powerful type of analysis, the detection of patterns and relationships that are not specified by the analyst but "discovered" and put forward as an item of possible interest. Advanced analysis is the closest you can get to a "crystal ball" to look into the future.

A comparison of the three analysis methods is summarized in Table 8-3.

There is another important comparison to be made with the three types of analyses and the frequency and quantity of use. Think of the three types of analyses as the tiers of an iceberg as in Figure 8-5. The bottom tier is query. It is clearly the most frequent type of analysis and used by many people in an organization. As certain analysts grow and evolve in their skills and comfort with the data warehouse they will want more capability. These people will move up to the next tier of analysis, the slice and dice capability. As the warehouse matures and evolves with more and more blissful data, some analysts will likewise mature and evolve to even more sophisticated capabilities, scaling the tip of the iceberg, with advanced analysis. Only a few people will reach this level, likely statisticians, data analysts, and expert business strategists.

REMEMBER

Queries are the most frequent type of analysis, used by many people in an organization, followed by slice and dice analysis. Advanced analysis is used rarely and only by few people in an organization.

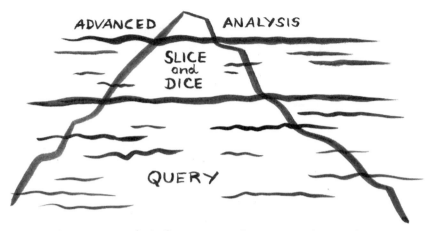

Figure 8-5 Analysis frequency and quantity of use iceberg.

What Defines Data Warehouse Success?

Data models are built to ensure that the data warehouse substantiates the requirements of the business and ensures that the customers' expectations on response times and performance are met. Capabilities such as OLAP, multi-dimensional analysis, and advanced analysis can provide answers to business questions. Thus the main customers of a data warehouse are those who utilize it the most. These customers are the business clients of the organization. Therefore, business clients have the final word on judging whether a data warehouse is a success.

Remember Ted's organization at the beginning of this chapter? It was fortunate to experience such success with its data warehouse. Like the happy customers in Figure 8-6 it was delighted with the enrichment provided by the data warehouse and had no difficulty declaring it a resounding success.

Not all organizations are so lucky; in some organizations, expectations of the capabilities and performance of a data warehouse are not met. This can be due to a situation or combination of situations that arise unexpectedly. Unmet expectations can lead to a partial or complete failure of the data warehouse. Some common situations of nonacceptance of a data warehouse are:

1. The business was made to fit the model. In such a case the true business need for the data warehouse was never determined. Without a clear goal or definition of the objectives of the data warehouse there are too many obstacles to overcome and the effort died a painful death.

Figure 8-6 Success can be measured by "delighted" customers.

2. The organizational culture was not ready and could not change to accept the data warehouse. A data warehouse requires enormous change. Business clients must be involved early so that they can modify their thinking and accept the changes one small step at a time. Organizational leadership, change agents, education, and training all play an important part in the acceptance of a data warehouse. Allow adequate time and budget for training. Even with intuitive tools business clients need time to be educated on the data, the overall business, and the business value of the data warehouse.

3. Certain functions and capabilities are unavailable or too complicated to use. Empowering business clients to create their own queries and reports against the warehouse is a major benefit of data warehousing. Everyone who uses the data warehouse should be comfortable with the capabilities and access tools so that they can get the information they need quickly and easily.

4. The response times to queries are too long. Expectations of response time must be defined at the start. On-line transaction processing (OLTP) queries have response times in seconds or subseconds as they access small amounts of data. Data warehouse or OLAP queries sometimes require accessing thousands, maybe millions, of rows of data. These queries will take longer. Business clients need to understand that data warehouse queries are usually measured in minutes, not seconds. There may even be some queries where the response may take hours (or even days), but these complex queries should be the exception and not the rule.

5. The availability of the warehouse is low. Poor availability could be caused by the number of hours per day or days per week the warehouse cannot be accessed. Business clients will want the warehouse to be available when they need it. It is reasonable for them to expect the warehouse to be near 100% available during regular business hours. If users of the data warehouse find it is unavailable too often, they may stop using it altogether.

6. Inaccurate or conflicting data. Cleansing and validating data is an ongoing effort to constantly improve data quality. If business clients often come across dirty data, or queries and reports provide wrong information causing bad decisions to be made, business clients will quickly mistrust the data and walk away from the data warehouse.

7. The warehouse's actual expenses exceed the estimated budget. Large gaps between actual costs and the estimated budget may be due to optimistic estimates, unexpected or higher costs, increased or changed scope, or just plain inexperience in calculating estimates for a data warehouse endeavor. Business groups need to get value for their investment and the warehouse must be cost justifiable to continue to obtain their sponsorship and support.

8. The warehouse was not delivered by the expected due date. Many of the same issues that affect actual expenses will also contribute to slipped deadlines and unmet schedules. The original expected due date may have been set prematurely without the benefit of a project plan or WBS, estimates may have been optimistic, scope may have increased or changed significantly, or resources may not have been available when needed. Business groups need milestones to be set and met to continue to see the value and payback from the data warehouse.

9. The warehouse is not scalable or flexible, that is, the data warehouse is restricted and constrained so it can't grow or change as the business develops and responds to market demands. As business clients become more knowledgeable and comfortable with the data warehouse, they will be dreaming up new ways to bring value to the organization. The data warehouse must be able to expand to handle new capabilities, new clients, and new or different business rules. If the data warehouse cannot expand as needed, it will quickly become an outdated system or a white elephant just waiting to be junked.

10. The warehouse is not cost justifiable, that is, the costs were higher than previously determined, the benefits came out to be lower than expected, or the payback period was longer than projected. Data warehouses need constant measurement of results, celebration of successes, and advertisement of benefits. A low return on investment (ROI) could be a problem with the endeavor's initial strategy. If so, re-evaluate the ROI and adjust benefits and costs with more current and accurate values. If the business value still cannot be justified, the data warehouse endeavor should be brought to a close.

You can see there are many areas in which a data warehouse could fall below expectations. To succeed, a data warehouse must provide the required functionality and capabilities with easy-to-use access tools. It must provide response times that are reasonable, it must be available during regular work hours, it needs to contain data that are clean and accurate, it must be delivered within the estimated budget and schedule, it must be scalable and flexible, it needs to be cost justifiable, and the culture of the organization must be ready to accept it.

Business clients have the final word on judging if a data warehouse is a success or not. Like Ted, if they are happy with the capabilities and performance of the data warehouse they will have no problem declaring the warehouse a success.

REMEMBER

Business clients must be happy with the capabilities and performance of the data warehouse to declare it a success.

What Is a Data Warehouse? (Revisited)

As we now know, a data warehouse is many things to many people. Now that we know so much more about data warehouses, we can look at Bill Inmon's[1] definition of a data warehouse again and understand what it is about. Dr. Inmon's definition is:

A data warehouse is a set of computer databases specifically designed with related, historical blissful data that assist in formulating decisions and taking action.

"A data warehouse is a subject-oriented, integrated, time-variant, and nonvolatile collection of data in support of management's decisions."

Key words in his definition are:

- Subject-oriented: The data are arranged so that related data often accessed together reside together in the warehouse. Some sample subject areas are customer, product, vendor, and order.
- Integrated: The data are blissful and clean, that is, inconsistencies are removed. Issues resulting from incomplete, inaccurate encoding, and physical attributes of the data are resolved.
- Time-variant: The data represent data over a time period. The data consist of a collection of snapshots taken from source systems at specified time intervals (such as monthly, weekly, daily, or more frequently), integrated, transformed, and stored in the warehouse.
- Nonvolatile: Once the snapshot of data is captured, transformed, and loaded into the warehouse, the data within the snapshot are not changed. Thus the data were accurate at that point in time. Only two types of actions take place on warehouse data:

    1. The data are loaded.
    2. The data are accessed for analysis.

Dr. Inmon's definition simply says that a data warehouse consists of data that are related by subject area, have been properly transformed, reflect snapshots of the past, and once loaded these snapshots in time do not change. The data are utilized for decision making support.

Recall my definition of a data warehouse as:

". . . a set of computer databases specifically designed with related, historical blissful data that assist in formulating decisions and taking action."

Both definitions work; use the one that works best for you. The key point to remember is that a data warehouse consists of blissful data. This blissful data provide the answers to making the right decision to drive strategic action. Let's summarize what we have learned about data warehouses:

1. A data warehouse provides meaningful, accurate, and useful data to all employees of an organization – it contains a single version of the "truth."
2. A data warehouse delivers many benefits. Its blissful data enables employees to better understand the business, leading to the enhanced ability to predict new trends and beat the competition, as well as the means to intimately know and thus better serve the organizations'

customers. By providing employees with the information they need for analysis and decision making support, an organization's data warehouse improves productivity per employee, which leads to increased profitability for the organization.

3. A data warehouse is maintained separately from an organization's operational databases so that it does not slow or negatively impact the operational systems.

4. A data warehouse is an entire environment of change, integration, enrichment, and flexibility.

5. Data marts are a type of a data warehouse utilized to solve a defined set of functions for departmental focus.

6. A data warehouse must support the integrated business rules, policies, and business of the organization.

7. A data warehouse contains data that come from operational systems and other sources within an organization. Transformation rules are applied to prevent dirty data being loaded into the data warehouse.

8. Metadata must be defined, collected, and made available to people in the organization in a metadata repository.

9. Organizational structures and cultures play an important part in determining the readiness of an organization for a data warehouse.

10. Sponsorship of the warehouse from business units is achieved by their understanding of the value a warehouse will bring to the organization. They view the data warehouse as an investment into the future.

11. The utilization of project management techniques is very important in data warehousing endeavors because of the high levels of integration, risk, and communication involved.

12. A data model is needed to pattern the data to be structured into the data warehouse. It ensures that business requirements are substantiated by identifying and documenting the relationships between data elements.

13. Warehouse capabilities, performance, and requests for expansion and growth from business clients are the factors that determine the success of a data warehouse.

Armed with this knowledge you can now go forth and conquer. Victory is within reach!

Remember

"A data warehouse is a set of computer databases specifically designed with related, historical blissful data that assist in formulating decisions and taking action." It:

- Contains a single version of the "truth."
- Enhances employee decision making and productivity leading to increased profits.
- Exists separately from the operational systems.
- Provides an environment of change, integration, enrichment, and flexibility.
- Includes data marts that are used to solve defined sets of problems.
- Must support the integrated business rules, policies, and business of the organization.
- Contains data from operational systems and other sources within an organization. Transformation rules prevent dirty data from being loaded into the data warehouse.
- Is utilized together with metadata in a metadata repository.
- Is more readily accepted by certain organizational structures and cultures.
- Recognized by business units as an investment into the future.
- Requires utilization of project management techniques for success.
- Utilizes a data model to ensure that all business requirements are substantiated.
- Is measured to be a success by the satisfaction and requests for new capabilities by the business clients.

REMEMBER THIS!

✔ A data model is a schematic showing the data in the warehouse, how the data relate to other data, and how the data should be structured. It is used to ensure that the data warehouse can substantiate all business requirements.

✔ Modeling the data correctly enhances data warehouse performance. A bad data model will result in slow response times, more complex queries, and unhappy customers.

✔ A data model consists of entities of an organization's business, the attributes of these entities, and the relationships between these entities.

✔ A query to a database or data warehouse provides the basis for analyses in understanding data. Response times to canned queries are quick and predictable, but response times to ad hoc queries can be in minutes and hours.

✔ Quick and easy access to data provided by queries enables employees of an organization to obtain information for analysis and decision making support.

✔ Slice-and-dice or multidimensional analysis enables viewing data from different points of perspective or angles to gain insights or discover data details that were previously unnoticed.

✔ Advanced analysis or data mining is the analysis of detailed data to detect patterns, behaviors, and relationships in data that were previously only partially known or at times totally unknown.

✔ Queries are the most frequent type of analysis, followed by slice-and-dice analysis; advanced analysis is used rarely and only by few people in an organization.

✔ Business clients must be happy with the capabilities and performance of the data warehouse to declare it a success.

✔ "A data warehouse is a set of computer databases specifically designed with related, historical blissful data that assist in formulating decisions and taking action." It:

- Contains a single version of the "truth."
- Enhances employee decision making and productivity leading to increased profits.
- Exists separately from the operational systems.
- Provides an environment of change, integration, enrichment, and flexibility.
- Includes data marts that are used to solve defined sets of problems.
- Must support the integrated business rules, policies, and business of the organization.
- Contains data from operational systems and other sources within an organization. Transformation rules prevent dirty data from being loaded into the data warehouse.
- Is utilized together with metadata in a metadata repository.
- Is more readily accepted by certain organizational structures and cultures.
- Recognized by business units as an investment into the future.
- Requires utilization of project management techniques for success.
- Utilizes a data model to ensure that all business requirements are substantiated.
- Is measured to be a success by the satisfaction and requests for new capabilities by the business clients.

Case Studies

CHAPTER 9

*Is There a Light at the
End of the Tunnel?*

AXIOM 9

Seek new heights by
agreeing to agree!

Have you noticed that some people move into a house, spend years remodeling it, and when they finally get it just the way they've always wanted, they sell it and buy a new one? A couple I know, Sam and Darlene, always had a remodeling project going on. For 7 years, they wallpapered, tiled, and painted. Weeknights and weekends were always spent on their house and yard. All Sam and Darlene talked about at work was their improvement projects. They spent all their free time together; with so much in common, everyone thought they had a wonderfully successful marriage.

But, once Sam and Darlene got their house and yard looking just as they envisioned, they put it up for sale and placed a down payment on a new house. They never moved into the new house, though, as suddenly and to everyone's amazement Sam and Darlene got a divorce.

While this story about Sam and Darlene didn't seem to end so well, it contains two lessons that can be applied to data warehouse endeavors. The first is that moving into a house doesn't mean the work stops there. There is always change and maintenance to be done. Similarly, once a data warehouse is established the work doesn't end there: Change, maintenance, and improvement must continue to occur. The second lesson is slightly more obscure. Think about "Who defines success?" In Sam and Darlene's case, obviously it was only Sam and Darlene who could define the success of their marriage. Others looking in could only "perceive" a successful marriage based on the large amounts of time the couple spent together working on the house. It is the same for a data warehouse endeavor: "Who defines success of the data warehouse?" The people who use the warehouse most frequently are the ones who should define it a success or not. Thus business clients are the ultimate final word in determining data warehouse success. Their clamoring and requests for expansion, additional capabilities, and improvements are the indicators of true success.

Therefore, the main criteria that count are those defined by the business. For this reason it is very important to make sure that the agreed-upon criteria for success are clearly defined in the game plan for the first endeavor and each subsequent warehouse expansion. Business clients measure success by the level of business value achieved by the endeavor. As they see this business value being delivered and as they grow in knowledge and understanding of the organization's business, they evolve into a near idyllic environment of constant change, integration, enrichment, and flexibility reached by only a few organizations today.

In this chapter, I present two case studies: one from an organization well on its way to the blissful state of data warehouse success and the other from an organization that ignored the warning signs and fell into the many pitfalls of data warehouse failure. Although the first organization (I call "Looking Good Company") is only in its very young days of business intelligence, it has set a strong foundation for its warehouse to expand and grow into the future. On the other hand the problems at "It Ain't Broke (Don't Fix It) Company" are so huge that the case study contains two sections; the first section covers the overall problems in the organization and the second section discusses the problems within one of the business units I have named "Parts-for-Profit."

As we go forward into the future, keep in mind that data warehouses are all about change, integration, enrichment, and flexibility. A data warehouse of blissful data allows an organization to be ready for global market changes and fierce competition, to remain flexible to sales downturns and upswings, to be able to attract new and retain existing customers, and to be quick to take intelligent action. Such organizations thrive. Organizations that are not prepared to face change and be flexible will languish. Blissful data and data warehouses are the swords of battle for the future. Draw your swords and be prepared to battle to victory!

Case Study 1: The Good

The Fortunes of Looking Good Company

A strong partnership between the business units and information technology (IT) results in an environment that enables business solutions to meet the organizational goals. The alignment of business and technology strategies culminates in the provision of effective transportation options and excellent customer service to residents of an urban region consisting of more than 3 million people, with millions more visiting every year.

Looking Good is a transportation agency responsible for a host of transportation services. Their vision is to provide leadership in creating transportation choices that enhance the quality of life. Their main goal—"Mobility!"

Challenge

Expand availability and convenience of current services, plan and implement new services to meet rising demand, and increase interaction and share best practices with transportation authorities of surrounding regions, vendors, constituents, agencies, and customers while improving cost-effectiveness of the organization.

Solution

Implement an enterprise data warehouse for analysis of company business by starting with key subject areas and identify and plan for additional opportunities.

Results

A pilot subject area was identified and the first milestone was reached in 45 days. The completion of the pilot in 6 months got the business clients very excited and clamoring for more capability.

In the Beginning

Looking Good was formed by the consolidation of multiple transportation agencies of the public sector. Each of these agencies had disparate data systems on various platforms with diverse infrastructures. Vast improvements were made in recent years to consolidate data and migrate to a robust and state-of-the-art technology platform. At about this same time, the organization came up with a 10-year plan to move the company into the future.

Although the disparate systems had been combined into a standard platform, the organization as a whole faced the dilemma of not really understanding what it had in its data banks. Little was known about the challenges faced by each of the business units and their short- and long-term business goals. Each line of business continued to operate in its own vertical stovepipe. Faced with rising transportation system demands and increasing costs, key IT personnel knew that it was up to them to provide the leadership to bring the business together. They were always on the lookout for new techniques to bring value to the organization. One such technique was the concept of data warehousing.

Norm, an IT specialist, got together with Phil, a business manager, to review the data requirements of the organization and perform a feasibility study for a data warehouse. In 3 months, with the help of other business personnel, the key subject areas of the business were identified. The availability and quality of data were assessed, hardware and software requirements were identified, and a high-level return on investment (ROI) analysis was completed. All results of the study were documented into a business case and presented to a senior management steering committee.

The steering committee members were interested but cautious. They authorized $300,000 for a pilot, with the stipulation that if the pilot was ruled successful by two or more business departments more funds would be allocated for additional phases to follow.

Kickoff

Norm and Phil were set up as coleaders of the pilot, with Norm the project manager and Phil the product manager. Two team members from IT and an additional business analyst made up the team. For the pilot they selected an employee payroll capability. The company recognized its employees as a valuable resource and enhanced payroll capability would provide a visible and viable solution. The company had grown from 10,000 to over 17,000 employees in just a few years and earning details for retirement calculation and labor contract negotiations were often needed for the grants, budget, human resources, contracts, and accounting departments. A preliminary study of data showed an operational system employee master, 4 years of complete history, as well as archived data going back for an additional 12 years.

The 12 business analysts to be involved in the pilot came from payroll, benefits, and contracts areas of Looking Good. Payroll department analysts often interacted with analysts from other groups. The contracts analysts would spend weeks collecting earning detail data to prepare for union contract negotiations. Without the proper earnings detail by employee by pay period, Looking Good chanced the risk of strikes, labor disputes, loss of grants, and contract default. Further, any retroactive payments that came out of the negotiations also required weeks of manual effort to identify which union members qualified for which amount of retroactive pay. The benefits analysts faced constant requests from retirees or employees about to retire. The level of pain and stress being experienced by these analysts was high. They looked forward to new methods to help them in their work.

The team set up the project objectives as follows:

- Create a single subject area data warehouse to provide earning details for current and previous employees by pay period in 6 months.
- Reduce preparation time for labor contract negotiations by 60%.
- Provide the capability to perform predictive modeling and analysis for union contracts and labor negotiations.
- Improve accuracy of employee earning details by 30%.

To meet the objectives, the team set up major milestones to be targeted as follows:

- Invite three "best in class" vendors to demonstrate software, evaluate, and select vendor for the data access tool in 21 days.
- Complete business requirements in 30 days.
- Extract and load active employee master information in 42 days.
- Data validation session with business clients by or before 45 days (major milestone with business clients).
- Extract and load active and inactive employee information (from master and 4 years of backup data) in 3 months.
- Data validation session with business clients in 3 months.
- Extract and load archived employee information (12 years history) in 4 months.
- Begin weekly data validation sessions with business clients at 4 months.
- Deliver end product in 6 months.

With such a strong bond between the business and IT staff, clear objectives, and well-defined strategies, Norm and Phil felt well prepared to face any unexpected events in this project. The assistant CEO was named executive sponsor of the data warehouse, and a kickoff breakfast was held for all the business units with an introduction of the overall warehouse benefits and goals, the pilot project team, and the pilot objectives.

Construction

Execution of the project plan began extremely well. The vendor selection for the data access tool and the business requirements were completed slightly ahead of schedule. But, unexpected hardware glitches caused PCs to crash often and upgrades were necessary. These upgrades were expensive and took an unexpected bite out of the budget. The executive sponsor approved the purchases. Data extraction, transformation, and validation for the first two iterations of data were completed with only some holdups and minor delay. The business analysts who attended the first data validation day were delighted with the query and analysis capabilities available to them. They requested additional validation days to become familiar with the access tool and the data. The project team enthusiastically agreed.

However, the archived employee information (12-year history) was laden with cryptic encoding and conflicting and incomplete data. Because much of this data went back to before Looking Good was integrated, a lack of documentation and expertise in these older files required the project team to spend significant amounts of time to track and analyze the cryptic meaning of the data. This was causing the project schedule to slip. Mindful of the looming deadlines, Norm called a meeting with the business analysts and explained that 20% of the remaining data was incomplete. He obtained their agreement to set a business rule to show such trouble records as "data unavailable." The team implemented this business rule and moved on to the next steps.

Data warehouse testing and additional data validation took place. The business analysts' expectations had been managed by Norm and Phil from the beginning of the pilot. This management of expectations paid off as the agreed-upon terms for success from the business plan were reviewed, discussed, and signed off on!

Outcome

The business clients had already been utilizing canned queries during the weekly data validation days. Four of the business clients had already moved to slice-and-dice analysis to perform predictive modeling and "what-if" analysis for union contracts and labor negotiations.

Although the data warehouse was deployed 2 months later than planned, the business clients were aware of the data issues and understood the delay. By the time the data warehouse was implemented they were familiar with the access tool and proficient with the query capabilities.

The warehouse provided the blissful data for queries and reports by the various business units. The benefits analysts could easily perform retirement calculations and provide retirement date comparisons for employees. By using the warehouse, contracts analysts were able to prepare for union contract negotiations in about 4 days instead of the 4 weeks previously required. Multidimensional database (MDDB) analysis allowed for comparisons and trends between salaries of union members over time to perform predictive modeling and analysis. By using data extracts, business analysts were able to identify employees eligible for retroactive payments at various levels in less than 20% of the time it previously took. The overall accuracy of calculations was improved. Preliminary estimates showed a 40% improvement. Understandably, the business analysts were delighted. All three business groups ruled the pilot a success!

Impact

By the first data validation day, the business clients were hooked. Business clients requesting additional validation days to become familiar with the access tool and the data are a clear indication that something was done right. These business clients were already talking to other business clients in the organization about the new capabilities afforded to them by the data warehouse. A second breakfast meeting called by the CEO took place to celebrate the completion of the pilot and spread the word of its success. The assistant CEO promoted the data warehouse and its benefits to the steering committee and funds were issued for the next phase.

Postmortem Analysis

What Was Done Well?

There were plenty of items that were done well. Some key items that contributed to project success were:

- Strong communication and partnership between the business and IT.
- The kickoff breakfast showing managements' involvement and support of the data warehouse.
- Starting small with a single subject area data warehouse with the plan to add on subject areas as additional phases.
- Involvement of the business clients began early, continued through the project, and intensified toward the close.
- Expectations were handled well by Norm and Phil.
- Problems were resolved quickly.
- Decisions were made to support the project objectives.
- The creation of a milestone chart with clear objectives set for every 30–45 days.

In summary, the Looking Good data warehouse pilot was a success because it had upper-management support, excellent communication, and business client involvement and the right decisions were made. It had a game plan with the right sponsors and right people involved.

What Could Have Been Done Better?

Although Looking Good has started off well, there were still some areas where some improvements would help them move toward the future:

- The preliminary high-level ROI analysis for the business case needs to be expanded into a more detailed analysis of the total benefits to be realized by the data warehouse. Included in this analysis would be the total cost of ownership for the data warehouse. Such an analysis would assist in obtaining larger amounts of funds being allocated for continued data warehouse growth and expansion without constant justification being needed.
- Project management disciplines for initiating, planning, executing, controlling, and closing should be utilized for subsequent project phases. As the warehouse expands the requirements for additional management of knowledge areas will increase. The knowledge areas of communications management, risk management, and integration management will increase exponentially.
- A metadata repository must be established. Once more subject areas are added to the warehouse, business clients will come to depend more on metadata.

In order to build a stronger data warehouse, Looking Good should perform additional ROI analysis, utilize all aspects of project management, and begin to build a metadata repository.

Lessons Learned from Looking Good

Many lessons can be learned from projects that go well, such as:

- The business must work in partnership with IT. There must be business client involvement early and consistently throughout the project.
- Don't bite off more than you can chew. To keep business clients interested and involved, show business value every 45–60 days.
- Research hardware configurations and requirements. Have the hardware infrastructure robust before beginning to execute the game plan.
- Never underestimate the problems with the data. Understanding the data for cleansing and transformation takes huge amounts of time.
- A data warehouse is an ongoing investment. To continue providing value, one must continue to invest in the data warehouse.

Lessons learned at Looking Good are that data warehousing success requires a strong partnering between business and IT, frequent milestones to show business value, robust hardware platforms, adequate time to identify and solve data quality issues, and continued investment.

Case Study 2: The Bad and the Ugly

The Trials of It Ain't Broke (Don't Fix It) Company

Even with CEO support, abysmal data warehouse projects can occur. The lack of integrated vision by the business units can lead to short-term goals of disparate independent data marts resulting in wasted efforts, misused resources, unrecoverable costs, ruined reputations, and unhappy clients.

It Ain't Broke (Don't Fix It) Company is a multibillion dollar company with global subsidiaries across North and South America, Europe, and Asia. It Ain't Broke has millions of customers and a sizable piece of the market share but could do better. Hence, the CEO of the U.S. sales operation set up a vision to gain an even larger portion of the market by targeting aggressive goals for attracting new customers and retaining existing customers. A preliminary study had uncovered that It Ain't Broke Company had no trouble attracting new customers but its customer loyalty factor at the time was only a dismal 19%. It's no secret in the business world that it costs a lot less to keep a loyal customer than to attract a new one. Therefore, It Ain't Broke could significantly improve its profits by keeping customers loyal to its products. The CEO of the corporation consigned his VPs to find and fix the reasons customers didn't come back to buy their second, third, or fourth product from It Ain't Broke.

Fortunately (or is it unfortunately for It Ain't Broke?), the VPs of the business units didn't have to look far. They found the reason for the lack of customer loyalty was the miserable level of customer service. Unhappy customers do not come back for more dissatisfaction. Improving customer satisfaction was a silver bullet to the company's bottom line.

Armed with this knowledge, the VPs looked around to see where service to the customer could improve. One of the first places they spotted was the customer service help desk. They found that customers experienced long phone delays before being able to speak to customer service personnel. In addition, these callers felt that they rarely received effective answers to their questions and perceived a lack of knowledge about the product from the customer service staff. Believing that the customer service desk was the root of the customer loyalty problem, it was determined that a customer data mart would provide the help desk staff with the necessary data to answer customer calls effectively. The IT group was tasked with creating a customer data mart.

The IT group set a goal of a customer data mart in 6 months. The 6 months quickly transgressed to 1 year before the customer data mart was finally realized. Oddly enough, there was no significant increase in customer satisfaction with the deployment of the customer data mart.

In the meantime, logistics services had also begun a data mart effort. This effort would assist in finding ways to improve the movement of products from one location to the next. But, huge data quality issues and growth restrictions severely constrained this endeavor. Other endeavors had also begun to mushroom in various parts of the company. Unfortunately, each endeavor had no connection (other than being in the same company) or communication with the other endeavors. There was no sharing of information, data, guidelines, or lessons learned. Many business unit efforts even bypassed the bottleneck (as they perceived) of IT and hired their own consulting firms to help implement vendor or packaged solutions. Each of these efforts did have one common characteristic: Each seemed to start out as a solution to be implemented quickly (4 to 6 months) and grew to take a year or more with questionable value being delivered to the organization.

What was happening here? Varying degrees of success were being achieved, but the objectives satisfied only narrow departmental needs. Without the cross-organizational view of the entire company, these objectives did nothing to support the overall company vision. These independent data marts were duplicating efforts, using a lot of time and resources, and costing the organization a lot of money. Without the centralized view of the company's data, It Ain't Broke will not be able to reach the levels of advanced analysis enjoyed by mature data warehousing organizations. With disparate views of the customer in the different data marts, It Ain't Broke would not know or understand a single customer. Without an understanding of the customer, the CEO may never see the significant leaps in customer service and customer loyalty factors that he was hoping to see. Without an enterprise data warehouse of blissful data, the business intelligence of It Ain't Broke will be severely restricted in its growth and potential flexibility to face the fierce competition of the future.

The Good, the Bad, and the Ugly at It Ain't Broke

Good

- The vision and commitment of the CEO to gain an increased portion of the market by setting aggressive goals for attracting new customers and retaining existing customers.

Bad

- The quickness of the VPs to hand off the problem to the first level of customer service – the customer service desk. This group interacted with only 5% to 20% of the organization's customers.

- An incomplete analysis of the problem: Customer dissatisfaction could stem from many other areas of service than a customer support desk.
- The philosophy of the VPs that a data mart was a technical solution and therefore the IT group's problem to handle.
- No sharing or communication of data, knowledge, business rules, and metadata between business units.
- The lack of leadership from IT to the business.
- The narrow vision of the business units to satisfy their departmental needs.
- The duplication and waste of resources in extracting and transforming the same data into the independent data marts.

Ugly

- The lack of a united vision and long-term strategy by the VPs.
- The lack of centralized and high-level sponsorship resulting in the short-term view of quick solution data marts.
- Decisions were made that did not support the overall company goal.
- A missing overall analysis of the problem.
- Lack of planning for long-term integration and benefits of an enterprise data warehouse. No specification of the overall goals, objectives, strategies, and ROI analysis of the solution.
- The multiple versions of the "truth" in the various data marts.

To understand better the barriers faced by business units at It Ain't Broke, an intimate look at one of the Parts-for-Profit business unit is included in the next section.

The Debacle of the Parts-for-Profit Endeavor

Challenge

Provide rapid, reliable, and accurate access to information to business analysts to support and enhance their tactical and strategic actions and drive the supply chain management efforts forward, thereby increasing customer satisfaction.

Solution

Use a reputable consulting firm to assist an in-house team in the creation of a centralized repository (a data mart) for analysis in 4 months.

Results

After 4 months, a data mart was nowhere in sight. Poor data quality, complex requirements, data extraction and transformation hold-ups, access tool snafus, and high project team turnover caused major delays. The data mart was finally deployed 2.5 years later.

In the Beginning

The Parts-for-Profit division of It Ain't Broke handles millions of stock keeping units (SKUs) or product parts per year. The operational system for these SKUs exists on three main disparate platforms and the integration of data from the different platforms was often complex, time-consuming, tedious, and error-prone. About 25 to 40 business analysts work diligently to support the departmental goals of providing outstanding customer service, reducing inventory and obsolescence, improving forecasts, and managing logistics and transportation, all for the most efficient costs. Their efforts require high levels of analysis and accurate information delivery with sound decision making.

Each month, these business analysts spent 2 to 3 weeks preparing the monthly forecast for service parts. They would spend hours, even days, pulling data from the different operational platforms, loading data into spreadsheets, and manipulating the data based on past history, trend analysis, experience, and sometimes pure guesswork. These analysts also had to react to sudden or unexpected demands, out-of-inventory conditions, and priority requests from important customers. An additional few days were needed to integrate the forecasts and check for consistency. It was always an anxious, rushed, and stressful situation to meet the monthly forecast deadlines.

Glen had worked as a business analyst for a number of years. He saw many areas for process improvement and used report writing software to pull information and format customize reports. This made life easier, but the manual processes and errors generated each month were still high. Glen was always on the lookout for a better way.

One day, Glen found out about the customer data mart endeavor going on at a different division of It Ain't Broke. He recognized that a data mart was the solution they needed at Parts-for-Profit to help them reach their goals for enhanced customer service, reduced costs, and process improvement. Glen went to the IT area to find out more about data warehousing, but they told him they were too busy at the time. Supporting and enhancing the operational systems was their priority. Glen was shut out in the cold.

Ron, a new corporate manager, started working in Glen's organization. Ron was interested in hearing Glen's ideas. Ron then took Glen's business case to the CIO. She was extremely supportive of the business case and saw their business need. She obtained $500,000 for Ron's organization to pilot a data mart for the organization. Glen was going to see his dreams realized!

Kickoff

Alan from IT was set up as the project manager. Alan set about creating his in-house core team, consisting of two senior business analysts (one was, of course, Glen); two extract, transform, and load (ETL) analysts to work with the data; and a database administrator. The project would be guided by an IT data warehousing governance group called the core competency center (CCC). In addition, an outside consulting firm was hired. Four resources from the consulting firm joined the core team. Ron was named the project executive sponsor. The team objectives were defined:

1. Create a centralized repository of SKU data for analysis in 4 months.
2. Reduce redundancy and time to create monthly forecast by 50%.
3. Obtain quicker response times for reports to support the decision-making process, resulting in better analysis and more accurate forecasts.

Glen, Alan, and Ron were optimistic the project objectives would be met as they felt that they had a strong core team, clear objectives, and solid technical support.

Construction

The initial steps were smooth. Glen already had the requirements from the different groups well mapped out. The business rules were captured into a business model and a data model was created.

As the team started into the second month of the project, things started to fall apart. Some of the roadblocks the team encountered were:

1. The data model revealed a complex set of business requirements; customization and special conditions were the norm, not the exception. These specialized conditions had to be embedded in the transformation logic.

2. Data quality was found to be "unbelievably poor" (Glen's words, not mine). These data problems had never surfaced in the operational systems. The core team had to backtrack to the actual processes to understand the special quirks and values in the encoding of the data. More than 80% of their time was spent tracking data quality issues.

3. Communication suffered. The consulting team created a data model without a complete understanding of the business requirements. Alan was too bogged down in data analysis issues to integrate the work of the team.

4. The access tool to submit queries and obtain reports was not a robust report writer. The business analysts had to work with the data access analyst (outside this project) to eventually obtain reports they needed.

The team tightened their belts and shifted into overdrive. They still felt that they could succeed. However, no major milestones had been set for the project other than the 4-month completion date. Therefore, the project team had no idea of how badly their schedule was slipping; they just knew they were behind.

By the end of the third month, things got ugly. Three people (75% turnover) from the consulting company quit! These people found it in their best interest to leave the consulting firm, not just the project. Replacing these people caused more delays. The CCC decided to jump in and started to demand schedule reports from the consulting firm staff. The in-house project team continued to struggle with data quality issues.

The 4-month deadline came and went. There was no data mart. The consulting firm made a request for 4 more weeks' of time and an additional 60% payout of the original fixed price contract amount. They were turned down and left the organization.

In the brainstorming session that followed, the CCC offered resources from their own organization, of course at a price. Ron felt his hands were tied, but having no other choice reluctantly agreed.

A development (test system) data mart completed construction 4 months later (a total of 8 months since the project inception). The CCC felt its obligation was complete and removed its resources from the project. It was now left to Alan and his remaining resources to validate the data and deploy the data mart to the production environment.

Outcome

Glen and the other business analysts continued to submit queries and create reports to view and validate data on the test system. They soon found that the canned queries created by the consulting firm were not what they had requested and were, in fact, useless. Glen had to work closely with other data access individuals to get the reports they needed.

Yet again, Glen's hard work came to naught as 2 months later, without any notification or approval from the Parts-for-Profit business unit, the CCC in an attempt to save on maintenance costs removed the OLAP access tool. Business analysts were told that they needed to switch to another access tool that had been purchased and maintained for a previous project. I'll call this access tool B1. The business clients felt the rug had been pulled from beneath their feet. Canned queries that had previously been created had to be recreated and retested using B1. To Glen's incredulity he found that B1 had less functionality and capability than the first access tool. With the inability to create some of their reports, many business clients called the performance of B1 "unacceptable." The business clients felt that they had been sabotaged by the CCC, and bad feelings prevailed.

Data quality issues continued to take a lot of time to resolve. For 20 more months, Alan and his team worked to resolve dirty data. That's right, another 20 months plus the 10 months that had already gone by. The project finally deployed 2.5 years after it began!

Impact

The Parts-for-Profit business unit was understandably unhappy with the events of its foray into data warehousing. Marginal business value is obtained from OLAP capability but the business unit is still unhappy with the limitations of the access tool. Therefore, the business unit has decided that no new growth of the data mart will occur until:

- An analysis of the root cause of the failure occurs.
- The total cost of ownership of the data mart for the next 5 to 10 years is determined.
- The ability of the data mart to grow to support the growth and expansion of the business can be assessed.
- The entire process is assessed to determine the value being delivered (the ROI).

Therefore, the future of this SKU data mart looks limited. Glen has obtained permission from his management to hire contractors and consultants to make some front-end Internet access improvements to the data mart. These improvements were implemented by bypassing the CCC and the development groups of IT.

Today, the business clients at Parts-for-Profit use the data mart for analysis. They have realized partial objectives, such as reducing the time to create the monthly forecast, but have no proper measurement to know if it is reduced by 50% or less. They are able to produce some reports more quickly, but the restrictions of the access tool severely limits the functionality they had hoped to achieve.

Postmortem Analysis

What Was Done Well?

Although it may seem like the SKU data mart project was as close to a project from hell as you could get, there were still some matters that were done well. Some of these were:

- There was a "real" business need.
- The request and drive for enhanced capabilities came from the business.

- The project team consisted of both business and IT personnel.
- Core in-house team members were motivated and committed.
- Objectives and requirements were well stated and clearly defined by the business.
- Business processes to utilize the data were defined in detail.
- Data validation and business client training sessions were emphasized.

In summary, the SKU data mart did have a real business need and the pain being experienced was very high, the core in-house team had strong business sponsorship and commitment, and a well-defined requirements document was prepared with the supporting manual processes behind it.

What Could Have Been Done Better?

Words of advice from one who's been there: Many lessons can be learned from a failure. Glen provides these lessons that he learned from the SKU data mart project:

1. Don't jump into a data warehousing effort unless you know where you are going.
2. Get the right sponsorship and assess total cost of ownership at the very start.
3. Perform an ROI analysis to determine the value for the investment.
4. Limit the size and scope for the initial attempt but keep options open for growth.
5. Assess data quality beforehand.
6. Do a manual process first with the data or you will fail.
7. Check references for consultants and vendors. Even a big name in data warehousing does not guarantee success.
8. Both the business and IT must work together. The business does not have the technical expertise to make it happen alone.
9. IT must pay attention to the business; they should make an effort to have some understanding of the business needs and requirements for performance and access tools.
10. A CCC must provide leadership and not be a bottleneck.
11. Key decision makers on the project must be BOLD: They need to be risk takers and change agents.
12. The project manager must be a skillful integrator, communicator, and risk manager.
13. A game plan or strategy to meet the objectives must be set early; this game plan must contain a method of measurement to gauge progress and important milestones to be targeted.

14. There must be teamwork and alignment between all team members (e.g., the data modeler and data access analysts).

In summary, the road to data warehouse (or in this case, data mart) success must consist of clear objectives, an analysis of the benefits, size, and investment (ROI analysis) of the effort, strong partnerships and commitment from various areas of the organization to sponsor the project, and the skills and efforts of the people doing the work.

Lessons Learned from It Ain't Broke

Numerous lessons can be learned from the It Ain't Broke organization:

■ Organizational culture and structure strongly influence the decision-making processes or its people. The stovepipe organizational structure at It Ain't Broke did not lend itself to the cross-functional solution of an enterprise data warehouse. This organization was not ready for an enterprise-wide solution.

■ Always keep the end goal in sight. At It Ain't Broke, the business units quickly lost sight of the end goal and reverted back to their own business objectives, which did not have a direct bearing on the overall company vision.

■ The business must work in partnership with IT. Business units by themselves do not have the knowledge to discern the intricacies of the advantages or disadvantages of the technical platforms, methods, data models, and tools to be used. IT needs the business comprehension to provide a viable solution.

■ Utilize a data warehousing sponsor to integrate efforts and facilitate communication between business units.

■ Have an overall coordinated plan. An enterprise-wide team of sponsors and people should be set in place to oversee and implement the plan. This plan must contain clear business objectives with the qualifying criteria for success. This team must also promote the end goal and benefits of acceptance of the plan to every business unit of the organization.

■ Do not underestimate the effort. A data warehouse is an investment, not only in its initial inception but also in its maintenance. An upfront ROI benefits analysis that measures hard and soft ROIs should be performed.

■ Always assess data requirements and quality of data.

■ Start with a visible and doable pilot. The pilot should show business value in 45–60 days with real results in about 6 months. Make each success visible to the organization.

■ Beware of shotgun approaches that solve only part of the problem – there must be a clear understanding of the entire problem before any attempts are made to jump in and fix a partial problem. Short-term bandages will cause problems and additional costs in the long term.

In summary, It Ain't Broke fell into many of the easy pitfalls of data warehousing. However, they are not alone; many organizations have gone the same route and are floundering to pull themselves out.

My recommendations to It Ain't Broke and other organizations in the same trap: Start anew. Armed with the knowledge you now have – take a step back, hire a consulting firm to assess where you stand, salvage anything you can, and start over. Yes, it will be expensive, but continuing with problems will cost more in the long run. Learning from failure sharpens your swords. Draw your sharper swords and be prepared to battle. This time to victory!

What Comes Next?

The future of data warehouses is already here. Early pioneers with successful warehouses have already stepped up to the next level, a level of business intelligence that helps drive the business. Many plans are in place at a variety of organizations. Some of the next steps of data warehousing you may see soon are:

■ A retailer uses data mining to determine the characteristics of the customers who buy certain products (e.g., teenagers buy a lot of hair spray and gel). Using this knowledge the retailer sends incentives to households with such customers or upcoming potential customers (such as preteens).

■ A financial institution sends a customer whose car loan has just been paid off an invitation to take out a new loan with an attractive interest rate for a car he may want to purchase for his college-age son or daughter.

■ A travel agency sends a special cruise discount on the occasion of a birthday or anniversary to customers who have booked cruises with them before.

■ A retailer monitors what products visitors are looking at on their website and how long they stay on that particular page. Although the visitor may not buy, a pattern of the visitor's interests and types of products she may purchase is established. Invitations to buy these types of products or related ones are pushed out to the visitor.

■ An organization determines the characteristics of customers who leave. The organization identifies other customers with these same characteristics as being most likely to defect. They send these customers special appreciation deals to prevent the possible defection.

■ Hospitals share information on symptoms, diagnosis, and treatment for diseases.

■ Government agencies use fingerprint scanners for identification to increase public safety.

Thus, data warehouses are the portals into the future. They provide the capability to "push" business out to the customer instead of waiting for the customer to come to a store or website. Data warehouses will become as prevalent to organizations as the microwave oven has become in homes.

As we move forward into the future, the field of business intelligence is evolving rapidly. New technologies and capabilities are emerging. Mature data warehouse organizations are moving to models where data in a warehouse are no longer static and can be updated. Organizations are obtaining more and more data. They are getting better at ensuring blissful data. Performance and response times continue to improve. The future looks positive and exciting. But, as you have seen in this book, technology does not make for data warehouse success. It is the people that count.

Remember, data warehouses are entire environments made up of hardware, software, special data, people, and processes. People make the hardware and software work. People implement the processes for attaining blissful data and the "ideas" for solving problems. People open the doors to business intelligence and make the organization successful. Organizations need people who are willing to change, seize opportunity, take risks, make decisions, and boldly take action. You are now armed and ready—with the knowledge you have acquired, go forth and discover!

Glossary

What Does That Mean Again?

Access. The operation of reading or writing data on a storage unit.

Ad hoc Processing. One-time only, casual access and manipulation of data.

Ad Hoc Query. An original or unplanned query that is used for in-depth analysis or to solve a specific problem.

Advanced Analysis (Data Mining). The analysis of detailed data to detect patterns, behaviors, and relationships in data that were previously only partially known or at times totally unknown.

Algorithm. A set of statements organized to solve a problem in a finite number of steps.

Application. A group of algorithms and data interlinked to support an organizational requirement. A common example would be a banking application that allows deposits, withdrawals, account openings, account closings, new loans, loan payments, etc. Computer hardware and software are often used to support these applications. A data warehouse can be considered an application.

Architecture. A term used to designate the structure/foundation of a computer system and its applications.

Baseline. The original approved plan for work such as a project. Usually used with a modifier, e.g., cost baseline, schedule baseline, performance measurement baseline.

Batch Environment. A computer environment where input is collected over some time period and then processed against databases at off-peak hours.

Blissful Data. Information that is accurate, meaningful, useful, and accessible to many people in an organization. Used by the organization's employees to analyze information and support their decision-making processes to drive strategic action.

Business Case. A "needs assessment" or justification to show why an endeavor is necessary to an organization.

Business Client. A person or process that works with a business application by issuing commands, queries, and requests to the application and receives messages in the form of data or reports back from the application. The user may trigger events to occur within the application. For example, a bank teller (the Business Client) opens up a new savings account for a customer. An "open new savings account" command is issued to the banking application and the application responds with the savings account number. Used interchangeably with the term Business User.

Business Intelligence. The set of products or services used to access and analyze data to turn them into information or knowledge enhancement. It includes decision support and data warehousing.

Business Rule. A policy of the business; can contain one or more assertions that define or constrain some aspect of the business.

Business User. (See Business Client.)

Canned Query. A standard or predefined query that is used frequently by one or more persons.

Change Agent. A person or process that brings about or implements change.

Data. Individual values of something known, conceded, or assumed for the basis of an argument or inference.

Data Mart. A type of data warehouse with data specifically designed for a defined set of functions.

Data Mausoleum. A data warehouse without blissful data, i.e., difficult data access and poor data quality inhibit people from using it.

Data Mining. Analysis of detail data to discover relationships, patterns, or associations between values.

Data Model. The specification of data structures and business rules needed to support a defined set of functions (sometimes called an Information Model); usually depicted in a diagram consisting of entities and relationships.

Data Modeling. The activity wherein subject areas of data and relationships between them are depicted in a diagram.

Data Steward. A person with responsibility to improve the accuracy, reliability, and security of an organization's data; also works with various groups to clearly define and standardize data.

Data Warehouse. A set of computer databases specifically designed with related, historical blissful data that assist in formulating decisions and taking action.

Database. An organized collection of data.

Database Management System (DBMS). A computer-based software system used to establish, access, and update data.

Decision Support. The analysis activity through which data are used to enable making decisions on facts versus guesses or intuition.

Decision Support System (DSS). The automated process to provide facts and information to facilitate decision-making activities. Usually DSS involves the analysis of many units of data in a heuristic fashion.

Deliverable. Any measurable, tangible, verifiable outcome, result, or item that needs to be produced to complete a project or a phase of a project.

Denormalization. The technique of placing data often accessed/used together in a physical location that optimizes the performance of the system (see Normalization).

Dependent Data Mart. A data mart that obtains its source data from an Enterprise Data Warehouse.

Dirty Data. Data that contain errors or cause problems when accessed and used. Some examples of dirty data are:

- Values in data elements that exceed a reasonable range, e.g., an employee with 4299 years of service.
- Values in data elements that are invalid, e.g., a value of "X" in a gender field, where the only valid values are "M" and "F."
- Missing values, e.g., a blank value in a gender field, where the only valid values are "M" and "F".
- Incomplete data, e.g., a company has 10 products but data for only 8 products are included.
- Spelling inconsistencies, e.g., a customer's name is spelled in several different ways in different locations.
- Cross-table inconsistencies, e.g., a customer's address shows a state and zip code that do not match the city.

Drill Down. To delve deeper into data by going from a summary value to more detailed values.

Enterprise. 1. An undertaking of some scope, complication, and risk. 2. A business organization.

Entity. A distinguishable, person, place, thing, event, or concept about which information is kept.

Extract-Transform-Load (ETL). The process of collecting, combining, and integrating data from many source systems to a single platform, be it a DSS, data mart, or data warehouse.

Failure (Project). The product or service is not delivered or completed within the time and cost allotted, or the product does not meet expectations.

Functional Organization. An organizational structure in which staff are grouped by specialty (e.g., production control, marketing, engineering, accounting).

Game Plan. The who, what, when, why, and how the endeavor will be accomplished. Contains the charter, goals and objectives, approach, risks, scope, schedule and cost baselines, milestone chart, people, organization, communication plans, and criteria for success. Sometimes called a project plan.

General Management. Consists of the planning, organizing, staffing, executing, and controlling the operations of an ongoing enterprise.

Heuristic. The mode of analysis in which the next step is determined by the results of the current step. Used for decision support processing.

Independent Data Mart. A data mart that obtains its source data from operational systems or other external media.

Industry User. (See Business Client.)

Knowledge Worker. A person who users a systematic procedure (which may include computer applications) regularly in his/her day-to-day work.

Known Unknowns. Some facts, events, or relationships are known but others are uncertain. For example, it is known that one or more snowstorms will hit the Northeast during winter months, but the time, location, and severity of the impact is unknown.

Mainframe. A large computer often used for processing transactional or operational type systems.

Metadata. Any information about data. Used in conjunction with business rules to understand the contents and processes of the data warehouse. 1. Business metadata define data elements, e.g., its format, coding standard (inches versus centimeters, etc.), and meaning of the element. 2. Database metadata define the various databases and tables of the data warehouse. 3. Application metadata is the definition of terms and functions specific to various functional groups.

Metadata Repository. A database or storage medium where Metadata are stored and easily accessed by people in an organization.

Milestone. A significant event in a project, usually the completion of a major deliverable.

Multidimensional Analysis. The ability to look at data in more and more detail, as well as from different perspectives or angles.

Murphy's Law. A famous eponym attributed to an Air Force officer in the late 1940s, Captain Edward Murphy: "If it can go wrong, it will go wrong."

Normalization. The process of removing inaccurate, inconsistent, redundant, and/or overly complex assertions from a data model.

On-line Analytical Processing (OLAP). The capability to view data in different ways, organizing the data by various dimensions to perform analysis, query, and reporting interactively.

On-line Environment. An interactive process in which results from a query or update are obtained immediately.

On-line Transaction Processing (OLTP). Any software capability that applies transactional updates and inquiries interactively.

Operational Data. The data used to support the daily functions of an organization.

Operational System. The processing of day-to-day operational data. Usually contains both batch and online environments.

Organizational Culture. 1. The shared methods in which people of an organization think and behave. 2. The "personality" of an organization.

Performance Domain. A broad category of performance in the field of project management. These are initiating, planning, executing, controlling, and closing a project, as well as professional responsibility.

Process. A series of actions performed by people to bring about a result.

Project. A concerted effort of work for a specific period of time to produce a unique end result.

Project Management. The application of knowledge, skills, tools, and techniques to project activities to meet project requirements. Differs from General Management.

Project Manager. The person responsible for managing a project.

Project Plan. (See Game Plan.)

Project Responsibilities. Who decides what on a project.

Project Roles. Who does what on a project.

Punch Cards. An early storage medium on which data could be stored on 3 × 7 paper cards, which allowed the data to be input into a computer.

Query. A request for information based on the value of certain fields against a database or a data warehouse.

Relational Database. A method for storing data in multiple tables, where relationships exist between tables.

Relationship. A connection between two entities that signifies the presence of a business rule.

Response Time. The amount of time that elapses after a query is issued and before the resulting data are sent back to the requestor of the query.

Reverse Engineering. The process of analyzing a subject system with two goals in mind:

(1) to identify the system's components and their interrelationships; and,

(2) to create representations of the system in another form or at a higher level of abstraction.

Risk. The probability of uncertain events occurring, causing positive or negative effects on the objectives of an endeavor.

ROI. Return on investment. A commonly used financial measurement of the payback of an investment. Tangible benefits are referred to as *hard ROI* and intangible benefits are often referred to as *soft ROI*.

ROI Analysis. The determination of the benefits and costs, usually calculated as a percentage over the time it takes to earn back the investment (in dollars) made.

Scope. The sum of the products and services to be provided by a project or project phase.

Scope of Work. Same as Scope.

Source/Source System. The starting location from where data is obtained. Operational databases are usually the *source* of data for data warehouses.

Sponsor. Individual or group that provides the cash or funds for creating and maintaining a project or the data warehouse.

Stakeholder. Individuals and organizations that are involved in or possibly affected by the data warehouse project activities.

Stock Keeping Unit (SKU). An identification, usually alphanumeric, of a particular product that allows it to be tracked for inventory purposes. Typically, an SKU (pronounced with the individual letters or as SKYEW) is associated with any purchasable item in a store or catalog.

Subject Area. A collection of related data values that is meaningful to the business or industry. Customer, product, revenue, and vendor are examples of subject areas.

Subject Matter Expert (SME). An individual with a large amount of knowledge about one or more areas of subject matter in an organization.

Super User. A business client with advanced or a large quantity of knowledge of the business, also known as a knowledge worker.

Transaction. The series of steps that take place to either access or update data in a database.

Transactional System. An online or batch system where data are accessed or updated by transactions.

Transformation Rules. The scheme or method used to convert codes to a common structure that is understood by all clients of the data.

Unknown Unknowns. A fact, event, or relationship that is not even thought of at the current time. In theory there are "zero hypotheses" and no premise to go by. In reality, there is some sort of a hunch, an educated guess, or an instinct.

Update. To change, add, delete, or replace values of data stored in a database.

User. (See Business Client.)

War Room. An area where project teams often meet to brainstorm problems and challenges. Project material and charts are posted for easy access and visibility.

References

(1) Inmon, W.H. *Building the Data Warehouse.* John Wiley & Sons: New York, 1992, 1993.

(2) Milne, A.A. *The World of Pooh.* Dutton Children's Books, Penguin Books USA: New York, 1957.

(3) www.sas.com/news/success. SAS Institute: Cary, NC.

(4) Tracy, B. *Victory.* AMACOM, American Management Association: New York, 2002.

(5) Fulghum, R. *All I Really Need to Know I Learned in Kindergarten.* Ballantine Publishing Group: New York, 1986, 1988.

(6) Klebnikov, P. "The resurrection of NCR." *Forbes,* July 9, 2001.

(7) Eckerson, W.W. "Resuscitating data warehouses." *Resource Guide 2001.* The Data Warehousing Institute, 2001.

(8) Lautenschlegar, B. "Enterprise data warehouse and the network effect." *DM Review* 11(2), 2001.

(9) Johnson, S. *Who Moved My Cheese?* G.P. Putnam's Sons: New York, 1998.

(10) Kotter, J.P. *A Force for Change: How Leadership Differs from Management.* The Free Press: New York, 1990.

(11) Matthews, A. *Follow Your Heart.* Seashell Publishers: Queensland, Australia, 1997.

(12) Dyche, J. *e-Data: Turning Data into Information with Data Warehousing.* Addison-Wesley Longman: Reading, MA, 2000.

(13) DMReview.com Editorial Staff. "The high cost of dirty data." *DM Review Online,* February 2002.

(14) Stackpole, B., "Wash me—poor data quality is no longer a little problem." *CIO Magazine* Feb. 15, 2001.

(15) English, L. "Mistakes to avoid for DW data quality." *DM Review* 12(6), 2002.

(16) Trompenaars, F. *Riding the Waves of Culture.* 2nd ed. McGraw-Hill Trade: New York, 1997.

(17) Hall, E. *The Hidden Dimension.* Anchor Books, a division of Random House: New York, 1990.

(18) Hall, E. *The Silent Language.* Random House: New York, 1990.

(19) Geertz, C. *The Interpretation of Cultures.* Basic Books: New York, 2000.

(20) Lawson, J. *The Worlds' Best-Loved Poems.* Harper & Row publishers: New York, 1927.

(21) Daggett, D. "The Financial Impact of Business Analytics." Press release. IDC Oct. 28, 2002.

(22) www.project-training-uk.freeserve.co.uk.

(23) Project Management Institute. *The PMI Project Management Fact Book.* Project Management Institute: Upper Darby, PA, 2001.

(24) Project Management Institute. *Project Management Professional (PMP) Role Delineation Study.* Project Management Institute: Upper Darby, PA, 2000.

(25) PMI Standards Committee. *A Guide to the Project Management Body of Knowledge.* Project Management Institute: Upper Darby, PA, 2000.

(26) Lewis, C. *Alice's Adventures in Wonderland.* Seastar Books of North-South Books: New York.

Index

Margaret Chu is a founding partner of OuterCore Professional Development, LLC, a company that provides leadership and project management consulting, training, and development. She is also an active member of the Project Management Institute (PMI[R]) and is an officer of the Los Angeles chapter. As a certified project manager or Project Management Professional (PMP[R]), she has led and managed a variety of Information Technology projects, including decision support and data warehouse challenges in aerospace, insurance, and sales and marketing companies.

She was born in Sri Lanka (previously Ceylon) and grew up between Ceylon and Hong Kong, eventually moving to California, where she now lives in Fullerton. Since receiving a degree in Computer Science from the University of California, Los Angeles (UCLA), she has worked in the Information Technology field for more than 20 years. Her distinctive qualifications come from lessons learned firsthand from a variety of projects. She is familiar with the people issues brought about by change and leadership in the workplace.

Additional information about OuterCore Professional Development may be found at www.outercoreinc.com. Margaret Chu may be reached at mchu@outercoreinc.com.